THE NATURAL RIDER

A Right-Brain Approach to Riding

MARY WANLESS

With illustrations by Christine Bousfield

Summit Books
NEW YORK LONDON
TORONTO SYDNEY TOKYO

Summit Books
Simon & Schuster Building
Rockefeller Center
1230 Avenue of the Americas
New York, New York 10020

First published in Great Britain by Methuen London Ltd., 1987

SUMMIT BOOKS and colophon are trademarks
of Simon & Schuster Inc.

Designed by C. Linda Dingler
Manufactured in the United States of America

10 9 8 7 6 5 4 3 2 1

Library of Congress Cataloging in Publication Data
Wanless, Mary .
    [Ride with your mind]
    The natural rider: a right-brain approach to riding/Mary Wanless; with illustrations by
Christine Bousfield.
    p.   cm.
    Previous ed. published as: Ride with your mind. 1987.
    Bibliography: p.
    Includes index.
    1. Horsemanship—Psychological aspects. 2. Imagery (Psychology) I. Title.
SF309.W265 1988
798.2'3—dc 19
ISBN 0-671-50766-4

Acknowledgments

I would like to thank Helen Davies, Helen Poynor, and Otto Reinschmiedt for their support during various phases of this project. I am also extremely grateful to Ann Mansbridge of Methuen, who had the courage to take me on, and who was able to send me back to my typewriter feeling even more inspired.

I am indebted to Pat Burgess and Cheryl Milner for helping me to clarify my thoughts about jumping, and to the following for permission to use quotations: Richard Bandler and John Grinder, *Frogs into Princes* (Real People Press, 1979); Baron Hans von Blixen-Finecke, "The Swedish Way Part Two: How the Horse Moves, and the Effects on its Training," *Horse and Driving*, January/February 1984; Chris Bartle in "Nerves of Steel" by Jenny Musto, *Horse and Rider*, May 1985; Neil French-Blake, *The World of Show Jumping* (Pelham Books, 1967); W. Timothy Gallwey, *The Inner Game of Tennis* (Random House, 1974); and *Inner Tennis* (Random House, 1976); W. Timothy Gallwey and Bob Kriegel, *Inner Skiing* (Random House, 1977); Charles Harris, *Fundamentals of Riding* (J. A. Allen, 1985); Erik F. Herbermann, *The Dressage Formula* (J. A. Allen, 1980); Reiner Klimke, *Basic Training of the Young Horse* (J. A. Allen, 1985); Maxwell Maltz, *Psychocybernetics* (Pocket Books, 1960); Denise McCluggage, *The Centred Skier* (Bantam Books, 1983); Wilhelm Museler, *Riding Logic* (Methuen, 1983); Lucinda Prior-Palmer, *Up, Up and Away* (Pelham Books, 1978), *Four Square* (Pelham Books, 1980), and *Regal Realm* (Pelham Books, 1983); Lucy Rees, *The Horse's Mind* (Stanley Paul, 1984); Molly Sivewright, *Thinking Riding, Book One* (J. A. Allen, 1979); William Steinkraus, *Riding and Jumping* (Pelham Books,

ACKNOWLEDGMENTS

1971); Sally Swift, *Centred Riding* (Heinemann, 1985), published in U.S. under the title "Centered Riding" by David and Charles (1985); and John Syer and Christopher Connolly, *Sporting Body, Sporting Mind* (Cambridge University Press, 1984).

In memory of the late Dan Aharoni, and of my horse, Cat Weazle, who were my two most long-suffering teachers. And with thanks to the many pupils and horses who probably taught me far more than I taught them.

The important thing in equestrian science is not so much the gleaning of new facts, but to discover new ways of thinking about existing ones. . . .

—CHARLES HARRIS

Contents

Introduction

There are many ways to think about riding, and many reasons for doing it. From pony-crazy children to top-class competition riders, each individual views horses in his or her own way. For some people, horses are very dear and special friends; for others, they are business investments, or playthings, or the means toward some higher achievement. But whether you regard the horse with awe or love, it is impossible to escape the sheer power of his presence, the phenomenal influence he exerts on the lives of all of us who decided at some stage that we wanted to become riders.

This book is primarily aimed at the serious riders who have made that decision, whose curiosity has led them to explore some of the finer points of riding, beyond the ability to sit astride the horse and push-pull him into action. Many would-be riders are lured onto the horse's back by the thought of peaceful rides in beautiful countryside, and once there, they realize that they have bitten off more than they can chew. While some rush to the nearest indoor riding school to equip themselves with more effective tactics, others carry on, proudly proclaiming that they have no need for riding lessons, perhaps occasionally pausing to wonder what the attraction might be in endlessly repeating circles. Of those who go to riding school, some gain the expertise they sought, but some do not, and they can spend years wondering why other riders are so much more effective. Whatever your curiosity, this book may give you some answers, and if you find, like me, that having a rather crude, argumentative relationship with the horse reduces the pleasure you feel when you go out riding, then I'm sure you will welcome any increase in your skill.

There have been times when I have wished that an uncomplicated approach to riding could have been enough to satisfy me—I would have saved myself endless problems, as well as the blood, sweat, and tears that went into solving them. But it was not enough, largely because I did not trust the horse enough to just sit on his back and let him get on with it; I needed the expertise which would allay both my anxiety and our arguments. I had also had instilled into me from an early age that if a thing's worth doing, it's worth doing well—so I *had* to become a good rider.

As a child I loved the excitement of riding: I did not worry if I bumped and bounced a bit, and although I was slightly envious of my more talented friends, I had no pretensions about my ability—and no ambition to become a great rider. But there came a time when I was told about bringing horses "onto the bit," and if I wanted to be classed even as *reasonably* decent, this was obviously what I had to learn to do. Unfortunately, my attempts only brought me up against bigger problems than I had encountered before, and the horse and I seemed less (rather than more) comfortable together. But at the same time as I was struggling myself, I was also being exposed to more and better riders and, as my horizons expanded, I gradually realized that riders I had once defined as "good" actually had far less skill than I had credited them with. Meeting really skilled riders showed me that the rider can have far more influence on the horse than I had ever imagined possible. Often, when I was riding a horse who seemed rigid and unyielding, a better rider would take over, and I would watch the horse become far more graceful in his movement, more proud in his carriage, and more *willing* in his whole demeanor. It was as if the rider was a sculptor, and the horse was the clay: when I rode him he was completely inflexible, but in the hands of one of these good riders he became a malleable medium, ready to be molded into whatever shape and movements the rider chose for him.

Prior to this time, I thought that dressage was something you could do if you were lucky enough to find one of those mythical horses who naturally looked right. Of course all the horses I rode had ewe necks, or hard mouths, or were stiff to one side; and these difficulties seemed inherent, inevitable, and insurmountable. My friends and I dreamed of the day when we would be privileged enough to ride a "real" dressage horse. These dreams collapsed around my feet when I finally saw all sorts of rather nondescript-looking horses, each with an impressive list of "problems," transformed before my eyes into beautiful dressage horses. Enthralled by these magical changes, I determined that my seat would one day have such an effect. But the harder I tried, the more the ease and grace I so envied seemed to elude me, and gradually I settled into a state of frustration and despondency. I had reached the plateau which besets so many riders, where increased effort seems only to lead to diminishing returns. The pastime which had once given me so much pleasure gradually became a source of misery, and my career as a "serious" rider finally became *so* serious that I decided to give it up.

This proved to be a great turning point. Comparatively soon, I let myself be persuaded back onto a horse again, and it was immediately apparent that my whole attitude had changed. I did not care anymore about how good or bad I was, and with this great burden gone I perceived myself and the horse quite differently. I began to notice things I had previously been blind to, and very soon this had a transformative effect on my skill; my interest in riding returned, and with it came a new sense of excitement. I began taking lessons from some of the best riders in Europe. While they mostly challenged me, they also said, "Yes, that's right," to the basic feels I was getting. Once again I was on a quest, only this time each day brought some new learning, and I quite often experienced those magical rides for which I had previously just longed and which I had merely watched from the sidelines.

This experience awakened my curiosity about the whole learning process, and I began wondering why some riders learn and perform so easily while others seem doomed to struggle. I figured that talented riders must be doing something different from everyone else, and I set out to discover just what that was. I had always suspected that good riders did not always do what they said they were doing (or perhaps they were also doing other things which they were not talking about), and I was relieved to discover that researchers in America had found this to be typical of anyone who shows outstanding ability in any skill. Then, while learning dance, I found a new approach to body skills and learning which resonated with my own. It seemed that a revolution was taking place in the teaching of other sporting disciplines, and the new techniques had been born out of experiences similar to mine. Backing them was a theory which immediately made sense out of my own discoveries.

It's actually quite common for any breakthrough within a specific discipline to come from outside that discipline: it has to, in a way, because the experts are already thoroughly versed in all the knowledge that lies within their prescribed boundaries. The Wright brothers were not aeronautical engineers but bicycle mechanics, and Louis Pasteur was not a physician.. Both made enormous contributions to science by crossing frontiers, and offering new knowledge to fields beyond their own. My own research took me away from traditional riding dogma into neurophysical reeducation, which covers body awareness, postural alignment, and movement tuition; and then to Zen philosophy, the martial arts, and sports psychology. In these fields, teachers and trainers have developed an overall philosophy about learning how to learn, which they can then apply to the specifics of any particular discipline. Throughout this circuitous journey I kept riding, discovering the potency of my new knowledge, and coming full circle—back to the writings of the great masters (people like Podhajsky, Müsler, Decarpentry, and Seunig), which I could then understand far more fully. Part of the moral of my story may be that we only truly understand what we have discovered for ourselves. We all benefit enormously when we take a more active part in our own learning process, and the many pupils I have taught using techniques of unlocking mind and body have been as excited about their own abilities as I have.

I hope this book can help to point you in the right direction, so that you too may notice the "keys" which suddenly unlock at least one part of the riddle of riding. It is to some extent a presentation of work in process—and as my learning continues I am sure that I shall have new ideas to add. Nevertheless, I believe its principles are sound, for it is merely a new look at an old skill, providing a more useful way to talk about what talented riders have been experiencing throughout the centuries, but could not find the words to explain to the uninitiated.

This book is full of simple explanations—analogies which illustrate a point. Think of them as maps or models designed to help you find your way around a certain territory. But take care; very often we mistake the model for the "truth," and this is like confusing a map with the territory it represents. You may well use other maps to describe the same territory, and if a map of yours differs from a map of mine, that does not make one of them "right" and the other one "wrong"; it simply means that they are different. Analytical knowledge has its limitations, so instead of pursuing it for its own sake I am more interested in creating models, which are far more useful because they directly affect learning—improving our practical ability, so that both horse and rider can maximize more of their potential.

In this book I leave out a lot of technical information about riding. I do not describe how to mount or hold the reins, nor do I give descriptions of the various school movements. I assume that most of my readers already have a basic knowledge of riding, and that those who do not can look up anything they need to know in a more conventional textbook. Throughout, I refer to the rider as "she" and the horse as "he," and in this I mean no disrespect to male riders or female horses. As you use this book I encourage you to take time over the dismounted exercises, to think through the Awareness Questions and Imagery sections, and to take some of the ideas with you into your riding. Chapters 1 to 3 will give you information about your brain and your body, teaching you how to cooperate with them and use them far more effectively. Chapters 2 to 12 deal more directly with the experience of riding as perceived by riders at different levels. Even if you are an experienced rider, the earlier chapters provide a wealth of useful ideas, offering a grounding which you may never have had. This basic lack could well explain the difficulties you currently experience—as well as giving you an insight into the problems of friends and pupils. More novice riders may find the middle chapters (especially 6, 7, and 8) rather complex; so if they do not make sense to you now, come back to them later, and instead of skipping over the words, actively involve your imagination so that you ask yourself, How might that feel?

The ideas I present here are very new to the horse world, and may seem rather strange. But I encourage you to greet them with an open mind, because suspending disbelief can open the door to dramatic changes. If you set out to find where my arguments fall apart, I guarantee that you will find places where they do. (It is an easy matter to disprove any theory by using the wrong technique at the wrong time, and with the wrong attitude.) So do yourself the favor of regarding these ideas positively, focusing on those which have the most meaning for you, and building up your learning from a basis of *what works* for you. My intention is to show you how to teach yourself—and other people—far more creatively, and I believe that each of us is ultimately our own best teacher.

Through this book, I hope to encourage an attitude which enables each individual to get more satisfaction from her riding, gaining access to the natural abilities which so many of us have blocked. This in turn makes life more pleasant for her horses, enabling them, too, to use more of their natural ability. Future discoveries may embellish or supersede those presented in these pages, and it is almost certain that they will yield even more useful models, which will show the learning potential of the average human being to be even greater than I have suggested here—and probably far greater than you have even imagined.

Mary Wanless
London

1 The Mind

Riders very often blame their bodies for problems which really belong in the mind—or at least in the body-mind system. Only in our language can we separate the two; in reality there is no clear distinction, and your mind has tentacles which reach out to and influence every conceivable part of your body. If you need proof of this, try the following exercise: Stand in a room where you have plenty of space, with your feet about fifteen inches apart. Extend your right arm out in front of you at shoulder height, and swing it around behind you, twisting your body so that you can follow it with your eyes. When you reach the point you cannot comfortably go beyond, stop, and take note of the spot that your hand points to. Now do the same with your left arm, and again note the spot which marks the full extent of your range. Return to the right arm and repeat the movement several times. You should find that your range increases considerably, allowing you to twist around farther each time. Pay attention to the bodily sensations you have as you do this, and then, *in your imagination only,* replay those sensations several times for your left arm. Now, swing your left arm once in reality. You should find that your range of movement has increased considerably—probably as much as in your right arm after a series of actual physical repetitions!

The full implications of this may not immediately be obvious to you, but suffice it to say that the way you use your imagination influences your body. This happens (for good or ill) whether you are aware of it or not, and you can easily learn to use your mind in ways that improve your riding performance dramatically. By directing your attention to specific body parts, and imagining them as heavier, or lighter, for instance, you change their way of functioning. You can even imagine (bizarre as it may sound) that you have two bolts passing through your backside down into the horse's back —rather like plastic toy cowboys and Indians—and find that this image, once planted in your mind, causes an immediate and significant improvement in how you sit to the trot. It has for almost everyone I have suggested it to!

Most people, however, believe that their ability or inability as a rider is determined by their body shape. The truth is that all of us have the physiological equipment required for riding, and what counts is *how we use it.* I had an eye-opening experience many years ago when my very elegant teacher, whom I admired immensely, took me along as groom when she went for a lesson with her teacher. It did not go well, and after we had loaded her horse, she climbed into the truck looking weary and distraught. Eventually she sighed and said, "How I wish I had his legs." Suddenly I realized that she perceived her limitations in much the same way that I perceived mine, and that I was not alone in my despair or my frustration. I now know that all riders share this inevitable part of learning, and I regard frustration very positively, because without it, in a situation where everything is already perfect, there is little motivation for new learning. Problems arise, however, when frustration involves so much discontent with oneself, and so much envy of others, that it blocks the learning process altogether: in their inextricable way, body and mind together produce the problem.

During the course of my riding career, I must have spent an enormous amount of time bemoaning my lack of talent. I blamed the problem on my body, which would never do what I wanted it to, and I saw myself as a victim of nature. Some of my teachers saw me that way too, but all of us were under the mistaken impression that talent is a *thing* which the rider either has or has not. Since then, I have come to believe that talent is not a thing but a process. Our ability is determined not so much by what we have, but by *what we do with what we have,* and this is the province of the mind.

I now believe that talent is a certain way of approaching learning, so that you perceive what happens between you and the horse, discover what works and what does not, and choose to do the things which work. If you want to be a competition rider, then your courage, the speed of your reflexes, and your ability to stay calm under pressure become paramount. But even these are not fixed, immutable quantities. When learning is effective it develops your confidence, your perceptions, your speed and timing; it brings out the best in you.

I take the philosophical stance that the oak already exists inside the acorn. Given the right conditions it automatically grows into an oak tree, fulfilling its inborn potential. Given the right conditions the rider can also fulfill *her* inborn potential, learning how to make optimum use of muscles, senses, and mind. But riding with any finesse is not easy; it requires very subtle coordination, and what appear to be opposite character traits—authority and sensitivity, for instance. In learning, most of us soon come across some seemingly insurmountable obstacles in our physique or personality: we are too impatient, or too lenient, or we have a habitual stiffness in some body part which will not go away. (These, you will soon discover, are the least of your difficulties.) Not everyone wants to put in the time and commitment which are required to overcome such obstacles, and most people specialize in the facets of riding which come most easily to them. Of those who *do* tackle the difficult parts, some struggle more than others, and almost all struggle more than is necessary. But when each rider goes at her own speed, she can experience the satisfaction and delight that go with traveling a very challenging path, and learning its lessons. The excitement of success need not be reserved for the "talented."

Children naturally tap far more of their innate learning ability than adults, who often overestimate the difficulties of learning, and interfere with their inherent ability so much that they can seem stupid and incapable when they are actually far from it. Contrast the experience of a child learning to walk with that of a rider. Given the chance, the child will choose to watch children slightly older than herself, who can show her what she needs to know. As she watches, without analyzing, she becomes able to imitate their movement. Trial and error do the rest, and as she moves toward her desired goal she just discards movement patterns that do not work. Instead of trying and trying again, she takes the feedback that what she is doing is not working as an indication that she should try something else. Fortunately she cannot yet speak, so she is saved the agony of telling herself, Now, I must bring this leg forward, roll my weight from the heel to the toe, ease my weight from the other leg, and be careful not to wobble.... The rider, however, as she learns new movement patterns, all too often comes around a corner telling herself, Inside leg on the girth, outside leg back, now I must be careful not to collapse... Then, having ridden a bad corner, she comes along the next time, and does exactly the same thing again! Meanwhile she is getting more impatient with herself: Come on, you idiot, get it right this time. Can't you even get the proper bend? She becomes engrossed in a kind of internal warfare, between the "I" who does the insulting, and the "me" who does the riding; and this takes all her attention. While she's thinking, and listening to the voices inside her head, she is blocking the information from her body—her "feel" sense—that could transform her ability.

The rider does indeed have a more difficult task than the child learning to walk. The human body is reasonably well designed for walking, and may even be preprogrammed to produce this movement pattern as a motor response. But it is not well designed for riding, and certainly not preprogrammed for it. This makes riding an exceptionally demanding skill. But even here, the principle still holds that the child's way of learning, using imitation and experiment, makes the learning process easy and efficient, whereas the adult's way is fraught with difficulty. It inhibits, rather than utilizes, the brain's natural abilities.

These two examples—the child's and the adult's way of learning—actually represent two completely different ways of using the brain, and each is a mode of consciousness related to one of its two hemispheres. The brain is shaped rather like one half of a walnut, and its two sides are joined by nerves which allow some flow of information between them. For reasons not completely understood, the left hemisphere controls the right side of the body, and the right hemisphere controls the left side. Where they differ is in their way of solving problems. The left hemisphere processes information in sequence, by adding one part to the next—so it adds letters to make words, words to make sentences, and sentences to make paragraphs. It has always been held in highest regard because it governs speech and reasoned, rational thought. When people suffer injury in the left hemisphere there is often a loss of speech, and a gradual deterioration in logical thinking. When corresponding parts of the right hemisphere are damaged, there is a deterioration in coordination and visual perception—so the people concerned cannot dress themselves or recognize friends.

The abilities of the right brain have gone unrecognized through the ages, because it does not store or communicate its knowledge through words. It processes information by looking at *wholes,* so in recognizing a face it does not add the hairline to the forehead, to the eyebrows, to the eyes, and so on; instead it draws a conclusion from the whole face. It then stores this information as an image, and on a future meeting it recognizes the face again by searching through its store of images until it finds the one that fits. The right hemisphere also appreciates and recognizes art and music, perceiving detail of color, texture, and sound. In riding, we are most concerned with the right brain's ability to perceive information through the body's kinesthetic sense. This is the sense through which we feel skin sensation and recognize heat, cold, and pressure, and through which we perceive internal sensation, get feedback as to how the body is arranged in space. Receptors in the joints and muscles continually relay information to the brain, monitoring which way up you are, where your arms and legs are, how tense you are, and so on. As you learn to ride, information is perceived through your feel sense and stored in the right brain as a series of "feelages"—feeling sensations which you can reproduce in your kinesthetic imagination, and recognize when you feel them again. Most people are far more familiar with visual images than they are with kinesthetic sensations, and part of the aim of this book is to increase your kinesthetic perceptions. This is extremely valuable, as the quality and quantity of right-brain feelages in a rider's store are the basic determinants of her present level of skill.

The left-brain way of solving problems, with its step-by-step procedure, is far more laborious than the right-brain way, where the answer often arrives, as if from nowhere, in a sudden "Aha!" Einstein and other creative geniuses have described how their discoveries came initially as an intuitive flash, and only afterward could they set about formulating the logical proof which justified their hunch. This ability to pass information between the two hemispheres, and to utilize the abilities of both, unlocks far greater potential than one of them used alone.

But the creative abilities of the right brain are undervalued in our culture, and Western thought has far greater regard for reading, writing, and arithmetic than it has for bodily skills, art, and "vision." In consequence, most of us receive a very one-sided education, and like an unused muscle, the right brain atrophies. With training, however, it can be brought back into full form—although people who have learned to use the left side of the brain almost exclusively are relatively unable (and unwilling) to use the right brain—even in situations where its mode of functioning is far more appropriate.

Many riders defeat themselves by trying to use a left-brain approach to solve a right-brain problem. They read every book on riding they can lay their hands on, they listen carefully to their teachers, and they amass vast amounts of theoretical information. They can quote at length from Podhajsky, Müseler, Decarpentry, and Seunig, but none of this left-brain knowledge changes their kinesthetic ability. They do not arrange their bodies any better, or perceive them any more clearly, so however much they know in theory, they still bump on the horse. But undeterred, and determined to find the key, they search for more books to read.

For years, I was one of those riders too. My thinking mind was sure it could teach me how to ride, whether I was on or off the horse. Put this leg here, and that leg there, it would say, and then it will work. So, dutifully, I tried putting this leg here and that leg there, and most of the time it did *not* work, even if I did manage to achieve my aim. When I concluded that I had no talent, it had never crossed my mind that I might simply be using a dud technique. Talented riders make the best use of their brains, and through this they make the best use of their bodies. They are the fortunate ones who naturally use right-brain processes, and this is why they progress so easily. In my own learning I had to change tactics, rather than trying harder, before I began to appreciate what skill really was.

An enormous amount about learning and communication was

discovered during the Second World War, when research into wea-
ponry led to the science of cybernetics. This explained what was
necessary to make a machine act purposefully, and when this
knowledge was applied to the human brain, it was realized that the
brain learns most efficiently when it acts like a class of machine
known as a servomechanism. One example of this is a self-guided
torpedo, which can automatically steer its way toward a goal. To do
this it needs to recognize its target, to have a propulsion mechanism, and to have sensory detectors which bring it information
from the target. This input informs the machine when it is on the
right course and when it makes an error, so that when it is getting
positive feedback, it keeps on doing what it is already doing and
stays on the same track. As negative feedback informs it that it is
too far to the right, say, its corrective mechanism automatically
moves the rudder to steer it to the left. If it overcorrects, the feedback mechanism causes it to steer back over toward the right, and
so it moves forward, through a process of making errors and correcting them, gradually groping its way toward its goal. With a
refined feedback mechanism, the machine need be only a little off
course before it corrects itself.

When a baby first learns to grasp objects you can clearly see this
feedback mechanism at work until, in time, she no longer has to
grope. For the sake of efficiency, the nervous system habituates
patterns of muscular use, ingraining neurological pathways in the
same way that one might make a pathway through long grass, and
keep using it in preference to creating another. Thus our responses
become "grooved," and relegated to the control of the unconscious
mind. In riding, the horse sets the rider a series of kinesthetic
problems to solve, and the skilled rider ingrains useful habits that
are an effective means of solving them. Her kinesthetic sense becomes so refined that she realizes immediately when things begin
to go wrong, and she can instantly improvise, applying an effective
correction (a half halt perhaps) which nips the horse's evasion in
the bud. A novice rider will take far longer to diagnose the problem, and will make many more trial-and-error responses before
putting it right.

The servomechanism is inevitably successful because it remembers and ingrains only useful responses; the ones which do not

work are discarded and forgotten. When the brain functions at its optimum it does this too. But in the stress of the moment a rider often says to herself, Oh no, I hope I don't do that again . . . and so, of course, she does! By paying attention to her mistakes she remembers and ingrains them instead of her successes. So she ingrains only a limited number of rather ineffective responses, and she loses the flexibility which allows her to improvise and meet the demands of a specific situation. Only when she finally discards these in favor of ones which satisfy the conditions posed in the problem will she experience a sense of "fitting," the "Aha!" which tells her that problem and answer together form a complete whole, rather like two pieces of a jigsaw puzzle. The more effective the learning has been, the more options the brain has to select from, and when it scans its store of feelages in any new situation it is far more likely to find an effective one which solves the problem and makes a "fit."

The brain is continually receiving input from all the senses, but rather like a radio, it can only "tune in" to one at a time. So when you become entrenched in your internal dialogue you completely miss the kinesthetic feedback which sets this learning process in motion. This must be one of the most pervasive ways in which riders completely block their inherent ability—and lose faith in it too. Once the most useful feelages are ingrained and automatic, on the other hand, it becomes possible to ride and talk at the same time: I do this often when I demonstrate to a pupil. But when the work gets more difficult and demands more of my attention, I find myself drying up in mid-sentence. I notice that I am not speaking, I do not want to speak, and I am so absorbed in my riding that I cannot find words. In her book, Drawing on the Right Side of the Brain, Betty Edwards reports the same phenomenon, and it is typical of the kind of concentration that is required to perform a right-brain skill with any finesse. We see it often in young children and animals, who are so absorbed in their play that they do not notice distractions, or time passing. Most riders have stories of occasions like this, when the internal chatter stopped, when their whole being was focused on the task at hand, when time seemed to stand still, and circumstances conspired to produce one of those exceptional rides; but rarely do they attribute this experience to the

quality of their concentration. We all long to perform like this—
perhaps it even explains why we ride—and these moments in
which we surpass ourselves become treasured memories, which spur
us on when the going gets tough.

We cannot live all the time in this state of heightened awareness, and we can no more force ourselves into it than we can force
ourselves to go to sleep. Usually, it creeps up on the rider unawares, and the moment she thinks, I wonder if I can do that
again? All I did was to... she has split herself into an "I" and
"me," and ensured that she returns to an inferior left-brain way of
functioning. The right-brain awareness mode is as elusive as the
proverbial will-o'-the-wisp, and trying, forcing, and grasping at it
ensures failure. Riding is very seductive, in that good rides lure us
into attempts to produce the same experience again, even though
we often attribute our success to the horse, or luck, or other circumstances beyond our control. Other athletes have more difficulty attributing their slumps and winning streaks to the ball, or
their opponent, but the horse all too easily becomes the scapegoat,
who is blamed for the bad and gets credit for the good, so that the
rider never has to take responsibility for either. The performers
who learn the most from their mistakes and successes are those who
treat them—at least partially—as their own creation.

Riders have been particularly slow to recognize the importance
of mental training, perhaps because of their reluctance to recognize
the true extent of its influence. When I rode my first correct half
halt, it "just happened" (a phrase many riders use), and as the feel
and shape of the horse changed underneath me, I knew I was experiencing the magic for which I had been searching in vain. But I
had no idea how I had done it, and could only attribute my success
to luck, fate, or the horse. To reproduce the feeling, I first needed
to see that "magic" has a structure, with underlying rules of cause
and effect which demystify the enigmas of riding. Instead of having
to believe in external powers which make things "just happen," I
was able to own that power for myself.

If there is a magic ingredient in successful riding, it is this right-
brain concentration, and the most skillful performers are consistent
in their ability to enter the awareness mode. Although none of us
can make this happen, we can get to know useful pathways into it,

just as we can get to know attitudes and rituals which make sleep more likely. One renowned rider I know begins each session by humming to herself as she is riding, and this blocks the internal dialogue, leaving the right brain free to get on with the job. (When I tried this while typing, my left-brain interference was reduced so much that my speed literally doubled; there was a new depth to my concentration, which left me unaware of time and distractions.) But this quality, which is the epitome of the awareness mode, is not there in our normal attempts to concentrate. I must concentrate, we tell ourselves, but as Timothy Gallwey states in *Inner Tennis*, this leads to *trying*, not concentration. When people say, "I ride so much better when I don't concentrate," they usually mean, "I concentrate so much better when I don't try."

Many people think that the opposite of trying is giving up; but in fact, trying *leads* to giving up, and the opposite of trying is *letting go*. The left brain (egotist that it is) does not like to let go, and when riders realize that trying does not get them very far, they often find themselves trying not to try . . . and so the diversions go on. In true concentration we become so fascinated by something that our attention is drawn to it as if by the object itself, rather than by our act of will. As Gallwey again suggests, ordering yourself about while riding is about as ridiculous as sitting in front of a good film and telling yourself to watch the screen. The orders are superfluous when you are sufficiently interested in what you are doing—so if you want to concentrate on something it helps to find what is interesting about it. Good tennis players, for instance, do not tell themselves to "watch the ball." Instead they look at its seams, or see which way it is spinning, or watch the patterns of light and shadow on it. This produces in them the attentiveness of a young child playing, along with its resulting high performance. Very few riders are able to focus the mind and stop the internal dialogue, yet this is one of the most fundamental skills of riding. Some of the old Zen masters compared training the mind to training a horse: if you force it, it will fight you; it responds best to tact and patience. But when you have a willing, attentive partner, the rewards are enormous.

In *The Inner Game of Golf*, Timothy Gallwey discusses two other modes besides the awareness and the trying modes: the panicking and the unconscious modes. In one you frazzle your brain cells, and in the other you let them do their own thing; but either way, you do not tend to be in the optimum state for riding. Historically, there have been huge rifts in the horse world between people who adopt these different approaches. "Cowboy" riders who are naturally brave and who just want to have fun on horses enjoy riding in the unconscious mode, and cannot see the point of riding lessons or schooling. They are content to use push-pull tactics, and they laugh at the people who waste their time, energy, and money going round and round in circles. The academic riders often despise their uneducated contemporaries, but mostly they spend their time in *abortive* attempts to improve their riding, trying hard—as indeed they must when they use a left-brain approach to solve a right-brain problem. They have often not given much credence to the masters, the brilliant riders who work from the awareness mode, although now, fortunately, this rift is closing. The masters themselves have little conception of how differently they use their minds and bodies, so it is hard for them to understand why other riders have so many difficulties. Often they keep to themselves, and have little patience with the established system for teaching and learning, or with ignorant riders who seem to ask such stupid (left-brain) questions.

Finding the awareness mode is far more difficult for some people than others, and one of the determinants is the way in which we talk to ourselves. I would not dream of talking to another person in the critical, derisive way I used to talk to myself, continually judging everything I did. In her book, *The Centered Skier*, Denise McCluggage points out that it is useful to begin your comments (if you must make them) with "Aha!" as in "Aha! I notice you are x-ing." As she says, that is a far cry from, "Idiot! There you go x-ing again!" and it will make you far less judgmental. In the old days, riding a bad canter transition would soon make me believe that I was having a bad day, and then I would start calling myself a bad rider and a bad person. On the odd occasions when I rode well, I became a good rider and a good person. My feelings of self-worth were at best shaky, as they went up and down with my performance, and I could only feel good about myself if I rode well. But a child does not think she is bad if she falls over in the process of learning to walk. Instead, she uses the fall as useful information to help her stay upright next time. Her mother can watch her fall without thinking that she is bad, or that she is a bad mother. Her self-worth is not dependent on her daughter's performance, so she can watch her with interest and some concern, but in a detached way which allows her to learn without interference.

The pure awareness that sees what *is*, without judgment or distortion, is fundamental to the learning process. I used to abhor my mistakes so much that I felt almost squeamish at the thought of my legs which kept wobbling, or my arms which tensed every time something went wrong. When riding, I went by the textbook rules about how my body should be, and I made determined attempts to fit myself into the right mold. Only when I stopped trying to re-arrange my body did I start to notice where it already was. This had an instantaneous effect on my performance, because building from a base of *how you already are* allows change to happen, whereas *trying to become something you are not* is a frustrating, impossible process. In terms of how the body works, this has a sound neuro-logical basis: the nerves which send impulses between the brain and the musculature work rather like the wires of an old-fashioned telephone exchange. Once the rider has ingrained specific neuro-logical pathways, her attempts to change her responses are rather like an engineer's attempts to reroute a set of tangled wires. Before he can begin, he has to discover where each one is going at the moment, and once he has this information, change is relatively easy.

Many of us waste enormous amounts of energy hating and fight-ing our bad habits, but the more we try to erase them, the more firmly they implant themselves, and the only solution is to change tactics, and to make friends with them instead. The more we take an interest in them and observe them without judgment, the more likely they are to reveal themselves to us, often in a moment of sudden insight, when we realize what has been happening. This breakthrough immediately gives the rider more feeling in her body, and more choice about her coordination. Instead of being the vic-tim of her own unconscious neurological wiring, she becomes the engineer who can redesign how she uses it.

The most skillful performers are those who began by ingraining useful coordinations, and who learned, like the servomechanism, through a process of refinement which bypassed their conscious awareness. This gives them right-brain knowledge. The vast majority of riders have read the books and know how they ought to be doing it (even though their bodies won't cooperate); they have left-brain knowledge. But when you are relearning—rerouting the inefficient neurological pathways which run all your responses—you end up with whole-brain knowledge. With each breakthrough the right brain communicates with the left, increasing your awareness and enabling you to talk more clearly about your experience. But without this the left brain has, literally, no idea what the right brain is doing, and the rider's verbal account will be a stilted, inaccurate version of her right-brain skill. Ironically, this is just as true for skillful riders as it is for the ones who are caught in the grip of those interminable bad habits.

This explains why riders who have struggled in their own learning tend to make the best teachers. The ones who are naturally talented get frustrated by their pupils' problems: they have so little understanding of them that, ultimately, they end up either reciting the dos and don'ts or tearing their hair out and shouting, "Why can't you do it like me?" But since they do not know how they actually do it, they cannot explain as well as those who have discovered more. These talented teachers often use metaphors, which solve the communication problem by speaking to the whole brain. They are bilingual, with words for the left hemisphere, and images, feelings, and atmosphere for the right. You are probably familiar with the age-old idea of holding the reins as if you were holding fledgling birds which you must neither squash nor allow to escape. I encourage my pupils to make up their own metaphors: one of the ones I like best was made up by a child who discovered that she sat to the trot much better when she imagined having two bolts which came from the saddle up into her backside—just like the plastic cowboys and Indians. I have found this helpful to many people, but some other images will be far more individual. In her book *Up, Up and Away*, Lucinda Prior-Palmer states, "Frequently to this day I find that someone might have been telling me something for literally years, but it will only sink in when another says exactly the same thing in a different way, maybe merely by using a fresh smile."

Sally Swift's book *Centered Riding* is a very rich source of images: she suggests, for instance, imagining that your body is filled with ice cream, which melts and dribbles down into your legs and out through your feet. These next chapters will give you many more ideas and, however bizarre they may sound to your left brain, I can assure you that there are bound to be some which are just right for you, speaking so powerfully to your right brain that your muscles know just how to respond.

Researchers have investigated the problems inherent in teaching and learning, and realizing the uses—and limitations—of imagery, they have evolved the concept of "modeling." The function of modeling is to arrive at descriptions of skills which are useful in teaching others, and modelers build up their descriptions by paying attention to what skilled performers actually do, rather than what they say they do. They claim that "if any human being can do anything so can you. All you need is the intervention of a modeler who has the requisite sensory experience to observe what the talented person does—not their report— and to package it so that you can learn it."*

In effect, modelers make recipes. Given the finished product— in this case a first-rate rider—their task is to work *backward,* discovering what has to be happening for her to produce such amazing results. Then, when they have discovered what ingredients are needed, in what quantities and what order, they work *forward,* testing the recipe by producing other first-rate riders, until they can consistently produce the same results in anyone. My own experience was that conventional recipes did not get me where I wanted to go; I blamed myself (I did not have the right ingredients) rather than querying the recipe. I now believe that we all have the necessary components; the difference between the more exceptional and the average rider lies in how they use them. Modelers evaluate their recipes according to what *works,* not what is *true.* Knowing one recipe does not mean that you know them all, and there are, no doubt, many ways of arriving at the final result. A modeler's pupil will not instantly have the years of experience which give the masters their finesse; but she can very quickly grasp

*Richard Bandler and John Grinder, *Frogs into Princes* (Real People Press, 1979).

the *structure* of that experience, so she knows how it is made up. With a practical understanding of its underlying components, she is no longer dumbfounded by the mysterious ability of the talented. Instead she comes to believe, as I do, in the words of the famous German rider and author Wilhelm Müseler: "Feel is no black magic, and anyone can acquire it to a considerable degree."

2 The Body

One of the major disadvantages of our left-brain education lies in our conviction that the body *should* obey when we tell it what to do. It takes only a short time in the saddle for most of us to realize that this does not work too well. The left brain arrogantly concludes that the body is not behaving itself, so we tell it louder, scold it harder, and become so entrenched in this internal warfare that we never stop to wonder if there might be another way. Even those who do question what they are doing rarely realize that the only answer is to completely reverse their tactics, and *listen* to the body instead of ordering it about.

While you are reading this, pay some attention to how you are sitting. Does one buttock contact the chair more closely than the other? Where are your feet positioned on the floor? How are your arms resting? Is one shoulder higher than the other? Is your head on one side? The answers to these kinesthetic questions are obvious as soon as you ask them, but until you ask you do not consciously know. In riding, at the stage when you do not know how to do something too well, you have to keep reminding yourself about it, intervening with the conscious mind until the body learns to position itself automatically. Inevitably, your awareness of a body part will fade a few moments after you have reminded yourself— and new priorities will vie for your attention. So you can only bring the part back into consciousness by reminding yourself again, or moving. (This is known as The Principle of Adaption!) By now you have probably forgotten about your buttocks and shoulders, and if you were riding, the chances are that you would have forgotten about them too. This would not matter if you had already ingrained a useful way of placing them, and could rely on your unconscious mind and "automatic pilot" to hold them there; but by relying on automatic pilot alone, you miss many opportunities for new learning. The riders who learn the most do so because they are continually looking for new ways to refine their perceptions and streamline their skill.

However, becoming aware of your body while riding is actually far more challenging than this simple exercise suggests. As a beginner, you probably have found yourself at a complete loss to control its various parts, and since then, you may well have reached the plateau where there seems to be no choice but to resign yourself to the fact that it rarely does what you want it to. But these difficulties you have are merely symptomatic of a far greater problem: that of bringing the body back into full conscious control, which is possible, but not easy. All adults have distortions in their body image—the way in which they perceive themselves. Young children do not: they have far greater body awareness than adults, and are more in touch with their movements, sensations, and needs. But in the process of growing up, as they learn to inhibit their spontaneity and conform to the demands of an adult world ("Sit down," "Don't wriggle"), they do so at the cost of their own perceptions. Gradually these become blunted and distorted, so that a gap develops between the body as it is perceived and as it actually is. Through the process of growing up, some body parts are overused while some are underused; as they become rigidly fixed, their owner becomes habitually insensitive to messages about the muscular tension which holds them in place, and eventually her awareness of these parts fades. The net result is that some body parts are not sensed at all, while others are sensed indistinctly, or as distortions of the body's actual reality.

As these tensions gradually contort the body, it loses the ability to correct itself. Instead of stacking our various parts neatly one above the other, therefore, we work *against* gravity: backsides stick out behind us, while shoulders tip forward to compensate; knees lock, and necks tighten. Our muscles fight their way to a precarious equilibrium, and when the body is in motion we often work against ourselves—as if we were treading on the brake and the accelerator at the same time. But however strange this may sound or look, it comes to feel like "home"—so comfortable and familiar that what is wrong is sensed as "right" and what is right is sensed as "wrong." Over time we become so alienated from ourselves that we no longer know what we are doing; but worse than this, *we do not know that we do not know!* So, despite our conviction that we are standing straight, sitting square, and not yanking on the horse's mouth, our bodily sensations are not to be trusted.

If all this presents a rather daunting picture, take heart from realizing that the body can, in fact, still unravel itself. Learning to "hear" kinesthetic feedback allows you to feel and know yourself again; so as you recognize your neurological "wiring" and get improved feedback from muscles and joints, the gap between what you *think* you do and what you *actually* do decreases. Parts of the body which have partially or completely ceased to respond to voluntary control then become available for use, and instead of using crude, large-scale movements, you become capable of many more distinctions. In *The Centered Skier*, Denise McCluggage describes this as "breaking up chunks of habitual movement as a gardener breaks up clods of earth with a hoe." It gives you much more finesse, a catlike economy of movement and effort. The sensations produced by good functioning are pleasurable in themselves, so when the kinesthetic sense and nervous system are given the chance of experiencing more pleasurable states they begin to choose them, and to protest at deviations from this new norm. A well-aligned body moves with ease and grace, it is well lubricated and efficient: it looks good, it feels good, and it lasts much longer.

It was through riding that I gradually realized how numbed my physical sensation had been, and many of my pupils have echoed my words: "I feel as if I used to ride (and live) under an anesthetic!" Each of us can choose whether we make the best of a bad job, working around our kinesthetic limitations, or whether we develop the tools to do a good one. So being a natural rider does not mean doing what comes naturally. It means changing what you are doing, often in ways that initially feel very unnatural, until the body has regained its natural poise and sensitivity.

The process of learning is far more refined than most teaching techniques acknowledge, and all too often we see teachers and pupils practically doing battle. The teacher says, "Give up that bad habit!" The pupil says, "But it's home . . . you can't evict me!" The habit is the outward and visible sign of a whole system of interactions; grabbing at it is rather like grabbing at the free end of a knot and trying to pull it undone. Instead, you have to know how it is intertwined, so you can separate causes from symptoms, and begin with parts that are ready and able to change. The body's neurological wiring will only unravel itself in a certain time and in a certain order: one cannot tell or force a muscle to give up its tension—one has to lure it, and convince it that it is safe. In skillful performance the effort is matched exactly to the task, and no superfluous muscles are involved. But when they are, this is a sign that the body (in its own peculiar wisdom) is trying to make up for some other part which is not doing its job. These muscles know that their role is important, and they will not give up their (supposedly) excess tension until other muscles have been persuaded to take over. Once they do, all sorts of "bad habits" just melt away.

Another dimension of this problem concerns parts and wholes. The body works best when it organizes its various parts around an objective, so skillful riders simply pay attention to the result they want to achieve without worrying about the means to the end. This gives them an animal-like quickness and sureness—the ultimate in skillful performance. (Can you imagine, for instance, how well Bruce Davidson would fare if he rode around Badminton thinking about his knees, heels, hands, and so on?) In learning, you have to pay attention to the *means whereby* you do something, inhibiting your old reactions and substituting new ones, breaking up those "clods" of habitual movement. A left-brain, piece-by-piece approach can be to your advantage, as long as you recognize its limitations: if you pull the pieces out for inspection all you will be left with is a load of loose wires. Paying attention to individual body parts interferes with the coordinative functions of the brain, and leads to some rather stilted performances (to put it mildly). This has often been called "paralysis by analysis," and it is the fate of the centipede in the old rhyme:

> The centipede was happy, quite,
> Until the frog in fun
> Said, "Pray, which leg comes after which?"

>This set his mind in such a pitch,
>He lay distracted in a ditch,
>Figuring how to run.

Thus if you focus on parts you lose the whole, you lose the connectedness and the flow, and you never develop your right-brain sense of "fitting." But you can only solve the puzzle and undo the knot by starting somewhere; otherwise you struggle hopelessly because your body lacks the subtlety to give you the results you seek. So you have to move between the two, fitting wholes into parts and parts into wholes, because if you lose sight of one of them, you get hopelessly stuck.

Ultimately, the details of the coordination involved in riding are unknowable. The hip joint alone is surrounded by some twenty muscles, most of which also affect the back, the knee, or the belly. There is very little hope that I, or anyone else, will ever know exactly which muscles are responsible for which aspects of the rider's coordination (and even if I was right in my assessment that someone needed more tone in her abductor longus and less in her gluteus medius, I would not help much by telling her!). So instead of pursuing this line of research, it is more useful to rely on the right brain, which is continually telling muscles to tighten or relax, making adjustments according to conditions within the body, and according to sensory feedback which describes the feel of the horse's movement. Computations about timing, speed, and degree are made unconsciously by the automatic mechanisms of the brain, and only a tiny proportion of the total pool of messages which come from the body ever reach consciousness. In a state of higher arousal (the awareness mode rather than the panicking mode), more messages get through, which explains why attentiveness can avert many a potential crisis, and why it would not be safe to ride a cross-country course in the reverie which makes hacking so delightful. So however aware we may be, we can only touch the tip of the iceberg—and thank goodness, as dealing with all that consciously would be an impossible task!

There is an enormous gap, therefore, between what we are aware of and what "really" happens. When we attempt to describe our experiences in words there is yet another loss of detail, for our senses are far more subtle and refined than language. Our eyes, for instance, can recognize many more shades of blue than we will ever be able to name. But the more conscious we are of our surroundings, the richer our speech will be. The Eskimo language contains over seventy words for snow, basically because their survival is so intimately connected with snow, depending so much on their ability to perceive and communicate fine differences in it. Skiers, too, use a terminology which makes distinctions the average person would not notice. It is not that Eskimos and skiers have different sensory apparatus from the rest of us; they have simply been attentive, developing their sensory acuity and then adapting and extending their language, so that they can communicate accurately to each other.

Eskimos and skiers seem to have had little trouble reaching a consensus which allows them to describe the quality and texture of snow. But—in the English language anyway—distinctive states of being in riding seem, so far, to have defied labeling. In some European countries, where there is a much stronger tradition of dressage riding, riders describe the feel and quality of the horse's movement using a whole vocabulary which we do not have. In Great Britain and America, our terminology is vague and imprecise: the term "on the bit," for instance, means different things to different people, and it covers a multitude of sins. Often, a rider's longing to work her horse on the bit is so acute that wishful thinking wins the day, and it is no easy task to match what the horse feels like with what he looks like when he is *really* on the bit.

In the process of discovering what feels and looks "right" we are all struggling with:

1. What we think we do. (Our limited, and possibly distorted, kinesthetic perceptions, coupled with the feedback we have been given by teachers. These two are often at variance.)
2. What we actually do. (As far as the details are knowable. This often conflicts with our own perceptions, and sometimes with our teachers'!)
3. What we know we should do. (Our theoretical left-brain knowledge about riding, gathered from books and our teachers, often not 100 percent accurate.)
4. The corrections we think we ought to make, and try to put into

practice. (Again, popular misconceptions and inapplicable generalizations can send us barking up the wrong tree.)

5. The changes we actually need to make to bring our functioning into line with the most efficient classical way of riding—according to the ideals of whichever school we follow. (This requires us to expand our kinesthetic perceptions to perceive the body as it actually is. This increases our physical sensation, returns the body into our conscious control, and renders it a far more effective tool for riding.)

Dealing with our own unique kinesthetic difficulties is one problem, but perhaps a more difficult one is posed by the misconceptions, generalizations, and inaccuracies which send riders looking in the wrong direction for the answers. In riding there are few absolute rules which are true for everybody, and many confusions arise from the attempt to fit all riders into the same mold, without recognizing the uniqueness of each individual's problems. Most teachers talk in sweeping generalizations, making rules which are supposedly never violated. But the more we generalize from our experience, the more likely we are to produce statements which are wrong in certain circumstances. For instance, most riders know that they should push their heels down. I am not convinced that this is a useful direction to give to anyone (as pushing down on the stirrup tends to push the rider's backside up and out of the saddle), but when the rider has already pushed her leg forward and out of a shoulder-hip-heel alignment, pushing more is the last thing she needs to do. What is a useful correction for one rider can be completely wrong for another, and also completely wrong for the first at a different stage in her training. As she learns by trial and error and gropes her way toward her goal, the rider inevitably overcorrects, and sometimes even has to change tactics.

The contradictions and paradoxes which leave most riders hopelessly confused make sense when seen from the more detailed perspective of a body and how it works. Instead of talking in generalizations, we need to define the variables which are different for each individual. Then we can make a framework to fit each person, like a map on which we put crosses saying "You are here." Only then can we define the different adjustments which each individual needs to make if her body is to become an effective tool for riding, perceiving information, acting on it, and responding to the nuances of different horses and situations.

It is very easy to understand how these inaccuracies and generalizations arise. Since all riders make different adjustments to put their particular body into the optimum state for riding, they will all describe their experiences differently. Each of them is highly likely to make the assumption that everyone else is the same—and, of course, nobody is. Add to this the discrepancies between what both skilled and unskilled riders say they do (their left-brain knowledge) and what they *actually* do (their right-brain knowledge), and it is no wonder that we spend so much of our time wallowing in confusion.

All this may paint a rather gloomy picture, and it is certainly true that learning to ride is an extremely challenging, complex task. But I am optimistic because I have seen, time and time again, how easily people can let go of habits and limitations which have previously seemed insurmountable. What this requires is a new kind of teacher-pupil relationship, and a new understanding of the process of change. Instead of trying to weed out bad habits in their pupils, teachers need to discover much more about the body and how it works, so that they can recognize underlying patterns and distinguish causes from symptoms. Pupils, for their part, learn far better when they become willing to experiment, casting off their feelings of "rightness" instead of staying with the safe and familiar, and thinking, But surely she can't mean *that*. Yes, change does feel peculiar, weird, sometimes even unpleasant, and instead of just offering eviction orders, teachers will benefit enormously by using more subtle means to lure their pupils away from home. To be effective, the learning process requires the active participation of both parties; instead of being the one who shouts and the one who listens (or does not), teacher and pupil then work together, without judgment, pooling their resources to unsnarl the wires and solve a very fascinating puzzle.

Let me give you an example from my own learning. Last summer I sometimes rode a very big German mare, who had extremely powerful and extravagant paces. This, coupled with her temperament, meant that I found her extremely difficult, and although at times she produced magnificent work, it was not without struggle. There were several occasions—as I was struggling—when I had a very new feeling in my back. It was seemingly the result of my inability to sit her well, yet I had a hunch that it might somehow be more correct. It was as if I had let the feel of her movement go right up my spine. Since I had absolutely no idea what had happened (and I could not produce the same feeling of my own volition), I simply filed it away for future reference. Earlier this year I went away to train for a while, and every day I worked on the lunge. The person helping me was continually saying, "Your seat's good, it's well in place. But something isn't quite right. It's as if you're pushing too hard." Expecting the push to come from my pelvis or lower back I kept scanning them in my mind, searching for where it might be—but I had no success. Then, on my last day a miracle happened (do not ask me how or why it chose that time). I suddenly let go of a tension in my upper back, just between my shoulder blades, and there was the same feeling I had had in the summer. "That's right!" said my teacher, and I surprised her by insisting that I practice both the new feeling *and* the old one, moving between the two so that I could learn more about them, and produce each one at will. Then it was time to come home.

After that, the snow fell and the ground froze. Because I have no access to an indoor arena I spent my time writing rather than riding, but I was using mental rehearsal (which you will learn about later) to help ingrain the new feeling. Then, a few nights later, the strangest thing happened. I lay in bed on my stomach—something I normally do not do. After a while I realized that I was in a profound state of relaxation, more relaxed than I usually get, and the new feeling was centered in my upper back. A few experiments showed me where the old familiar tension was—of course, it was the same feeling that I had released in my riding. I realized that it was a part of my normal stance, something I have taken with me when I sit, walk, ride—and lie in bed. Now I do not need it any more; it is superfluous. I now understand why I have often experienced some aching there at times when I have been particularly stressed (for instance, in driving long distances). Now I have the choice to let go of it—at least sometimes—and no doubt this will gradually get easier. I love the new light and relaxed feeling it gives me, especially when I am lying in bed, and I cannot wait to get back on a horse again.

This is typical of the way that change happens (for me anyway), and viewing your riding in the light of your normal posture and movement can lead to some profound discoveries. A useful by-product is that I now have more information about how the body works and some ideas about how I could help riders with a similar problem. But of course I cannot make the change for them. I can choose my timing, point out a direction, give them clear feedback, and involve their perceptions . . . but ultimately, *they* have to leave home.

This kind of understanding is a long way from the kind of generalizations we frequently use. Relaxation and tension are often assumed to have an on-off relationship (you are either relaxed or tense), but in fact there is a continuum between the two, in which each individual muscle can have varying degrees of tone. Inactivity (for instance, being immobilized in a cast) causes muscles to lose tone, and as they become more flaccid, they become relatively unable to act. This will inevitably lead to compensatory tension elsewhere, and in parts of the body which are tightly held the muscles eventually become locked into a state of extreme contraction. It is then impossible to separate one from another, so they react as one mass. It is often assumed that a horse and rider should be completely relaxed, but in fact it takes a certain amount of tone in the muscles to hold the body upright, so "completely relaxed" means "lying flat out." It takes even more tone to run, jump, or stabilize the body on top of a moving horse, and for every task there is an optimum amount of effort, which uses the minimum number of muscles to the maximum advantage, doing the job in the simplest way. With too little tone, the body loses stability and control; with too much it wastes energy and may even work against itself. In riding, as in everything, there are both good and useless tensions: some things must be allowed to happen (through relaxation), and others must be made to happen (through muscular work). We get into trouble when we try to "make" things which have to be allowed, or try to "allow" things which have to be made.

I had an example of this when I was training recently. The

person lungeing me kept saying, "Your leg isn't long enough, relax it more." So I kept searching for ways to let it drop—to no avail. Then I found a way of making it lengthen, which felt to me like something I had to *do,* a precise muscular effort just in the angle where the outside of my thigh came into my body. "Well done!" she said, "You relaxed your leg!" Throwing out tension altogether is like throwing out the baby with the bathwater, and it has some disastrous consequences. Without it the rider cannot support her own body weight, and it weighs heavy on the horse (just as it weighs heavy on you when he leaves you standing with a hoof pick in one hand and the weight of his whole hind leg in the other!). Moreover, the rider slides, like the proverbial sack of potatoes, into whatever position the saddle and gravity arrange for her. Only when she carries herself on top will she persuade the horse to carry himself underneath her, so that instead of dragging his limbs along the ground, he finds a catlike poise, spring, and efficiency. Despite all this power underneath them, the most skillful riders sit extremely still; they have the tonal quality of a hunk of raw meat or putty which has been glued onto the saddle. Many of the riders I meet lack this stillness and body control because they have insufficient tone in their working muscles, and when they assume that the answer to the problem lies in more *relaxation,* they put themselves into an even more difficult position. It is as relevant to say that the horse and rider should be relaxed as it is to say that a ballet dancer or gymnast should be relaxed. It is true in the sense that unnecessary tension will hamper their concentration and coordination, but it is not true in the sense that their posture and precise body control are dependent on a certain (optimum) tension in the working muscles.

Many riders are told that they are stiff. If my experience is anything to go by, this can mean a life sentence, a prophecy of doom. Like many others, I assumed that the cure (if indeed there was one) might lie in hours and hours of sitting trot without stirrups; that somehow it might be possible to wear away the stiffness by attrition. Most riders are still stiff at the end of their lessons, using the same jarring, inefficient coordination they were using at the beginning—because practice makes perfect not what you *think* you are practicing, nor what you *should* be practicing, but what you are actually practicing! Practice turns out to be a wonderful way of ingraining your bad habits even more. Often, as riders do this, their friends and teachers look on, seeing and accepting their idiosyncrasies as an inevitable part of them—the silhouette which is so distinctly theirs. The most exciting part of my work is seeing this change, seeing ugly ducklings turn into swans, released from their restrictions by a new movement pattern—the breakthrough which changes their silhouette instantaneously (not by attrition), just as mine changed on the lunge that day.

Most riders and teachers assume that the primary cause of stiffness is too much tension in the pelvic region; but I have found that this is rarely so, and calls to "Relax!" are certainly not effective. Instead, the problem is more often too much *flaccidity*, and it is interesting to note that some of the most skillful riders have unusually high muscle tone in the pelvic region. But flaccidity inevitably provokes compensations, leading to stiff shoulders and arms which react as one mass, and/or legs which cling onto the saddle. Think of it this way: the major shock-absorbing joints of the body are the hip joints, which lie lower down than the point of your hip and slightly higher up than the projecting bone you can feel on the outside of your thigh. The weight of your upper body passes down the back of your spine, which at the level of your sacrum (the lower back) fuses with your pelvis. This means that your weight passes down through your pelvis to its lowest point—the two seat bones. Meanwhile the upthrust from the ground and the horse's movement passes up the front of the thigh bone and thus into the hip joint itself. So if your hip joint lies on the same horizontal level as your seat bones, which it might if your back were very hollow (try experimenting with this idea as you sit in a chair), the upthrust would meet the downthrust, and clunk . . . there would be no give. But if your hip joint lies *above* your seat bones there is the possibility of some leeway, and you can absorb the horse's movement. Since the hip joint is so hard to feel and locate, I suggest to riders that they think of bringing their seat bones toward the underneath of their pubic bone. This requires some considerable muscular effort, which changes the whole orientation of their back and pelvis, bringing them toward the front of the saddle and holding them there. Some other changes in the pelvic region make this

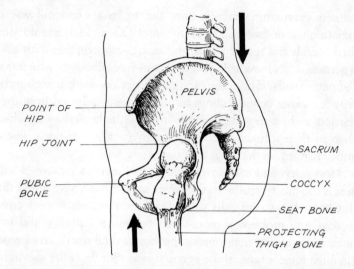

1. The downthrust of your weight passes through the spine and pelvis to the two seat bones, while the upthrust from the ground and the horse's movement passes up the front of the thigh bone into the hip joint.

even easier (they are explained in the dismounted exercises of the next chapter), and this muscular reorganization frees the rest of the body from its need to compensate.

I have seen an enormous number of riders unstiffen themselves with remarkable ease. Like everything else, riding is relatively simple once you know how to do it; it is finding out how that takes the time, and this can be a relative nightmare. (How I envy the youngsters I teach, who can start out doing it right!) Like any new movement pattern, this pelvic change takes time and attention to ingrain, and it will break down under stress and fatigue, so it is important not to overdo it. But careful work will soon make it feel "right" and normal, increasing its ease. Stiff riders usually hollow their backs, locking their hip joints, while supple ones release them. So, in riding terms, suppleness relates not to the ability to wrap your feet round your ears—you do not have to be particularly flexible to ride—but to your ability to provide adequate shock absorption, staying with the horse whatever he might do underneath you. As rider and horse become more supple, the ease, power, and range of their movement increase, and become more *durable;* so the rider is able to keep her seat on more impulsive gaits, and the horse is progressively able to hold his good carriage as he moves toward collection, extension, and more pronounced bends.

This whole discussion has hinted at another area of confusion, which concerns strength and power. The strength of a muscle is related to the amount of weight it can support when contracted, but power is the ability to *use* strength, and this requires the cooperation of muscles which pull or relax so that movement can take place. Most riders assume that more strength (i.e., more contracted muscles) will make them more powerful; but their effort inevitably involves parts of the body which do not need to be involved, so in fact, their coordination is hampered, and their power and efficiency are *reduced.* At best, much of their effort is wasted, and at worse, they work against themselves and provoke the horse into battle.

Assuming that more is bound to be better is really a case of overkill—using a sledgehammer to crack a nut. Horses are so huge and strong that it is tempting to believe that sledgehammers must be appropriate, but when riding degenerates into a battle of strength, the horse most certainly has the advantage. Taking up a strong contact and booting the horse in the ribs tends to produce equally crude reprisals, and it certainly is not an effective way of bringing him onto the bit. In contrast, he becomes malleable when the rider becomes, in the words used by trainer Erik Herbermann in his book *The Dressage Formula,* "an inseparable part of the horse, in no way disturbing his body movements." When riders sort out the good from the useless tensions, and match the effort to the task, they are often amazed at how little effort is involved—and it is the specific, precise effort of holding their body in a certain alignment. ("What?" they say. "But I feel as if I'm not *doing* anything!") Effectively, this means that when you are in control of your body, your body will be in control of the horse, and you need never resort to bashing him about.

As riders become more skillful and discover the value of subtlety, their body use takes on a new quality, like that of the martial artist. The aim of the judo, karate, or aikido student is to utilize the power which is housed in the center of the body. Like the horse, the human being has her power source in her pelvis—deep in your belly (about an inch below your navel) lies your center of balance, energy, and control. It is not in the limbs, or in the head —even though it suits our egotistical left-brain view of life to think of the head as headquarters. All good athletes begin their movement from their center (whatever the detail of their particular skill), and you can distinguish them easily from the ones who block their power flow with muscular tensions, or who flail about with their limbs. The most efficient and beautiful movement has the magical quality of "effortless effort"; the athlete is "centered," "grounded." Her body, in the words of Denise McCluggage, is "receptive to any *possible* change, but not tensed by the expectation of any *particular* change." It is catlike, poised, and powerful... poetry in motion—just like our ideal for the horse. (One of my old teachers used to sit in rapture as he watched his cat climb in graceful slow motion up the stairs. "Ah," he used to say, "if only we could get the horses to move like that....") Powerful riders use their strength solely to keep the integrity of their body alignment, establishing it by generating sufficient tone in their working muscles; once they have done this, there is little more to do. This ultimate in bodily use is always coupled with the right-brain awareness mode, an attentive, relaxed, concentrated mind, so body and mind are united in a harmony which transcends the internal dialogue, and allows us the fullest expression of our inborn gifts.

3 Dismounted Work

Ever since I first began riding, I have been fascinated by the paradox that the riders who most easily get the horse going seem to be the ones who do the least! For years, I would watch good riders in utter amazement, wondering how they created so much impulsion, how they shaped the horse, and how they sat so still. But this paradox remained a mystery to me, and riding lessons seemed to shed very little light on it. In fact, when I finally began to understand, it was through a mixture of observation and experiment. I scrutinized the bodies of my teachers and my pupils; I asked them questions; and I rode myself, monitoring my own body until I could begin to match how I and other people felt with how we looked. Many of the answers, as I now see them, came from this process, and also from other sources outside the whole sphere of riding— mostly from movement and body awareness teachers, and from sports psychologists who have been doing similar work in other fields. They all taught me a tremendous amount about body-mind dynamics, and encouraged me to take my own insights seriously, even when they conflicted with the traditional dogma I had learned from riding teachers.

After I had thought about ways of adapting and applying this learning to riding, I realized that I could usefully teach riders the basics of muscular use and body-mind dynamics in dismounted sessions. These can take much of the strain out of learning (as well as minimizing the stress on your horse), and can help you to get the best out of the comparatively short time you spend in the saddle. Many of the problems of riding are best solved *away* from the horse, and the exercises in this book provide a baseline you can come back to when your mounted work is not going well. They may break some of the destructive cycles you can so easily get caught in, and they divide the skill of riding into learnable-sized hunks. They also spare you the trauma of trying to follow how-to instructions while you are actually riding; it is far easier in the comfort of your living room! Practically everyone who has done these exercises has reported that you can carry over many of the ideas into your riding, often with dramatic results. Besides offering specific guidelines on how to organize your muscles, these exercises also show the phenomenal way in which right-brain imagery affects the body: they illustrate the difference between *letting* something happen and *making* it happen. Perhaps most important is a gentle attitude toward yourself and learning, which allows you to start asking the right questions, and looking in the right place for the answers.

The first prerequisite for effective riding lies in finding the state of relaxed concentration—a calm but alert mind, and muscles which have just sufficient tone to hold the body in balanced equilibrium, without it sagging or being overly tense. The optimum tone needed to stabilize the body on top of a moving horse is actually far greater than that needed to sit in a chair; initially, though, we are going to use this more passive relaxation as a backdrop against which to train the mind. However reluctant you may feel, I encourage you actually to *do* these exercises rather than just reading about them (although you may need to read through each complete section before you begin doing the exercises it describes). To be effective, this chapter requires your active participation. Your left brain will tell you not to bother, that it is not worth the effort, and that it is far more important to keep reading and finish the chapter as soon as possible. If you listen to it, you will miss a lot.

These exercises can be done sitting in a straight-backed chair, or better still, kneeling astride a big floor cushion, which you can squash into a suitable shape. Failing this, a number of smaller cushions may do, or you can kneel with just a cushion or two between your backside and your calves. When you have settled yourself, close your eyes, and take some time to feel your body. Which parts feel comfortable, and which feel tense? Which parts can you not feel at all? Pay particular attention to your breathing: which parts of your body rise and fall with each breath? Does the air go right down into your belly, or is it mostly in your chest? Stretch yourself up as tall as you can, and feel how this affects your breathing. You will probably find that you now breathe only into your upper chest, because the way you have hollowed your back and pulled in your stomach creates a ring of tension, rather like a tight belt, which refuses to let the breath pass down into your belly. When you have experienced this, let yourself slump, so that your chest collapses and your head drops forward. Again, your breathing is very restricted, and only in your chest. Now experiment with moving very slowly between these two postures, and seek out the "middle place," where your back is almost straight, rather than hollowed or bowed, and where it offers support to your whole torso.

Your spine naturally curves forward at the small of your back (the lumbar region) and at your neck, and slightly backward on the level of your pelvis (the part of the spine known as the sacrum) and your rib cage (the thoracic area). When you slump, or stretch up, you exaggerate its curves, reducing the efficiency of your breathing, forcing the body out of alignment, and causing the stresses and compensations discussed in the last chapter. While it is impossible to eliminate these curves altogether, imagine your spine like a strong, stable column—perhaps like a broom handle, with some inset pieces of very firm rubber—which passes from your tailbone, up through your back and neck, into the back of your head. This should help you to drop your chin and lengthen the back of your neck—a place where many of us cramp up as we ride. F. M. Alexander, founder of the Alexander Technique,* believed that tension in the neck is reflected throughout the whole body, so it is a particularly important place to release. To help you, imagine someone pulling you gently upward by a handful of hair—or do it yourself —taking the hair from just behind the top of your head, but as you feel yourself lengthening, *resist the temptation to pull in your belly and hollow your back*. Instead, keep your waistline expanded (in true Humpty-Dumpty style), and as your ribs come up and away from

*Many riders have found it extremely useful to have Alexander lessons. For a list of qualified teachers, write to: N.A.S.T.A.T., P.O. Box 148026, Chicago, Illinois 60614-8026.

your hips, do not go beyond the point where your belly begins to draw in. Many people find this idea rather strange, as they feel that the only way to be an acceptably-shaped human being is to pull in their belly; but try it anyway. Paradoxically, even though you may feel squat and round in this position, you will look erect and elegant. The ring of tension caused by pulling in the belly is a very common misconception, and it explains the apparent inability of many riders to ride efficiently. Interestingly, I have never before seen drawing in the belly mentioned as a fault in British riding books—instead it is often advocated by teachers—but it *is* given special mention in the German manual *The Principles of Riding.* From my observation, it seems to be a much more common fault in Britain than elsewhere in Europe.

Let us come back now to your breathing. Sitting in this position may already have helped you to breathe more fully into your belly, and we need to encourage this tendency even more. If you can remember back to the days when you learned chemistry at school, you can probably recall the conical flasks which have a long narrow neck leading into a big, round base. Imagine one of these inside you, with the neck passing down through your rib cage, and the bulb beginning beneath your ribs and filling out your belly. Now breathe so that air flows down past your ribs into the container in your belly, and feel it fill out with each breath. You are now using your diaphragm as you inhale, and this gives you a far greater lung capacity than when you lift your chest and merely fill out the upper part of your ribs. The diaphragm is a very powerful muscle which forms the base of the lung cavity. When relaxed it curves upward like a mushroom, and each intake of breath pulls it down, creating a vacuum in the lungs which automatically draws in air—without any effort from you. As you exhale, it returns upward, pushing the air out. The movement you feel in your belly is not actually air, but the action of muscles which pull the diaphragm down. Nonetheless, the conical-flask analogy is a useful one, and you want to think of the movement in your belly as the originator of the gentle expansion which occurs in your rib cage whenever your lungs fill with air.

*German National Equestrian Federation, published in England by Theobold Books, 1985.

When you are riding, and stabilizing your body on a moving horse, you have to add one more idea, which gives you the optimum tone needed to sit in equilibrium. This is the mobilization of the very powerful muscles which lie beneath the diaphragm, within the abdominal cavity. Babies use them a lot as they first learn to roll over and sit up, but as we get older and become relatively so much stronger in our limbs, we tend to forget about them. However, they are really the main power source of the body, and we move our extremities much more efficiently when we begin any movement from here—with an awareness of our center. Place the palms of both hands beneath your bottom ribs, and spread your fingers out over your belly. Now bear down as if you want to defecate, and feel what happens beneath your hands. You should feel the muscles press out against your fingers, particularly under your ribs, and in a ring around the edge of your belly (more here than around your navel). Hold this posture for a while, so that the muscles press out even as you exhale. It feels like hard work (and shocks a lot of riders who are expecting to be completely relaxed),

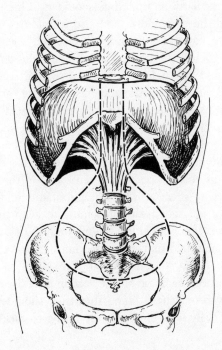

2. The rib cage has been cut away to expose the diaphragm and the imaginary conical flask in the abdominal cavity.

but it is actually far less of a strain while you are riding and in need of the greater oxygen supply which this gives you. In fact, you naturally organize your belly like this when you sweep, or do other tasks which require the power of the pelvis to be transmitted throughout the whole body.

When I showed this to a woman whose job involved lifting heavy weights, she immediately said, "Oh, this is how we were taught to lift things safely, so that we wouldn't hurt our backs." These muscles have a similar protective role in riding. Although riders always think solely about the back, I have found that the back and front of the body function as polarities—like north and south, you cannot have one without the other—and I have found that teaching riders about the *front* of their body has immediately helped them sort out difficulties in the *back* of it. Tension in one of these areas is always reflected in the other, and we will discover more later about how engaging the abdominal muscles organizes and protects the back, and has a profound effect on the horse too.

Return now to a more relaxed vertical posture, still breathing into the belly. The chances are that you are still holding some unnecessary tension, particularly around your shoulders. One of the best ways of relaxing the body more (and also learning more about it) is deliberately to increase the tension before you release it. So do this now, with each body part in turn, holding the tension for a count of ten, and then relaxing. Begin with your scalp and face; then your neck and jaw; your shoulders, rib cage, and upper arms; your lower arms and hands; your solar plexus and the small of your back; your belly; your buttocks and pelvic floor; your upper legs; and your lower legs and feet. As you tense each body part, notice what happens to your breathing, and feel it deepen and return to your belly as you release. If you tense any of these parts as you ride, it is going to affect your breathing too, and monitoring your breathing is a very good way of helping to keep the body free of excess tension. (Do not belittle the importance of this simple exercise: one woman found that she tensed her hands every time she tensed any other part. Another, who did it sitting on a chair, discovered that her heels came up off the floor in response to any other tension. Many people have found that their shoulders join in indiscriminately. Why wait until you are riding to tackle these problems? You could do it on the train, at the office, or while washing the dishes. The possibilities are endless!)

When they have done this exercise, most people find that they feel comfortably relaxed, yet solidly stable. Keeping your breathing and awareness focused in the center of the body gives you the natural poise and strength of a martial artist, and this makes you far more difficult to knock off balance. Once you have attained this aspect of relaxed concentration, it is easier to turn your attention to the mind, ridding it of all extraneous thoughts—the monkey-like chatter which takes your concentration away from each present moment. Begin by focusing your attention on your breathing, feeling the rise and fall of your belly, and each time you find your head filling up with thoughts, let them flow away from you—as if down a river—and return to the sensation of the breath. Then begin counting as you exhale, and each time you reach ten, begin again at one and continue for as long as you want. This is a very good exercise in relaxed alertness, because if you get too carried away, you will "come to" again as you find yourself counting twenty-five, twenty-six... etc. The way you have to monitor yourself here parallels the attentiveness you need while riding.

After a while, stop counting and open your eyes. But instead of focusing them on a specific point, use your *peripheral vision*, so that you take in as much as possible of your potential field of view. (If you are not clear about the difference, interchange the two different ways of looking until you are; you should find that using your peripheral vision will allow you to see more than 180 degrees.) The way you are wired neurologically means that when you focus your eyes on a specific object, it is practically impossible for you to stay in touch with your body sensation... and this makes riding with any finesse impossible. Many riders continually check on their horse's head position by looking intently at his ears, and as soon as they do this, they become unaware not only of other riders, but also of their own kinesthetic sensation. Like the ring of tension, this is one of the most pervading and damaging stances. So, next time you ride, take some of these ideas with you: arrange your spine in the "middle place," breathe into your belly, engage your abdominal muscles by bearing down, and use your peripheral vision. Experiment with these at walk on a long rein, because they are the

foundations you will use when you become more actively involved
in shaping the horse.

The next set of exercises is designed to help you find the more
active posture which draws your body into the alignment that has
such a magical effect on the horse's carriage. Most riders experience difficulty because either they can get their seat into the right
place, in which case their leg rides up, or they can get their leg
into the right place, in which case their back hollows and their
seat slips back. Placing the seat and the leg both at the same time
often seems impossible, but once you have discovered how to do it,
you have solved the most perplexing riddle of riding. I call these
exercises "specific muscles exercises," because they help you learn
how to "press the button" in your brain which activates a particular
muscle. They are intended to develop new neurological pathways,
rather than to develop your muscular strength and endurance (although they can be used for that too). If you have a significant
layer of fat, do not be put off when I ask you to feel for a particular
muscle with your hand; I have yet to meet anyone who has not
been able to find the underlying muscles, although it may initially
take some perseverance.

By way of an introduction, lie on your side on the floor, resting
your head on your arm, with your hip and knee joints at angles
similar to the ones you would have if you were riding. Then, check
whether your back is straight, and confirm your feeling by using
your hand to feel if there is a hollow in the small of your back.
Imagine your spine like a broom handle again, and lie for a while
in this alignment. Now, aim your buttocks and seat bones slightly
down toward your feet—which is the equivalent (if we rotated you
90 degrees) of pushing your seat down into the saddle. What happens to your knees? You will find that they bend more, and come
up slightly, and your knee and hip joints close more. These work as
reciprocal joints, in other words, they both like to have the same
angle, and normally we stand with them both open at 180 degrees,
and sit with them both closed at 90 degrees. In riding they like to
show the same angle too, so as soon as you push your seat bones
down, your knees will come *up*. Now, reverse the procedure: lie on
your side again as before, and draw your seat bones slightly forward
and up, into your buttocks. (You might like to imagine each seat

bone being pulled by a piece of string which passes through your belly.) Notice that your seat bones are drawn forward slightly, while your hip and knee angles open slightly, so if you were riding, your seat would be drawn forward in the saddle at the same time as your knee would descend. This is an alien concept to people who have grown up with the idea of pushing down into the saddle, but in my experience this pushing leads to all sorts of problems (imagine the poor horse's back), and drawing your seat bones into your buttocks gives you, surprisingly, a firmer, stiller seat.

Repeat the exercise with the fingers of your free hand placed firmly on your upper seat bone, and feel for a hard pad of muscle which moves in toward the bone as you move it forward. (You may have to contract it strongly and press in hard before you feel it.) This is your hamstring muscle, which runs down the back of your thigh, and it is a riding muscle which works at high tone. As it contracts like this, it provides the hard pad of muscle which you sit on, and which many riders mistake for the seat bone itself. As you repeat this movement, notice that it makes you feel as if you are drawing your seat bones closer together. This is, in fact, an anatomical impossibility; you are simply feeling changes in the use of your muscles. Nonetheless, it is a very useful image. Common sense—and popular theories about riding—suggest that you gain more stability by drawing your seat bones as far apart as possible. In practice, I have found that this is not so. Meanwhile, test the two ideas for yourself: change your way of lying so that you keep your

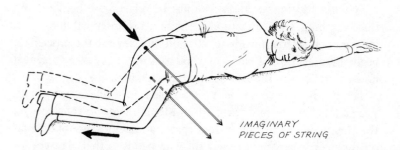

IMAGINARY
PIECES OF STRING

3. The hip and the knee are reciprocal joints, so that as you draw your pelvis forward your knee will descend.

knees together, and widen your seat bones and buttocks as much as possible. As you do this, you will find that your back hollows, and that your seat bones point backward rather than forward. This mirrors the way that many people ride, and by hanging on with their thighs they actually lose stability in their seat.

Change position now, and lie flat on the floor on your back. Take some time to close your eyes, breathe into your belly, and feel your body. Which parts of it touch the floor? If you could trace the edges of the areas of contact, what shapes would they make? How much of your back, your thighs, and your calves touch the floor? How far off the floor do you imagine the small of your back to be? Gradually slide the soles of your feet up toward your buttocks until they rest comfortably on the floor, with your knees and feet about fifteen inches apart, and your knees pointing toward the ceiling. How does this affect the small of your back? Slide your feet up and down several times, feeling for changes in your back. With your knees bent, can you arrange your pelvis so that the whole of your back makes a clear contact with the floor? You have now brought yourself into the position of having your back straight, which as we have said before, is the optimum position for sitting in equilibrium. Spread your hands over your belly as you did earlier, and re-create the feeling of bearing down. How does this affect the contact your back makes with the floor? You should find that the area of the small of your back presses more firmly into the floor; in horse parlance, this is known as "using your back." Lie like this for a while, and breathe into your belly. You will probably feel this position as quite stressful, and you are right—your body is doing far more muscular work than it does if you just lie relaxed on the floor, and the breathing feels unnatural because it is intended for much greater effort. After a while relax again, and reverse the procedure: begin by pressing the small of your back into the floor, and feel how this reflects in the muscles of your abdomen.

For the next exercise, lie on your back in a relaxed way, with your knees bent toward the ceiling. Mentally, locate your coccyx, the tiny bone at the base of your spine, and get a sense of how far off the floor it is. Then, slowly tilt your pelvis so that your coccyx lifts off another inch. What happens to the contact your back makes with the floor? Repeat this movement several times, and feel how rotating your pelvis also makes you reach into your knees, moving them slightly away from you. Basically, this is the same exercise as the one you did lying on your side, only now you can feel how rotating your pelvis also brings your back into clearer contact with the floor. Rest again, and then repeat the movement, adding in the feeling of bearing down: you should feel that this presses the small of your back even more clearly into the floor. Together these coordinations give you a very clear and powerful way of using your back. To complete the exercise, place the middle finger of each hand onto your seat bones, and do the same movement, feeling for an exaggerated contraction of your hamstrings.

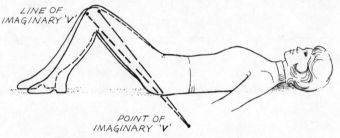

LINE OF IMAGINARY 'V'

POINT OF IMAGINARY 'V'

4. As you rotate your rib cage and push into your knees, the small of your back presses more firmly into the floor.

We now need to look more closely at the muscles forming the front of the thigh. Lying on your back again, lift one knee right up toward your chest (but do not strain to do it). Now, press your thumb deep into the angle between the front of your thigh and your body, and gradually lower your foot back down toward the floor. At some stage, you should feel a tendon (rather like a piece of taut rope) press out into your thumb. Lift your knee slowly up and down several times, feeling for this tendon, which serves the function of attaching the muscle bulk of the front of your thigh into the projecting bone of your pelvis. (Actually, there are two tendons lying quite close together here, and if you poke around you may be able to distinguish them, and feel their points of insertion into your pelvis.) Lower your foot to the ground again now, and feel whether you can keep the tendons sticking out against your thumb even as your foot reaches the floor. Practice until you can stick the tendons out against your thumb at will, without having to lift your leg. Notice how this moves the muscle bulk of your thigh from the outside toward the center, making the thigh more triangular in shape. As a finale, begin from your resting position, isolate the tendons at the front of the thigh, and, keeping them in place, rotate your pelvis slightly to bring your coccyx up off the floor. Feel your knees reach away, your hamstrings contract, and the small of your back press into the floor. Then bear down and keep breathing!

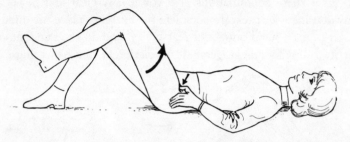

5.   Feeling for the tendons which lie in the front angle between the leg and the body.

After doing these exercises, we need to look at some theory about how the muscles work. In normal movement, the muscles at the front of the thigh and those at the back form a partnership. As the front muscles contract to pull the knee forward and up, the hamstring muscles relax and lengthen to allow it maximum free movement. As the knee moves back and down, the muscles reverse roles, contracting at the back of the limb, and relaxing at the front. Notice that the pelvis, to which all these muscles are attached, is the fixed point, while the knee is the moving point: the knee is so much lighter and more mobile than the pelvis that it is easiest for the muscles to work this way. If the knee becomes the fixed point, however, they can be used to move the pelvis, as they do when you stand up from a chair.

In skillful riding, the muscular use in the thigh is slightly unusual. First, the knee is the fixed point, while the pelvis needs to be sufficiently movable to go with the movement of the horse. This in itself presents a problem, because it is far easier to move the knee toward the pelvis ("gripping up") than it is to pull the pelvis toward the knee ("sitting deep"). The knee is relatively mobile, and the pelvis is incredibly heavy, so of course all beginners will find themselves riding the "easy" way until they develop the strength and technique to do it the "difficult" way. Second, the leg and body only become stable when *both* the muscles at the front of the thigh *and* the muscles at the back of the thigh pull the front and back (respectively) of the pelvis toward the knee. Very little body movement is involved in riding, and the muscles mostly have the function of pulling on the joints to exert forces which stabilize the body and hold it in place. If the forces exerted by these opposing muscle groups were equal to each other, the body would be completely still, but when the force of one group slightly overcomes the force of the other, there is just sufficient movement to "go with" the horse. Kinesiologists call this "slow tension movement" and it is the basis of many skills in which steadiness and accuracy are required—ballet and gymnastics, for instance. It makes the body so stable that it can make not only tiny adjustments (the type you would use in threading a needle), but also large, quick changes in speed and direction. You use muscle contractions which do not result in movement whenever you push or pull against a heavy, immovable object; but in riding, as the horse moves under you, the forces you exert have the effect both of pulling you into a deep, stable position, and of encouraging the horse to rearrange his musculature, so that he changes shape underneath you. Sitting in this way makes the rider (who appears to be doing nothing) fantastically effective, although the effort of maintaining these forces is tremendously taxing—as you probably found when you were lying on the floor.

I believe that this explains why so few people ever get the hang of dressage riding. First, many riders push their seat bones so hard into the saddle that they become two pressure points, which cause the horse discomfort even through the padding of a saddle; and so, of course, he retaliates by hollowing his back. Second, it is far easier to stabilize yourself by inadvertently pulling on the rein than by mobilizing your thigh and pelvic muscles as you have just done in the floor exercises. Third, you automatically expect to relax the muscles at the back of the leg as you contract the ones at the front (which leads to the "armchair seat"), or to contract the ones at the back of the leg while you relax the ones at the front (which leads to the "fork seat"). Using both at the same time while holding the knee as the fixed point is something we rarely do, and it does not come easily: in fact it is such a surprising contortion, and so far away from "home," that few riders would ever dream of doing it!

Still greater stability and accuracy are gained when we introduce two more opposing muscle groups: the *adductors* of the thigh, which lie on the inside and pull the legs in together, and the *abductors*, which lie on the outside of the pelvis and the upper thigh, and which pull the legs apart. To feel these in practice, lie on your back on the floor, and take some time to settle yourself. Draw your feet up toward your buttocks as before, but this time cross one leg over the other, and put one hand so that it lies flat between your legs. Squeeze your hand between your legs, and you will feel the action of your adductor muscles. If you bring your hand right up to your crotch, you can feel the tendon which sticks out on each side as your muscles act, and which connects them into your pubic bone. Find out if you can keep each tendon sticking out as you return your foot to the floor; and then learn to stick them out at will.

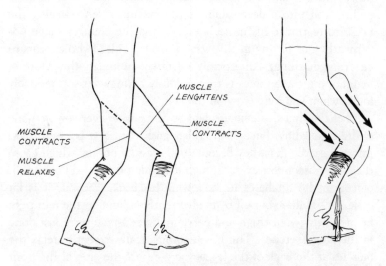

MUSCLE
LENGHTENS

MUSCLE
CONTRACTS

MUSCLE
CONTRACTS

MUSCLE
RELAXES

6.   The use of the thigh muscles in normal movement and in riding.

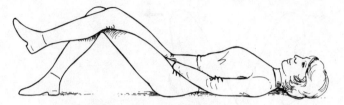

7.   Feeling for the adductor muscles of the thigh.

To feel your abductor muscles, lie on your back with your knees bent, and let them drop slightly outward. Then imagine that you would like your thigh bones, if they could (by magic) continue on past your hip joints, to meet at a point somewhere underneath you below the floorboards. Exaggerate this feeling and, as you do so, press your fingers into the muscles high at the outside of your thigh, and feel for the contraction here. You should also be able to feel the contraction of the muscles which lie just above your leg on the outside of your pelvis—abduction is a rather weak movement, and many people have rather flaccid muscles here, so you may have to press in deeply. You may also have noticed that your hamstrings have joined in, and that all these changes have again lifted your coccyx slightly off the floor, while pushing the small of your back even more firmly into it! As well as abducting the legs you have also been rotating them, and you will again find yourself feeling as if your seat bones have come slightly closer together (although this change, as we have already noted, is really a function of your muscles and not your seat bones).

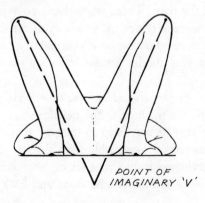

POINT OF
IMAGINARY 'V'

8a.   Finding the abductor muscles of the thigh. [The drawing shows the imaginary V shape which would be made by your thigh bones if they could continue, by magic, down through the floor.]

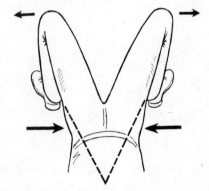

8b. The point of the imaginary V.

In riding, it is as if there is a critical width between the seat bones, which is slightly less than the width you would feel if you just left them to themselves. By making your thighs into a V shape like this, you draw your buttocks in closer together and open your legs. But riders often do the opposite: as they press their knees and thighs tightly into the saddle their buttocks spring apart, their backs hollow, and their seat bones point backward—as you found when you were lying on your side. As a result, their seat completely loses stability. The advantage of the correct V is that it provides another set of opposing muscle groups, which hold the body firmly in place and up to the front of the saddle, where the sitting space is narrower. (Indeed, without this narrowing of the pelvis, it is almost impossible to stay there.) It is as if the right side of the pelvis exerts a force toward the left, while the left side of the pelvis exerts a force toward the right. Then, when the force of one side slightly overcomes the force of the other, you have (as we said before) the possibility of minute adjustments in your balance, and this enables you to have a very subtle, precise influence on the horse's bend.

All that is left now is to activate the adductors and the abductors at the same time, and to add them on to the muscles you have used previously. As you do this, it may help to imagine that you want to make your thigh as narrow as possible from side to side; then rotate your pelvis slightly, reach into your knees, bear down, and exaggerate the use of your muscles at the front and back of your thigh. And there you have it: the contrast between a secure, effective seat, which is capable of fine adjustments, and one which is sloppy and out of balance. To get an even clearer idea of the difference between the two, sit astride a big floor cushion, and move from a normal posture to one in which you are pulled forward by all this muscular holding. The contrast in feel and muscular effort is immediately apparent, but only a trained eye would see it when *observing* a rider. The horse, however, would notice immediately.

The active seat is muscularly very hard work—although it feels far less stressful when you are actually riding. But even people who have had very little sensation in their pelvis report that they can feel much more when they draw their seat bones into place like this. It is a far cry from the relaxation most riders think they need, but when these muscles actually do their share of the work, there is no need for contortions in other parts of the body, and the rider can feel coordinated, graceful, effective, and even (as some riders would say) relaxed.

I want to move away now from locating and using specific muscle groups toward developing an overall feel for effective body use. These exercises are designed to help develop your kinesthetic sense, and your ability to use your imagination helpfully. It is important to realize that we all specialize in the way we use our senses: some people are highly visual, with a flair for color and design; others have a good ear for accents and music; while some are more aware of their body sensation—they may be good at dance and physical skills. Like the Eskimos, we can all train the senses in which we are not so specialized, but our natural inclinations affect the way that we imagine things. Most people imagine *visually*, by seeing pictures inside their head; some are not so good at this—their pictures are fuzzy or unstable, or they may not even have them at all. (People who imagine in pictures always think that everyone else does too, and those who do not are always shocked to discover that the rest of the world has access to a wealth of internal movies!) Those who are more specialized kinesthetically imagine by recalling the physical feelings which were evoked in them by an event, or a series of actions. To clarify the difference between the two, imagine yourself sitting comfortably on

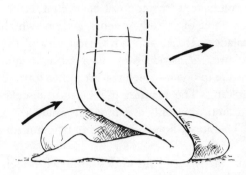

9. The change in posture which results from using the thigh, back, and belly muscles.

a bench at a fairground, watching yourself taking a ride on a roller coaster, seeing its structure and shape, and yourself sitting high up there. Then imagine actually *sitting in the car* of the roller coaster, holding on to the bar in front of you as you come up to the top of a rise and see that enormous drop. Notice the difference.

When you imagine something from the perspective of being inside your own body, you experience all the feelings of the event, and this is the most useful way to imagine yourself riding. If this does not come easily to you, and you tend to imagine yourself from the perspective of an outside observer, you need mentally to step inside your own body, so that you see the scene from inside your own eyes. (As you do this, pull the picture around you if necessary.) Then add in the feelings: so, as you imagine yourself riding, and can see the horse's neck and your hands holding the reins, can you feel your hands too? As you see your thigh resting against the saddle, can you feel the saddle too? Can you feel the movements of the horse's back underneath you? When you want to recall a situation vividly it helps to use all your senses, including also hearing and smell, but the primary one for us is the kinesthetic sense.

Here are some preparatory exercises. Raise your arms straight out in front of you, and then above your head, then lower them down. Now close your eyes, and do the same movement in your kinesthetic imagination, feeling the sensations you would feel if you were actually doing it. (Are you in fact doing this, or are you making a picture of yourself?) Keep experimenting with ways to step inside your body, and as the feelings become more full and clear, check them against some actual physical repetitions. Then try the same thing with jumping forward, lunging to the side, getting up from a chair, or any everyday movements. Now sit on the floor in a position you habitually use, and in your imagination create the sensations you expect to feel as you get up. Check these by doing it in practice. How accurate were you? Did you anticipate correctly how you would have to place your hands and feet, and so on? And what about all the changes in your weight? Was it more or less hard work than you expected? Again, move between your imagined movement sequence and your actual one, until your kinesthetic representation is full and accurate.

I hope that this last exercise showed you how inaccurate you can be when you make kinesthetic assumptions about how you do things. (One of my students actually fell over when she tried to put into practice the method which had worked in her imagination!) So if you have not paid much conscious attention to the way you ride, your kinesthetic recall could be equally inaccurate, and so could your fantasies about how you are one day going to produce the most fantastic half passes.

Being able to produce detailed, accurate kinesthetic representations of the feelings you experience as you ride can have a significant effect on your actual practical skill. The arm-swing exercise at the beginning of Chapter 1, a brainchild of the Israeli teacher Moshe Feldenkrais,* demonstrates this connection clearly. It may be helpful to repeat it now, making sure you are using your kinesthetic rather than your visual imagination. By concentrating more explicitly on the feelings of the movement, you may find that you can improve the result you get. How can this be? The answer is that the brain cannot distinguish between real and imagined performance. So, in imagined performance, it still sends tiny impulses along nerve pathways to the muscles, which contract almost imperceptibly. Neurological pathways are deepened and muscles are exercised in the same way as they are in actual performance, and they derive the same benefit—as your body has just shown with this increase in your range. One of the most famous pieces of research on this was done by the Australian psychologist Alan Richardson,

---

*Moshe Feldenkrais was a student of F. M. Alexander, who went on to develop his own "Awareness Through Movement" exercises. Some of these are available on cassette tape from The Feldenkrais Guild, P.O. Box 11145, San Francisco, CA 94101.

and it concerned performance at basketball free-throw shooting. He took three groups of people, chosen at random, and measured their performance at shooting. Then, over a period of twenty days, one group practiced for twenty minutes a day, one did not practice at all, and one spent twenty minutes a day imagining themselves shooting. At the end of this time their performance was measured again. The first group were found to have improved their scoring by 24 percent, the second group did not improve at all, and the third group, who had imagined shooting rather than actually doing it, improved by 23 percent.

Many other studies have shown very similar results, and mental practice is now used almost universally by athletes. In fact, the most successful ones have always done it anyway, but only now have sports psychologists realized that teaching the technique to less able performers could allow them to show some of the same talents. It has even been found that injured soccer players recover far faster if they use mental practice to exercise neurological pathways and muscles while they are laid off—and of course this has enormous implications for anyone who is sick or injured. It is a particularly helpful technique for riders, because it allows them to get the practice they need without running their horse (if they are lucky enough to have one) into the ground.

In an unsophisticated way, we all use mental practice. When you find yourself going over and over that awful refusal you had at the eighth fence, you are using it in a very damaging way, ingraining in your body the responses which led to this disaster. I often find myself doing this in dreams—at times with a clarity which has astounded me, and left me completely confused when I have finally woken up lying in bed! The detail you can experience in your mental performance is a good indication of the quality and quantity of right-brain feelages you have ingrained. Once there, these always benefit from further practice. Sometimes you can even ingrain new ones when you watch other athletes in action. It is well known that the standard of tennis played on public courts improves after television coverage of the Wimbledon tournament, simply because the players have watched skilled performers and then let their imaginations roam. Obviously, if you want to use this to your advantage, it pays to watch and imitate the best riders you can find!

Turning mental rehearsal into a far more sophisticated tool requires time and practice, just as it does to refine any skill. It is one of the best ways to prime the link between mind and body, because you improve your physical performance at the same time as you learn right-brain discipline, and train your mind to concentrate. Some exercises are best done at home, preferably in a quiet place which you can use at the same time each day, while others can actually be used during performance.

Begin by settling yourself comfortably, sitting with arms and legs uncrossed, and with support for your spine. Then take some time to relax, paying attention to your body and your breathing, until you dissolve any tension which could clog your body-mind communication. Choose a work session or competition which was particularly memorable for some reason, and mentally put yourself into that scene, remembering the weather, the time and place, other people who were there, and above all, yourself and your horse. Then replay the session. What are you most aware of, what is it that makes this time so special? Experience the scene as an observer looking, and also from inside your own body. How clearly can you feel yourself; which parts predominate and which are missing or numb? Take all the time you need to experience that time as vividly as you can, with all your senses, but stop before you reach the limits of your concentration and enjoyment. Usually two to five minutes is sufficient, and it is important not to turn what can be an immensely valuable and enjoyable exercise into a chore containing bad feelings which contaminate your actual performance.

In mental rehearsal, it is important to imagine yourself performing at a level of proficiency which you sometimes reach, and want to produce more consistently. It is not helpful to imagine that you are outstandingly brilliant, and to focus on goals you want to achieve, without paying attention to sensations you have as you achieve them. If you find that your rehearsals are vague or inconsistent, this is telling you that you do not yet have an ingrained way of performing that particular skill, and you need to go back to actual practice. You may even find that your replay skips bits here and there, or that you suddenly flip out of your body and have only a visual perspective. These gaps and inconsistencies are telling you what you *do not yet feel*; on the other hand, if you are more established in your riding, you may find that reviewing a session afterward can provide the missing link—the loss of balance, or the possible new coordination which, if you take it into your performance next time, can solve a problem that has been perplexing you.

In their book, *Sporting Body, Sporting Mind*, Christopher Connolly and John Syer give an excellent review of many possible uses and techniques for mental rehearsal, and I encourage you to investigate them further. When you have ridden well, do not miss the opportunity to replay short sequences, both in the moments immediately afterward and later, at home. When you are about to ride, particularly on a big occasion, do not miss the opportunity to prime yourself by previewing your performance. You can prepare yourself at home, and also in the moments before you begin a test, a jumping course, or an individual movement. As you come around the corner to position the horse for shoulder-in, preview it mentally (and make sure that what you are anticipating is your highest-quality work!). When you cannot afford enough riding lessons, when your horse is lame, or when you simply need more practice than he does, the answer lies in mental rehearsal.

This last section outlines some exercises I use to demonstrate the difference between effective and ineffective ways of using your strength. The first is about trying. When I use this in a dismounted workshop, I usually ask one of the participants to try to pick up a fairly large cushion. When she picks it up, I say, "That wasn't what I asked. I wanted you to *try* to pick it up." So she looks at me rather dubiously, and picks it up again. After several people have had a go, I usually have to demonstrate myself. So I place my feet on one end of the cushion, my hands on the other, and then heave with all my might—using a few grunts and groans for dramatic effect. Of course, however hard I pull, I cannot move it, but I do give a very convincing demonstration of *trying!* By definition, this includes an inbuilt force which works in direct opposition to the result you want to achieve, and the old dictum, If at first you don't succeed, try, try, try again, is to my mind bad advice. However much our society values trying, suffering, and using blood, sweat, and tears to achieve an aim, I am not convinced that this is the best way. Trying does not work because it involves mental strain

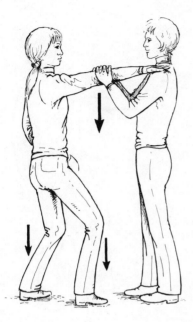

10. The stable body position for the aikido arm exercise.

and too many muscles; rather than trying harder in the face of failure, it is easier and more efficient to take this as feedback that your technique is not working—and to find another way.

This next exercise comes from the Japanese martial art aikido, and you need to do it with a partner, preferably someone of your own size. Stand at arm's length away from her, and rest your hand on her shoulder with the palm facing upward. Then, ask your partner to try to bend your arm, by clasping both hands together above your elbow and pushing down. Use all your strength to try to resist her, and (if she does not succeed fairly soon) keep this up for at least thirty seconds, or until you are exhausted.

Afterward, prepare yourself to repeat the exercise, but in a way which calls upon the power of right-brain imagery. Align yourself as before, but check that your knees are slightly bent, that your breath reaches into your belly, and that your feet have a clear, full contact with the floor. Imagine yourself as a tree, with roots extending down through your legs and feet into the floor, with the earth beneath. Then imagine a great source of energy in your belly, like a sun, which can radiate out through your whole body. Some

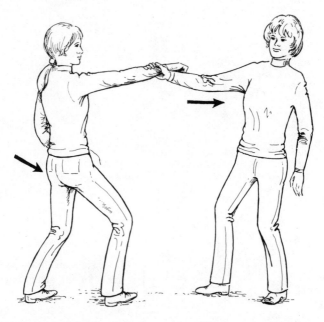

11. The stable body position which allows you to remain unmoved as your partner pushes or pulls. It is particularly important to stabilize the angle between your body and the leg which is farther back.

of these rays move out through your arm, and way beyond it, penetrating the walls of the room like a laser beam. You could also imagine this energy from your center as a powerful jet of water, rushing through a hose (your arm), and way into space. When you have a clear sense of these images, ask your partner to apply pressure to your arm again, beginning gradually. Instead of viewing the exercise as a battle of strength, treat it as an exercise in personal expansion: look beyond her, keep your knees bent, your hand open, and keep imagining the power which roots you to the earth, and rushes out from your center. As she begins to huff and puff, maintain your attitude of tranquillity, and imagine that your partner's efforts merely feed your current of strength.

How was your experience different with each of these attitudes? Change roles with your partner, and experience how it feels to be on the other side of the fence. If either of you have difficulty, you may need more time to align yourself with these images, and to summon your faith. This exercise shows that whatever we believe we can become, we do become, because (via our right-brain "programming") the body agrees with whatever is in our thoughts. As soon as you believe that your partner is bending your arm, she probably will bend it; but if you maintain your serenity, and your alignment with these images, she will find it considerably harder than she did before.

This exercise shows convincingly that more strength is not the same as more muscles: in fact it results from a physical and mental attitude of *expansion* rather than contraction. When we want to be strong, we tend to tense muscles indiscriminately, including, in this case, the ones which help your partner bend your elbow! Thus we become embroiled in all the self-defeating anguish that accompanies trying. We have to reassess our concept of a "strong" rider, and to realize that she gains her strength through using the minimum number of muscles to the maximum advantage, while magnifying their effect by programming the body with powerful right-brain images. This "attentive relaxation" gives far greater strength than forced resistance: it offers the serenity and power which lies at the core of my favorite paradox—the old Zen idea of effortless effort.

We now have one more exercise, which is the most directly analogous to riding. Again it is done with a partner. Stand with your feet about eighteen inches apart, and bend your knees so that your back is straight, and your backside as low as you can comfortably get it. Now rotate one foot outward 90 degrees, turn your shoulders to follow it, and raise the hand on that side to shoulder height, pointing it in the same direction as your foot. Make a fist out of your hand, and ask your partner to push or pull on it, to see if she can affect your posture or even force you off balance. To make the test more stringent, she can push or pull hard for a while, and then suddenly let go.

What happens? Most people find that their partner's pushes and pulls easily cause them to lose the alignment of their spine, so that they lean toward or away from her, and lose stability. If they manage to stay vertical, they usually do so by pushing or pulling back on their partner, and when she lets go, they are suddenly left floundering. Repeat the exercise again. This time pay attention to the way your feet contact the floor, to your breathing, and to your alignment. Lower your center as close to the ground as you comfortably can, and feel how this stabilizes you over your legs, weighting you so that you cannot be knocked over. Imagine yourself rooted like a tree, and powered with the energy of the sun. When your partner pushes and pulls, refuse to join in the battle: instead of pulling or pushing back against her, hold yourself rooted, stable and unmoved. When you do this successfully you will be unaffected even when she suddenly lets go. If she pulls so hard that you cannot maintain your posture, jump—this will keep the integrity of the body, and bring you closer to her so that you land in exactly the same alignment as before.

Your partner's attempts to push and pull you off balance are, for me, directly analogous to the way the horse treats you when you ride. Most often, we experience the horse pulling, but he can also, effectively, push you backward as well. This exercise shows the truth of the old adage, It takes two to pull, and perhaps it gives you an inkling of the way out of this trap. Good riders center themselves so effectively that the horse cannot disturb their alignment, and this allows them to become the *cause* of whatever happens in the rider-horse interaction, rather than being reactive—the victim of the horse's maneuvers. Of course, they only achieve this through learning how to maintain themselves in a stable posture (the one you learned in the floor exercises), while using the resilient strength that comes not from muscle contraction, but from the phenomenal power of right-brain imagery. My experience is that beginners can get the idea of this surprisingly quickly, but it then takes time for them to gain the faith and resilience that leaves them undisturbed by the varying rigors of sitting trot, canter, circles, lateral work, fast horses, slow horses, difficult horses, and so on. Once they are perfectly aligned and undisturbable, they gain the power and finesse of a master.

4 The Novice

As a practiced rider with many years of experience behind me, I now find it quite difficult to remember how I felt when I first ventured onto the back of a horse. In essence, though, we all experience a similar sense of disorientation whenever we first dabble with a new medium. On a horse, on skis, roller skates, a bicycle, or in a car, the rules which apply when you stand on your feet (and are taken for granted) do not apply anymore, and most people find that it is no easy matter to regain the fine body control which will enable them to be masters of a completely new medium.

Before I ever took to the saddle, my first encounter with a pony proved an unnerving experience, and made my prior expectations seem naive. As a young child I was in love with my picture-book ponies, and I dearly wanted to meet one in the flesh. So one day, at a friend's party, I climbed from her garden into a field where some ponies were grazing. I found some windfall apples, and followed the directions I had read in a book: with an apple placed on the palm of my hand I felt ready to face whichever one should come. The pony who approached me was actually quite small, but the closer he came, the bigger he appeared... until I felt so intimidated that I threw the apple at him and ran!

Even at the most primitive level, being faced with the unknown evokes the "fight or flight" reflex. But once on the horse's back, the would-be rider cannot do either; so, caught between the two, she freezes. Few riders go so far as to freeze completely, but all of them follow what sports psychologists believe to be a universal principle: When in doubt, tighten. The rider who doubts her ability (quite justifiably, as she has no right-brain information to tell her how to respond effectively to horses) is left at the mercy of survival mechanisms as old as man himself, and which are housed in the lower brain centers. As an involuntary reflex, she adopts at least some aspects of the "fetal crouch": she curls up her body to protect her chest and belly, which, as her ape-ancestors knew, are her most vulnerable parts. Her backside slips back, her legs draw up, and she tips forward. Her legs cling onto the saddle, clasping inward rather like a clothespin, and she clutches at the reins for security. Her toes clench up as well (a useful reflex for apes who dwelt in trees), and she also draws in her abdomen, hunching her shoulders and restricting her breathing so much that her sensation is numbed. Unfortunately, the instinctive logic that tells her that this is the safest way to be does not apply on horses. While she is using her arms and legs to cling on for dear life, she is actually fighting the horse's movement, and she interferes so much with his natural way of being that he too can take fright.

As we all know, these reflexes are far less prevalent in children than adults, and people vary enormously in their susceptibility to them. For the experienced, confident rider, the feel of a horse moving sensibly underneath her has become an accepted norm, and in an emergency her body reacts to bring her back to the normal feel. But the novice, who has no ingrained feeling of a norm, and no faith in her ability to cope, has nothing to return to—so her involuntary reflexes take over. It is this lack of faith that distinguishes adults from children, and in nervous riders it persists way beyond the stage when it is appropriate. I regularly see experienced riders who still regard a jog or a shy as a cause for alarm; this immediately arouses their involuntary reflexes, so the moment anything untoward happens, there they are, climbing up the horse's neck and clutching at the reins. I also meet riders who do not consciously feel frightened (or maybe they just will not admit to it), but their body behaves *as if* they are. Often they hold a remnant of the fetal crouch even in their unstressed riding: their norm includes a slightly tensed belly, restricted breathing, arms which pull back, and legs which grip up. Their adaptation to the horse's movement has not been complete, and their reluctance to go with him expresses itself primarily in the orientation of their pelvis and the contraction of their belly. Often these riders do not

12. The fetal crouch.

feel willing to surrender the rein completely; they prefer to ride "with the hand brake permanently on"—and sometimes they do not even realize that this is what they are doing. This body positioning actually gives them so little security and effectiveness that they have every reason for their lack of faith, and personally I have a lot of respect and sympathy for nervous riders (having been one myself). I believe that they are not as stupid as riding teachers tend to think—instead they are clearly giving the message, "My body isn't in the right place, and because of that I don't feel safe." Time and time again, I have found that nervous riders do begin to feel secure once they feel that *they* are the cause of whatever happens with the horse. Often, though, they do not discover an alternative to the vicious circle in which they are trapped—because they do not feel safe they adopt the fetal crouch, and because they adopt the fetal crouch they do not feel safe.

A little thought will show you that the most efficient responses (based on the alignment and tone which we built up using the floor exercises) are practically the complete opposite of the rider's involuntary reflexes (based on brute force, ignorance, and the fetal crouch). We can truthfully say that *everything the untrained rider instinctively wants to do while riding is wrong, inducing in the horse a response directly opposed to the one for which she was hoping.* Even without the stress which provokes the fetal crouch, the rider always finds it far more natural and easy to pull her hand back toward her belly than to advance the huge bulk of her pelvis toward her hand.

This, as you will discover later, is a vital distinction, and it is one of the few universal rules of riding that whenever the rider's seat cannot achieve an aim—be it control or the nuances of shaping a horse—her hand will inevitably step in and take over. This happens without her choosing it; in fact, it happens automatically whenever she *does not* choose the other way, and as a result, she completely loses the subtlety and precision which enable her to respond to the nuances of a particular situation. Although it is often said that one of the primary difficulties of riding is that the horse's reflexes are so much faster than those of man, I think the problem lies not so much in any inherent time difference, but in the fact that so few people train their learned responses to be 100 percent reliable. Only then do they become both causal and quick; the untrained rider who is reactive *necessarily* lags behind the horse, and then, nine times out of ten, she responds with her untrained, involuntary reflexes, which (of course) are wrong.

The amount of difficulty that a rider has in learning is determined to a large extent by her initial experiences. When these are particularly stressful her resulting high arousal can plummet her into the panicking mode, and reduce her ability to inhibit her involuntary reflexes. It makes no difference whether the threat to safety is real or imagined, or whether it is generated by an excessive desire to perform well: either way, it limits her conscious choice about how she will respond, and in the extreme she becomes the victim of "one-trial learning." Like someone who is frightened of spiders, she reacts to every situation in the same way; she loses the ability to improvise, and uses one fixed and ineffective response as her answer to every problem posed by the horse. In practice, it is more likely that she will ingrain a rather small repertoire of pretty ineffective responses, all based on elements of the fetal crouch; the real problem, though, is that *she does not even perceive the existence of alternatives.* She thereby loses so much flexibility that she becomes trapped within the confines of bad habits which (as her teachers will soon tell her) make her rigid, insensitive, and crude.

In the science of cybernetics, there is a law called "the law of requisite variety," which states that in any system of human beings or machines, the element in that system with the widest range of variability will be the controlling element. If this also applies to the horse-rider system, and I think it does, then whichever of them has the greatest flexibility in behavior will have the ultimate control. Horses are uncanny in their ability to assess a rider almost instantaneously, and when they have the edge on "requisite variety" they immediately take the upper hand and treat her like an idiot. You can often see beginners seething with frustration, humiliation, rage, and despair, as they kick more and they pull more, while the horse takes not the slightest notice. More advanced riders can be made to feel equally powerless by a horse they cannot bring onto the bit, or flex to one side. The problem in both cases (and with all bad habits) is that the rider is limited to doing *more of the same*. The answer, if you want to get a different response from the horse, lies in having the versatility to *do something different yourself*.

Any rider who is trapped within elements of the fetal crouch reflex (and that is practically every rider who is not yet a master) only finds a way out of her plight when her teacher takes seriously the real limitations imposed by her lack of choice. What she needs is a complete "rewiring," in which the old, habitual neurological pathways are replaced by new, more sophisticated ones. When I go through this process with a rider, I begin by offering her some new "wires," which bring her body closer to the alignment we built up using the floor exercises. This immediately frees other parts from their need to compensate, and it simplifies the more subtle aspects of unraveling the old tangled wires. The first thing I ask is, "Does it feel as if the horse is taking you, or as if you are taking him?" Strange as this question may sound, most people can answer immediately, and they almost always say, "He's taking me." At this point I offer an analogy: "In a way, riding a horse is rather like riding a bicycle. One of two things can happen—either you push the pedals round, providing the power for the bike, or, when you go down a very steep hill, you can no longer pedal fast enough, and you become a passenger. This is analogous to what's happening to you now. So how can you make yourself feel as if you're taking the horse, and being the one who organizes his movement?" I have found that people always respond to this idea in the same way. Instead of just kicking the horse (as you might expect), they reorganize their bodies so that the "pushing" comes from the bearing-down feeling we discussed in Chapter 3.

In riding dogma, we all hear a great deal about "riding the horse forward," and in my experience, the crux of a rider's ability—and her willingness—to do this comes from mobilizing the pelvic and abdominal muscles, much as she would do if she were sweeping a yard. This alignment and tone offers the rider a viable alternative to the fetal crouch, because it makes her causal rather than reactive. Without this muscular reorganization and its concomitant feeling of relief, she never believes the teacher's admonitions about leaning back and lengthening the rein; with it, however, she feels causal and therefore safe, even in more powerful gaits than she has previously been used to. Her right-brain sense of "fitting" then offers her a foundation on which to build, and a goal to which to relate, allowing the brain to function as a servomechanism. This is equally true in less dire cases, when the rider just does not feel quite right, and does not look quite right. The problem, even though it is less dramatic and more longstanding, almost always has the same basis; if it is given a new alternative, the rider's body can easily lead her away from her bad habits and into the realm of new possibilities, through which she increases her repertoire of useful responses and aligns herself with her goal.

Awareness Questions and Imagery

Below you will find questions designed to increase your body awareness, and suggestions, usually in the form of images, which will lead you toward more efficient muscular use. You can work with them both in a riding session and during mental rehearsal. First familiarize yourself with the images during mental rehearsal, then use them in actual practice. During the session, note the differences between your old familiar feelings and the new ones you are creating. How does the session match and mismatch the expectations you had before you rode? Afterward review it, using what I shall call mental rehearsal despite the fact that the exercise is taking place *after* the session. It is a rehearsal for the next time. Note the things you want to do differently. Then put these ideas back into practice.

• To what extent can you identify the fetal crouch reactions in your riding?

- Is the horse taking you, or are you taking him?
- If you find yourself wanting to hold him back, where in your body does this feeling of restraint seem to be focused?

When you feel tension in your arm and hand, this is bound to be accompanied by tension which pulls in your belly. Place the palm of your hand below your ribs, and spread your fingers out over your belly. Then deliberately bear down, and be aware of the effect that this has on your muscles. Can you maintain this feeling as you ride? How does it compare with your normal posture? While riding at a walk, move your spine between the two extremes of reaching up as tall as you can and slumping. Then find the "middle place," in which you can bear down while imagining that someone is pulling you up by the hair behind the top of your head: in a position of optimum alignment, your pubic bone, belly button, and sternum should lie in a straight vertical line. Imagine a big piece of hardboard nailed to the front of your body; as this can neither fold nor stretch, it will hold the alignment in place.

Most riders sit much too far back on the saddle, and this contributes enormously to their difficulties. In order to find the right place, lift your legs right up over the front of the saddle until they rest on the horse's shoulders. Then draw your seat as far forward as you can, so that you feel as if you are sitting on the rise toward the front of the saddle; keeping your backside in place, bring down your legs—or better still, have a helper replace your legs for you— and make sure that the muscle bulk of your inside thigh is pulled to the back away from the saddle. For most people, this is a huge adjustment which at first feels strange and uncomfortable, especially when it is coupled with the correct, vertical alignment of the front of the body. Staying here is not easy either, and to stop you from slipping backward you need to become aware of several factors:

- First, notice the positioning of your seat bones and your pubic bone: are they on the same horizontal level, or is your pubic bone higher up? The more you sit toward the front of the saddle, the more exaggerated this difference will be, and as you slide back they will come closer to the same level. To help you stay in place, imagine that you would like to draw your seat bones to-

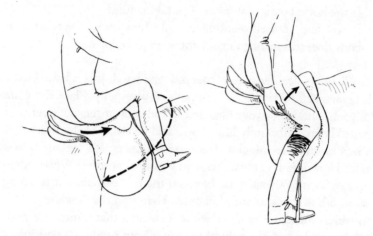

13.   Lift your legs up over the front of the saddle, and then scoop your backside up underneath you. If you do not have a helper to replace your legs for you, use your hand to pull the muscle bulk of your thigh *away* from the saddle.

ward the underneath of your pubic bone. (This is anatomically impossible, but still a useful image.) You could pretend that each one has a piece of string tied around it, and that these pass through your belly and emerge somewhere near the points of your hips. Someone is pulling on the pieces of string, so that they are drawing your seat bones forward and up into your buttocks. This will involve your hamstring muscles, and make it feel as if you are doing much more muscular work to hold yourself in place.

• Second, notice the distance between your seat bones. To influence this, think of making yourself narrower from side to side, just at the point where your legs come into your pelvis, as if you were pinching the two sides of you closer together. (This mirrors the floor exercise on page 63 and Fig. 8.) Imagine having a bolt passing through you, with someone doing up the nut, or think of a tight belt around you at this level. This "pinch" feeling draws your two thighs in closer together, so that they make a V shape, with the imaginary point somewhere just behind and above your backside. Ride at a walk, and experiment making the pinch feeling and then letting it go. How does this change affect your seat bones? Do they come forward or move back, do they move up or down, closer together or farther apart? Some people find it difficult to make the pinch feeling and to keep bearing down simultaneously. If you find this is the case, you will have to practice at a walk until you can coordinate the two. Also monitor your breathing: does the breath go into your chest or your belly? Check that you are bearing down as you inhale and exhale: if necessary, use the conical-flask analogy to help you, and feel the coldness of the air as it passes down that long tube.

• In each gait, can you make your breathing match the rhythm of the horse's movement? Try to prolong each in-breath and each out-breath to match his strides. Where do you look as you ride? Is your vision focused or peripheral? Whenever you find yourself looking down or staring out, shift your gaze above the horse's head, and maintain a broad field of view. If you are riding a safe horse in an enclosed area, try riding for short periods with your eyes closed, because this can help amplify your other senses, particularly your kinesthetic sense.

To the uninitiated, who have not yet discovered their limitations, riding looks deceptively easy, and the first surprise is its phys-

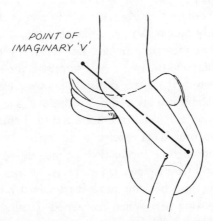

POINT OF
IMAGINARY 'V'

14. When you are sitting correctly in the saddle, your pubic bone, belly button, and sternum will form a straight vertical line, and your seat bones will be below the level of your pubic bone.

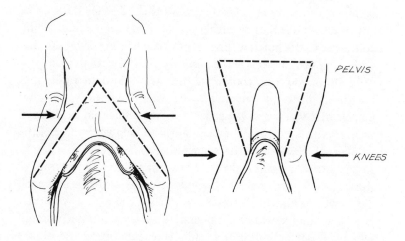

PELVIS

KNEES

15.   Making the pinch feeling draws your thighs into a V shape whose imaginary point lies above and behind your buttocks; when the rider draws her
knees up and in, however, as she does in the fetal crouch, the V tends to go
the other way.

ical discomfort, though few admit it. My brother is the only person
I have ever taught who has gone into the trot for the first time and
said, "Ouch, help! I don't like this, it hurts!" Most people are more
resilient—or perhaps they are just more in awe of their teacher—
and they usually turn rather pale, bite their lip, and pretend that
this is just what they were hoping for. Gradually the discomfort
becomes familiar, and the rider's next surprise is the realization that
she is completely at the mercy of this unknown creature. However
much or little she learns about riding technique, she soon discovers
(from bitter experience) that the horse is a herd animal, who likes
to stay with his friends. He prefers to go toward home than away
from it, and although he is remarkably generous, cooperative, and
forgiving, he still likes to have his own way; he uses subtlety to get
what he wants, and he wins most battles by ignoring the rider
rather than fighting her. When frightened he runs away, and he
has so little reasoning power that he cannot be bargained with.
(This is something that even some experienced riders seem not to
have noticed!) He may or may not have a sense of responsibility

toward the rider, but, even if he has, he will tread on her toes without noticing and will walk through a narrow gateway with no thought for her knees.

But the problem is not just that the horse has a mind of his own. His influence extends far beyond that, and once mounted, the beginner often feels as if her body no longer belongs to her: she is like a puppet, and the horse is pulling the strings. Every time she tries to move one part, another part moves as well, and however well developed her kinesthetic sense may be, it is no match for this situation. She is confronted with a task that is like trying to pat your head and rub your stomach both at the same time. But the even bigger problem is that she has *no idea of what it is that she is trying to achieve*—so her experience is rather like the kinesthetic equivalent of searching in the dark. Only when she discovers the rewards of being causal will she know that there is something to be gained from the correct coordination; yet some riders fumble around for years without discovering techniques which give them a sense of fitting. This is rather like playing the children's game of Hunt the Thimble, where the children, as they search, are given feedback that they are "cold," "lukewarm," "hot," or "boiling." In our case, all the feedback the rider ever gets is that she is "luke-warm." Some riders search for the answer in a variety of different places; others—the victims of one-trial learning—continually go back to the same one, only to discover that they are lukewarm, lukewarm, lukewarm.

While being a beginner most certainly has its frustrations, it also has its delights. I can remember the excitement of discovering ponies, the atmosphere of the stables, new sights and smells, and my eagerness to learn. Most of us want to recapture this feeling again later, when the thrill has worn off, and we need bigger and better horses and more daunting competitions in order to feel the same excitement. The mind and attitude of the beginner are precious tools which motivate learning. In Zen philosophy the "beginner's mind" is highly valued, in contrast to the attitude of the expert. The person who believes she already knows everything is not really open to new learning; it is as if she goes around with blinkers on.

Unfortunately, many pupils lose their beginner's mind when

they come under the influence of teachers who long ago lost their own, and whose attitude conveys the idea that "I had to suffer in learning, and you're going to have to suffer too!" But beginners often have a somewhat easier time. Classed as "bad" riders, they are given to the most junior, inexperienced instructor, who might perhaps still view them with enthusiasm. Some senior teachers believe that beginners are beneath their dignity, and not worth wasting time on. But to my mind, beginners present the teacher with an unrivaled opportunity in that they are virgin ground, in which she can cultivate a whole new set of reflexes and senses. When the beginner ingrains useful, effective coordinations right from the outset she saves herself a lifetime's struggle, whereas the longer she relies on her involuntary reflexes, the harder it becomes for her to change them. Though no longer beginners, those unable to overcome their difficulties are still classed as "bad" riders; but are riders at different stages in their development inherently better or worse than each other, and more or less worthy of respect? In *The Inner Game of Tennis*, Timothy Gallwey suggests that the unfolding/development of skill is analogous to a flower growing, and this means that we could paraphrase my question by asking, Is a rosebud worse than a rose? The answer is an obvious no. My own feeling is that the same is true of riders—that "bad," if we must use the term, needs to be taken as a description and not as a moral judgment. Each rider has her own integrity and is doing the best she can with the resources available to her; each one is equally deserving of our attention and skill.

The beginner's task is so overwhelmingly complex that the teacher has to help her by breaking it down into do-able-sized hunks. Gradually, these different pieces will be perceived as a unified action and ingrained as a right-brain automatic response which she does not even have to think about. But right now she has to adopt a more linear approach, paying attention, deliberately and step by step, to all the different body parts, inhibiting the movements of tensions that she does not want, and substituting the ones that she does. Psychologists have found that the conscious mind can pay attention to a maximum of seven hunks of information (plus or minus two, depending on the individual), but my experience suggests that at least three of these are taken up by merely being on a horse, and that any rider who can work effectively with four distinct pieces of input is doing extremely well! The teacher can aid this process by starting with the most basic building blocks, but even then, these are so interconnected that by the time the pupil gets to the end of the list something is bound to have gone wrong at the beginning, and she has to start all over again. After enough conscious repetitions she is able to go through the checklist far more easily, until the body begins to position itself automatically. So instead of thinking about hands *or* legs, she can think about hands *and* legs; the different units become integrated into one coordination—enabling the conscious mind to fill its seven (plus or minus two) spaces with some new information.

This early phase of learning may be easiest to remember if you ever learned to drive a car with a stick-shift gearbox. At one time it was probably all you could do to put your foot on the clutch, move the gear lever, keep a hand on the steering wheel, and look where you were going. Now, hopefully, these responses are smooth and effortless, and they feel like one action; as far as the right brain is concerned, they *are* one action, ingrained as a single motor pattern which it never needs to dissect. The pattern can be refined further by paying conscious attention to it, as you might choose to do if you are driving at speed, or under difficult conditions. You can also have a conversation or daydream at the same time, allowing your driving to proceed on "automatic pilot"—although an untold number of road accidents testify to the resulting loss in perception and speed of response.

In conditions which encourage the rider to stay in a state of relaxed concentration, and which are conducive to learning, it takes very little time for useful responses to become habitual. Each time the body chooses to do something a certain way, the likelihood that it will choose that way again increases; when fear, pressure, and fatigue are kept to a minimum, therefore, the rider can build on her learned responses rather than reverting to her involuntary ones. But it takes far more time for her to develop so much faith in them that she chooses them in more difficult circumstances, and can use them to convince the horse of her authority. In a very short time the beginner has "done" walk, trot, and canter, transitions and turns, and she may well ask, What more is there? In terms of quantity, there is little more to learn, but in terms of quality, she has only touched the tip of the iceberg. A good rider's mastery both of herself and of the horse is so great that the horse becomes a willing and cooperative partner, who responds to very light controls. At this early stage in learning, it is hard to believe that the answer to the problem of authority and control lies in subtlety and precision; but we do ourselves a great disservice when, having attributed our difficulties to the brutish nature of the horse, we then use strength to try to solve them.

Awareness Questions and Imagery

- You can recognize good riders by the way they sit—extremely still—and by the way they seem to have control over all their body parts, so that they do not bump and wobble about.
- Which parts of your body do you find most difficult to control?
- What unwanted movements would you like to be able to avoid?

It is usually best to focus on the center of your body (your pelvis, belly, back, and thighs) before you think about your arms and lower legs. So when you are familiar with the ideas in the previous section, gradually add these to them: Which part of your hand actually holds the rein? How do you prevent the rein from slipping through your fingers? Which part of your hand is turned up, and how is it angled? It is best to hold the rein so that you squash it between your thumb and first finger, letting these do the holding so that your remaining fingers do not have to grasp it tightly. To keep your hand the right way up, imagine that you are holding a wine glass, and that you do not want to spill any liquid. Your joints are aligned in the most efficient way when your elbow hangs close to your side, and the back of your hand forms a straight continuation of your lower arm—as if you had no wrist. This straight line should then continue down the rein to the horse's mouth.

In what way does this alignment feel different from your normal way of holding the reins? Ideally, you should hold the rein with no muscle pull in your arms. If you are tempted to pull your hands back toward your belly, it may be that your reins are too long, or this may be symptomatic of tension in your belly.

- How hard are you pressing into the stirrups? Do you think of pushing your legs straight down, or do you think of their going out around the belly of the horse?

Imagine that you would like your feet to rest on the stirrups in the same way that they would rest on the floor, i.e., taking support rather than pushing down. Are your toes open or curled? Which gives you a steadier lower leg, and a more stable base of support?

Many riders push their heel down so hard that their leg comes forward and out of alignment. By doing this, and by pushing their leg straight down, they also reduce the shock-absorbing effect of their joints.

Often it is more helpful to think of pushing your knee down, and your heel back, so that it points toward the horse's hind leg. It is perfectly adequate to have the sole of your boot lying horizontally. Your lower leg will be in optimum alignment when you can balance out of the saddle, as if at the top of your post. Try this initially in halt, holding the horse's mane so that you will not pull him in the mouth if you lose your balance. When you can stay in place without holding on, ask a helper to lead your horse, and try the same exercise in walk and trot. Ideally, you should be able to do it with the reins knotted on the horse's neck, and your arms held out sideways at shoulder height. The resulting feeling of security is well worth the effort of practicing. While standing still, imitate the action of posting to the trot, but do it slowly enough to allow you to discover whether there is any movement in your lower leg as you rise or sit. Does it swing forward or back? To help you hold it still, focus on the angle behind your knee, allowing this to open and close as you move your pelvis. Think of the rise taking your pelvis forward rather than up, so that your pubic bone swings over the front of the saddle. As you rise, the line of your thigh should point vertically down toward the ground, and your kneecap should roll slightly in toward the saddle.

- As some riders come down into the saddle, they barely make contact with it. (They look as if it is so hot that they dare not touch it!) Others thud down into it, as if it were an armchair. Which do you tend to do? As you land, is there a significant difference in level between your seat bones and your pubic bone?

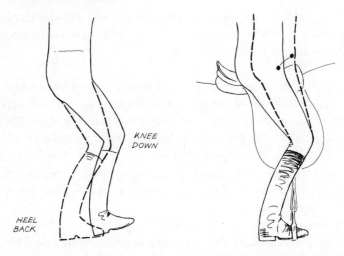

KNEE DOWN

HEEL BACK

16. If you think of pushing your heel down, you tend to push your leg forward out of a correct alignment; so instead, think of bringing your knee down and your heel back. At a posting trot it needs to remain completely still, while the thrust of the rise brings your pubic bone over the pommel, and makes your kneecap point toward the ground.

Can you keep bearing down and keep the pinch feeling both as you rise and as you sit?

If you hollow your back and draw in your belly you will find it difficult to contact the saddle clearly; as you keep bearing down, aim to feel the whole contact area underneath your thigh and buttocks as you land, and bring yourself as far toward the front of the saddle as possible. As you descend into the saddle, imagine that you are landing on eggs, which you must touch, but not break. This requires you to keep supporting your own body weight, rather than flopping down and surrendering it to the horse.

Riders vary enormously in their susceptibility to fear, the ease with which they gain faith in the horse, and their learned responses. Some find that the biggest difficulties in learning are posed by the self-defeating anguish of the internal dialogue; for others, the problem lies in their extremely vivid imagination. While riding along quietly these riders invent scenarios in their heads about how the horse is bound to buck when they canter next time, or how he will automatically be more difficult the moment they turn for home. The rest of the riders stroll along with no thought of these horrors; if they did imagine them, perhaps they would view them with excitement! Riders who are naturally bold all too often assume that everyone else should be like them and look down on those who are not. It is widely held that in the horse world riders are supposed to be brave; but who has more courage, the rider who feels no fear, or the one who, despite her internal quakings, overcomes the pull of the fetal crouch, and goes ahead anyway?

Fear serves an important purpose: it is intended to make us discriminating about situations and ensure our self-preservation. The problem is that most of us distort one way or the other, believing either that we can do it when actually we cannot, or that we cannot do it when actually we can. This lack of realism taints the performance of many riders, making them overcautious, or so bold that one could question whether they are brave or stupid: either the danger they perceive or their supposed ability to overcome it is illusory.

Physiologically, fear initiates the rush of adrenaline, which prepares the body for fight or flight, but if we can harness this energy, we can use it as the fuel for peak performance. Actors instinctively recognize this, and know that they will only produce their best work when they feel nervous before going on stage. With the aid of adrenaline perception is heightened and energy increased, sometimes to the extent that unathletic people perform the "impossible" —and there are true stories of people who have leaped over gates in the face of charging bulls, or lifted cars off their trapped children. These exceptional responses are evoked by *real* danger; but the woman who lifted a car off her son might well be a nervous wreck when he next comes home late from school, because she is then responding to an imagined situation (What if he's had an accident?)—her fear is based on fantasy rather than reality. When fear is based on illusion it becomes anxiety, which distorts perceptions, reducing stamina and fine body control. It also restricts breathing. In fact, the physiological and psychological aspects of anxiety go together; you cannot experience the effects of one without those of the other. So if you begin with an awful fantasy, you will soon find yourself with constricted chest muscles and a pulled belly, struggling to draw in air against your own resistance. Or if you begin like this, in the posture of anxiety, you will soon find yourself actually feeling anxious. But regardless of how the rider generates her anxiety, and regardless of whether she does it in response to a real or an imagined threat, its effects are the same: she becomes hesitant and overcautious, while her reactions are slowed and her timing is impaired.

The result, of course, is that she tends to *create* the situation she most fears. Her first reflex is to pull on the reins, but this can have dire consequences. Horses are claustrophobic in the sense that when they are restricted they always want to get away; they become far more likely to jig up and down, or to fight for their freedom. (Conversely, when they are unrestricted, they often decide that they would rather not bother!) As soon as the nervous rider begins responding to some imagined situation (What if the horse takes off with me? What if he bucks?), and she grabs the rein in fear, her mental image is far more likely to become reality. The paradox is that through her attempts to gain control, she actually loses it.

It has long been recognized that anxiety is infectious. Perhaps the horse can sense the rider's emotional state through picking up her mental images—a phenomenon which some people call telepathy or ESP. It has also been suggested, though to my knowledge not proved, that fear may produce a smell to which horses react. It may also simply be that the horse is exquisitely sensitive to the rider's body positioning and tension, so that his response is primarily physical rather than mental. This is the explanation that I favor, and as you will see later on, this remarkable sensitivity can work *for* us as well as against us, especially when our own perceptions are developed to a similar level of subtlety. Whichever explanation you favor, horses seem to behave *as if* they can read their rider's mind.

In her book, *The Horse's Mind,* Lucy Rees states, "It never seems to occur to horses that they themselves might be the cause of our tension; instead they look anxiously for hidden tigers that we can presumably see." A rider who has earned the horse's respect becomes, in effect, the leader of the horse's herd, and as such she takes on the role of "chief tiger spotter"; and if the leader is frightened, why should the follower not be? While the horse may be looking for "hidden tigers," another important factor is at work, for his reaction is at least in part caused or intensified by the frightened rider's inability to *demand that he pay attention to her.* I learned a lot about this when I had to exercise my teacher's rather exuberant young horse every day, at a walk on a long rein. There were distractions in the environment which he found more amusing than frightening, and I soon realized that I could not even afford to let him prick his ears and look at them, or I was likely to find myself hanging round his neck! My only chance was to send him so strongly forward that I commanded more of his attention than the distractions, and then I could channel his power to my own ends. For feedback on how I was doing I would look at his ears. When the ears are out sideways the horse is using his peripheral vision, and his attention is directed primarily inward and toward the rider; when the horse you are riding wants to cavort about, his ears can provide a very valuable guide, reminding you of the need to keep driving him forward. In the days before I really had the guts to drive a horse forward, I would stop myself from leaning forward and grabbing at the rein, but I had not made the next transition—*actively to intervene.* Instead, I would sit and wait, hoping that I could glue myself to the saddle for long enough, but perceiving myself rather like a human cannonball who was eventually bound to be expelled from her equine cannon. In waiting and preparing for the worst I froze into passivity and surrendered my power to the horse —giving him permission to do just what he liked with me.

Riders who are *not* scared of the horse's power are usually unperturbed about riding young horses, and taking them hunting and jumping. They nurture the horse through his fear or respond to his antics with a sense of benevolent outrage. Traditionally, dressage has been the domain of those who *are* frightened, because the horse is kept calm, controlled, and enclosed between four walls, so that the rider need never feel the effects of his power. But in fact, the best dressage can demand as much courage as outdoor work, because the rider deliberately evokes the horse's power, using it to enliven his movement and make him dance. Sometimes, in putting him through new work, she takes him right to the point where he might panic, and then the outcome depends entirely on her ability to keep herself centered, so that she can also center him. The courage needed to stay calm in the face of such a potential storm comes only with enough positive experiences in overriding previous "What if" fantasies.

But when you do feel anxious, what can you do to help yourself? Attending to the actual here-and-now situation is the best way of decreasing self-doubt, and encouraging the mind to become calmer. The first step is to become aware of your breathing, putting it into a rhythm which matches the rhythm of the horse's gait. Talking to the horse is effective perhaps not so much because of the soothing sound of your voice, but because it forces you to keep breathing, and without the constricted breathing of anxiety it is impossible to experience the anxiety itself. (You cannot talk and hold your breath at the same time!) I had a memorable experience once in a job interview, when I had to ride a very fresh thoroughbred in an unfenced, floodlit arena which was full of spooky shadows. I spent the first quarter of an hour dealing with my nervousness and his by forcing myself to count and breathe in rhythm. One false breath, I felt, would be the end of both of us—and when I finally got the job, I discovered that the horse was such a lunatic that my perception had not been so far off! By breathing into your belly and focusing your attention on your body you become very sensitive to minute changes in the horse's tempo, and you can respond immediately, refusing to let him hurry or jiggle you out of your chosen alignment, tone, and seat-bone movment. You thus remain *causal*, the leader rather than the follower, and you can nip many potential evasions in the bud. When once I had to retrain a horse who was a confirmed runaway, I found that I could trot him in tempo (and therefore in control) very easily, until I would ride diagonally across the arena and change direction when he would shoot off with me. Eventually I realized that the problem arose because I was hurrying my own change of diagonal, barely sitting for the second beat, and in my experience, momentary inconsistencies like this can be enough to trigger a frightened horse who wants to run away.

When you are anxious, the key to deflating the apparent danger lies in *disidentifying* yourself from your fear. You then become the watcher of it, rather than sinking into your terror. So, from a dispassionate viewpoint, you can then monitor your own body reactions: to what extent are you tempted to fall into the fetal crouch? Do you feel the moment when you first begin to tip forward and draw in your belly? Can you monitor your breathing and use this to help you stay in place? If you find yourself wanting to grab at the reins, can you resist the temptation, and maintain an alignment in which you are causal? In a situation like this, it can help to rest your hands on the horse's neck, and then, when you feel the temptation to pull, you must press your fingers into the neck instead. (This is much more helpful if you have relatively long arms and a short back; otherwise you may find yourself leaning so far forward to do this that you get off balance.) It is also very useful to press harder on the rein with your thumb, so that you squash it more firmly between your thumb and your first finger. You can do this *without* pulling, and it will not involve the muscles of your shoulders or your belly. I have found that whenever a rider (nervous or otherwise) gets caught in a pulling match with the horse, the pulling is merely symptomatic of other changes in her body; as she pulls on the rein, *she also tends to pull in her belly*. It then becomes impossible for her to release her hand before she has let go of her belly. The muscles of the fingers connect ultimately to the large muscles of the belly, and whenever the rider pulls, this connection is activated. Its universality certainly explains why so many commands to "Stop pulling!" go apparently unheeded, and why so many pupils find themselves thinking, "I'd love to, but I can't!" This effect mirrors the last dismounted exercise in Chapter 3, where your partner pushed and pulled on you. Only by bearing down and taking on the body quality which allowed you to be unmoved in that exercise can you become a truly stable presence on the horse. Imagery can help here too: imagine yourself rooted around the horse like a tree, or with the stability of an immovable rock, and the feeling of security this offers will make the fetal crouch far less attractive.

It may also help to talk to your fear. If this seems like a rather bizarre suggestion, realize that you are probably already talking to yourself about it; perhaps there is some internal dissonance between the part of you which says, "You shouldn't be such a coward," and the part which says, "But I don't think I can do it." Instead you should address your fear directly, and instead of criticizing yourself or being impatient and angry, speak kindly to it, as you would to a young child, or a dear friend. Even if you do not like its behavior, tell it that you appreciate its positive intentions for you—it has, after all, got you this far, and kept you safe all these years. Tell it that you have taken sensible precautions for your safety, and that you would like to go ahead with your riding. Ask if it would be willing to watch over you from a safe distance, and imagine it sitting watching, perhaps by the edge of the arena. Notice what it looks like, and make sure that it is settled comfortably there. Then tell it that it can ask you to stop at any time if it is still concerned for your safety. And tell it too, that you will not leave it behind, that you will come back and collect it later.

Another way of disidentifying yourself from your fear is by using the "numbering exercise." While you are riding rate the amount of fear you feel on a scale from zero to ten, where zero is "no fear at all" and ten is "absolutely petrified." Then, every few moments, say (aloud or to yourself) the number which corresponds to the degree of fear you feel at that time. Surprisingly, once a rider confronts and labels her fear, she almost always finds that it is smaller than she thought it was. Quite often, I do this exercise with people who *look* terrified, and when I ask them for a number they suddenly pull themselves together and become rather nonchalant: "Oh," they say, "it's only about three really!" All of us are reluctant to look our fear in the face, but turning away from it in our imagination allows it to grow; like ghosts in the cupboard, the objects of our fear retain their power over us until we shine light on them, and discover just how dangerous they really are. So the effect of the exercise is to show you the extent to which your fear is appropriate to the present situation, and how much it is generated by flights of the mind.

Timothy Gallwey, who has made enormous contributions in this area, suggests in his book *Inner Skiing* that fear has a real threat for its basis where danger, vulnerability, and inability are all present. In Chapter 1, I discussed his idea of the "awareness," the "trying," the "unconscious," and the "panicking" modes, and suggested that our ideal is to learn and ride in the awareness mode. He and many other sports psychologists refer to this as the "stretch zone," because in the most productive learning contexts the rider is continually monitoring her reactions, and stretching herself to use her learned responses in more and more testing situations. The point where fear becomes incapacitating marks the far edge of her stretch zone, and once she passes this and moves into her panic zone her safety becomes doubtful. (For some riders, the comfort zone, stretch zone, and panic zone are synonymous with walk, trot, and canter!) Ideally, we would all push this boundary forward by seeking out situations which provide just enough stimulus to evoke a heightened response without overwhelming us. Bit by bit we take more risks—crossing more difficult terrain, riding more excitable horses, or jumping more imposing fences—and each time we draw from ourselves the kind of responses which minimize the danger involved and enlarge our store of effective experiences.

Rarely do riders learn like this, or train their horses in the same way. Some people avoid situations which frighten them to such an extent that they become trapped by their own fear. If their horses act up when hunting, they stop going hunting. If they buck while cantering in company, they stop going out for fast rides with others. Soon riding out alone becomes so exciting that they only dare stay in trot, and after a while they retreat to the safety of the riding ring. Even there, the whole process repeats itself... until they only feel safe working alone at trot in an indoor arena. When a rider like this finally does break out from these self-imposed boundaries the horse finds it so strange and exciting that he does indeed act up; so the rider discovers how right she was to be frightened, and she retreats, terrified, back into the riding school. Once again her fears have become a self-fulfilling prophecy, and only with the encouragement needed to face them will she discover the true extent of her inability.

At the opposite extreme are riders who do not recognize their vulnerability. They tend to put themselves in situations which demonstrate it to them, and this can be to their detriment if they do not take seriously the feedback about their limitations that falls offer them. If we refuse to learn from our experience, it tends to repeat itself until we do, and one rather swashbuckling rider I know finally learned his lesson when he entered an Intermediate Horse Trial with practically no preparation, and paid the price with a broken pelvis. Riding is one of the highest-risk sports (statistics published in the November 1985 *Horse and Hound* suggest that it is even more dangerous than motor racing and mountaineering), and the nearest one can get to a guarantee of safety is adequate preparation, which builds up the strength and resources of both horse and rider.

Equally dangerous is the plight of some nervous riders who knowingly put themselves into situations which are overwhelmingly frightening. All too often they are encouraged by friends and teachers to be more adventurous than their abilities warrant, and it can take far more courage to say, "No, I don't feel ready to do that yet," than it does to face the horror. Some teachers go so far as to goad their pupils into jumping by making themselves even more frightening to the pupils than the jump. But which is more important, the person or what she achieves? While this technique often works, the line between brave and stupid is very fine, and difficult to identify, especially when voices inside and outside your head are saying, "Come on, don't be such a coward," "If she can do it so can you," "You can't possibly back out now. . . ."

Beneath such remonstrations, each of us has an intuitive right-brain sense of our own actual ability, which we often sense as a gut feeling. But rarely do we acknowledge or trust it, because it is overlain by all the ramifications of our fear of looking stupid, our desire to impress people, or our fear of letting them down. So when you are faced with a decision whether to ride a certain horse, or jump a certain jump, what should you do? You need to discover if your fear is based in fantasy or reality—whether you do not yet have the techniques you need, or whether you are simply undermining abilities which you already have. So listen to your internal dialogue as impartially as possible, and wait for it to subside. If you are tempted to go ahead with the task in question, talk gently to your fear, thank it for its help in the past, and ask it to sit aside and watch you. Then do a mental preview of your proposed situation, and if you can imagine it going well, it is highly likely that you can produce the same result in practice. If, on the other hand, your mental preview is catastrophic, it is important not to perform physically until you can change your mental concept of how you will fare.

Whatever our reasons for riding, and whatever environment we usually ride in, most of us, at times, confront our vulnerability. We also confront our ability to surpass ourselves, drawing from ourselves and our horses hidden strengths that we did not know we possessed. Perhaps part of the attraction of riding is this quest to find out what is real about ourselves—to find out what is brave and what is stupid—so that we discover in ourselves the kind of courage which dissolves problems, and which offers the exhilaration of success.

Awareness Questions and Imagery

- To what extent do you become embroiled in the kind of anxiety which tends to provoke the situations you most fear? If your mind tends to fill with catastrophic expectations you will inevitably have a tendency to become reactive rather than causal—thus ensuring that you fulfill the prophecy.
- If you arrange your seat toward the front of the saddle, bearing down, using the pinch feeling, and checking your breathing, do you still feel as anxious? Does this enable you to release any tension in your hand and arm, so that you take the horse, and do not feel the need to restrict him?
- Which of you has control of the tempo? You are not truly causal until *you* have. Being able to control the horse's tempo with your seat offers a great feeling of security, and, when coupled with the above, should help you to release any more residual tension in your arms and belly.
- In every gait, the movements of the horse's limbs cause movements in his back which the rider's seat has to follow. As he walks, does his back move one side at a time, or do both sides move together? Feel the lifting and dropping of each of your buttocks on the saddle—the result is rather like walking your seat bones forward, so as one moves forward the other is left behind, and it automatically becomes ready to move forward in

its turn. (This means that you never have to think of either seat bone moving backward.)

- As your seat bones go with the movement of the horse, how much movement is there in the back part of your buttocks and the lower part of your belly? Experiment by exaggerating this feeling and being extra still, so that your seat bones move within your backside and there is very little external movement.

Most riders who try this feel as if they are restricting the horse too much and becoming too tense; my experience suggests, however, that the most skillful riders limit their following movement like this, working at much higher muscle tone than most people. This makes them far more precise; the horse can no longer jiggle them about easily.

- As you go with the movement of the horse, think of your knee as the fixed point and your pelvis as the moving point. Does your knee tend to wobble about, or to slide up the saddle? At first, it is easier to keep it in place with a slightly shorter stirrup, and as time goes on you will be able to lengthen it and maintain the same effect. To help you, imagine that your knees are held in place by an imaginary iron bar which passes through the horse's belly.
- At a sitting trot the rider's basic alignment is just the same as it is at a walk. Can you sit to a trot without tipping forward and gripping up? Do you take the horse or does he take you? At a sitting trot, many riders lose their seat bone–pubic bond placement, and lose the bearing-down and the pinch, so that they fall forward into the fetal crouch. Then they cling on with their thighs (the inverted V), and bump around so much that they cannot feel the horse's back movements distinctly.

Before you go into trot, arrange your seat well and, if necessary, put one hand onto the front of the saddle. When you work without stirrups take care not to stretch your legs down so long that your back hollows and your pelvis rotates; if this happens you will find yourself sitting on your thighs rather than your backside. Deliberately hold your leg out in front of you with a rather closed angle between your thigh and your body. (Later, when your seat is more established, you will be able to lengthen your leg.) Locate the tendons at the top of your thigh (see Chapter 3), and make sure they are sticking out. If necessary, lift your leg to find them, and then make sure you can keep them sticking out as you lower your leg back into place. As you go into a trot, make sure that you are taking the horse. Then keep drawing your backside under you, and monitoring this front angle.

- How many steps of trot can you manage before you tip forward and start to bump? Sometimes the rider's seat bones bump out of the saddle at a sitting trot, but more often, her seat becomes unsteady because of movements in the layer of flesh which lies between her seat bones and the saddle. This makes her buttocks behave like two bouncy rubber balls, and she will only sit well when this layer of flesh is *compressed* the whole time. To hold it like this keep focusing your attention here, and make sure that you are continually bearing down.
- Can you tell whether the horse's back moves one side at a time or both sides together? This may be a long-term project, but your goal should be to feel the horse's back's movements in trot as clearly as you feel them in walk. In order to do this, you may have to work holding the saddle, or, preferably, on the lunge. Remember that doing this will almost certainly require much more muscular work than you are accustomed to. (This is despite the fact that your friends will probably tell you how relaxed you look!)
- At a canter, the same basic alignment is required as walk and sitting trot. At a canter, does your backside stay in the saddle, or does it bump out of it? Do your shoulders stay still or do they rock? Which parts of your body support your weight? Does it rest primarily on your backside, your thigh, or your stirrup? Do you take the horse or does he take you?

Many riders become passengers in canter, and they tip forward, clinging on with their thighs and pulling in their bellies. When this happens their backsides bump out of the saddle in each stride and their shoulders rock forward.

To help you sit well, arrange your seat carefully before you begin, taking hold of the saddle if necessary. Initially, make sure that you do not stretch your legs down too long, or press hard into the stirrup. As you go into canter, let your lower back rock forward a little in each stride, so that you can allow the horse to come up underneath you in the third canter beat.

- Does this enable you to sit better? Is there still some unwanted movement in your shoulders and the back part of your backside?

Many people feel what I call a "splish-splosh" canter, in which the horse's back seems to move forward and backward underneath them in each stride. You want to make it feel more solid than this; aim to go with the movement of his back so that you feel only a forward movement. This will require you to keep bearing down, and to maintain a clear pinch feeling, along with your seat bone–pubic bone placement.

When you can sit well in canter, you will have no problem in feeling the horse's back movements, and identifying his leading leg. If you still find it difficult, however, work holding onto the saddle or, if possible, on the lunge, and keep returning to your basic pelvic positioning.

5 The Riding School Rider

I look back on this phase as one of the happiest times of my riding life. I lived for ponies, and was always desperate to go to the stables. When I could not actually be there, I spent my time talking about ponies, dreaming about ponies, reading about them and drawing them: they dominated my whole life—or at least, I wanted them to. I would practically move heaven and earth to get to the stables early enough to ride a pony up from the field bareback, and I worked for hours in the hope of a free ride. Like most stable helpers, I was exploited, and I loved every minute of it.

Every summer I went on a riding holiday, and to smell slightly dirty stables and musty hay still evokes memories of beautiful countryside and my favorite ponies—like most kids I liked them big, fast, and preferably both. Even Colonel Podhajsky, the famous director of the Spanish Riding School, admits in his book *The Riding Teacher* that what he most wanted as a child was to ride his father's biggest hunter. It seems that none are exempt from the thrill that goes with riding a "special" horse (and from the disappointment that ensues when someone else is allowed to ride it instead). Whatever horse I rode, I preferred trail rides to lessons, and I judged a teacher and a lesson by how many times we cantered, and whether or not we jumped. I knew (because I had been told) that I tipped forward, bumped at the canter, and did not have my heels down; this did not worry me as long as I rode my favorite ponies, and was challenged enough to be excited and not frightened. It only became important later, when just having fun with ponies was not enough, and instead I became involved in the more serious business of bringing them onto the bit.

By the time the rider has had only a few lessons, she already has her own ingrained ways of riding. Although the habits she has developed are rather crude and ineffective, this does not deter her from using them, and unless something drastic happens they will probably determine how she rides for the rest of her life. From a purely objective viewpoint, it seems amazing that human beings are so reluctant to give up habits that do not work. B. F. Skinner, a psychologist studying human and animal behavior, was once rather jokingly asked to design an experiment to determine the difference between a human being and a rat. So he had his students build equivalent mazes, scaled for rats and human beings, and he taught the rats to run theirs for cheese, and the humans to run theirs for five-dollar bills. The experiment showed that the humans were slightly better and faster at learning than the rats; the real difference, though, came when they stopped baiting the mazes with cheese and money. After a few experiments the rats stopped running, but the humans kept going. They even broke into the laboratories at night—and they kept on doing it!

On the basis of their ingrained habits, the teachers define their pupils as good, bad, or indifferent. In classes the good riders go at the front of the ride on the best horses, the mediocre riders go in the middle on the mediocre horses, and the bad riders go at the back on the most uncooperative and difficult horses. When they all ride sets of geometrical shapes, they display the "Chinese whispers" effect: there is a gradual decrease in accuracy until, toward the back of the ride, the shape of the movements becomes so ill-defined that it is barely possible to recognize what they looked like at the beginning. The teacher's primary job is to keep the pupils active and interested, and if they actually improve, that is an added bonus. Many of them spend their lessons practicing sitting badly, so that instead of improving, they just ingrain their bad habits even further. Some of them enjoy it, as I did, and keep going back for more. Others give up.

Very soon after she first sets foot in the stirrup, each rider develops her own approach to learning. Some are intent on trying hard, others on looking good, or on being "the best." Some are extremely dedicated, others could hardly care less. In riding school lessons, the front of the ride is usually occupied by the most stylish riders, who demand the right to ride the most prestigious horses. They often think they know it all, and they enjoy telling everyone else. Their true competence is not so important to them as looking good—they are the type who survey themselves in every window they ride past, and who will go on to buy the type of horse that completes their image. They will enjoy showing off on it, but are unlikely to test their true competence by entering competitions. They are careful riders.

Those who go on to be competitive will be so from the very first moment, and will fight furiously over the horses they want to ride. They like to show the rest of the class how bold they are, and they spend whole lessons willing the teacher to let them jump higher than everyone else. No challenge is too great for them and, although their style often leaves a lot to be desired, they always get away with it. Their guts and determination leave the rest of the class speechless with admiration—or muttering angrily because they perceive these people as heretics who are not doing it "right."

Following behind are the riders who really want to be good, but who are struggling with their own sense of inferiority. They wish they had the guts and style of the better riders, and they make up for their lack of ability with sheer effort, which ties their bodies up even more, and feeds the critical voices screaming away in their heads. At the same time, they are longing for the chance to ride the better horses, and living in the hope that maybe this will one day solve all their problems for them.

Bringing up the rear are the fearful, mousy ones, who ride along in a daze, wondering what is happening to them, and why their horses cut in around the corners so much more than anyone else's.

There are also the sometime riders, the relaxing executives, who do not really mind not being good, but who want to meet their friends every week, have a good laugh at each other, and finish the day over a beer at the bar. Boyfriends tag along behind girlfriends, and all of them work up a decent sweat, feel better for some good fresh air, and take pride in feeling that they got their exercise for the week.

Some riders do not want to be there at all. Some are under parental threat that they will not be able to watch television if they do not keep up with their riding; others are only keeping up with the Joneses. One way or another they are a motley crew, a rare assortment for any teacher to deal with. Still others have decided that the discipline of school riding is not for them so they go hacking instead, and enjoy sitting on the back of a horse without having to concentrate.

The riders who stay in the school are the motivated, determined ones, who want to be good (in whatever way they define it). Often they are the tryers, and their learning is accompanied by doses of frustration, anguish, and exuberance that testify to the importance which the sport has for them. Riders who get bitten by the bug of riding find that it takes over their whole life. To the horror of their non-horsey friends, they spend Monday, Tuesday, and Wednesday analyzing their last week's riding lesson, and Thursday, Friday, and Saturday contemplating the next.

In *The Inner Game of Tennis,* Timothy Gallwey devotes a whole chapter to "Games People Play on the Court." "That something else other than tennis is being played on the court is obvious to the most casual observer. . . . Not only can the full spectrum of emotional response be observed . . . but also a wide range in the motivations of its players." Like riders, some tennis players want to look good, while some do not care what they look like at all. Some brag about their ability, and some talk continually about how useless they are. Many great dramas are also acted out in the riding school, as riders—be they riding school pupils or horse owners—defend themselves from the threat they perceive in the horse, or their own poor performance. While some are battling with their horses, others are preserving the status quo, obeying all the rules and getting *their* satisfaction from the knowledge that even if they cannot do anything right, at least they can keep their shoulders, hips, and heels in a straight line.

My own attitudes to riding have changed enormously over the years. After my innocent youth, in which I enjoyed messing around with ponies, I became a rider who tried hard, and who desperately wanted to look good. I took examinations and entered competitions in my attempts to prove my competence, and I became ambitious. Later I became disillusioned when even my successes did not seem to make me feel better; but meeting really skilled riders revived my enthusiasm, and I became almost religious in my dedication to this new ideal. I shunned competition, but still had to prove myself. Yet another turning point came when I gave this up, regaining some of the innocent enjoyment of my childhood. My disillusionment with external rewards led me to search for viable *internal* rewards, for a skill that is worth having. This quest has brought me face to face with the internal obstacles which limit my performance, and as I transform these, I gradually develop my ability to work from a right-brain mode, drawing on more of my untapped ability and refining my perceptions. This brings me into a far more dynamic interplay with the horse, and he becomes my teacher, offering me feedback which affects the way I look at riding, at him, and at myself. The visible result of this (at least some of the time) is correct work—or even blue ribbons—but more important is the satisfaction that results when the horse and I work together, confronting the difficulties offered by our physiques and personalities, easing our way through them, and playing what Timothy Gallwey calls the "inner game." Lucinda Prior-Palmer, in her book *Regal Realm*, pays tribute to the same idea when she says, "If it was all about winning then I probably would not enjoy it . . . it is about building partnerships with animals. It is about them finding themselves and the rider finding himself through the mutual trust and confidence they develop in each other."

But rarely do pupils in riding schools—or even horse owners—see riding in this light, and it is unusual for a teacher to work with her pupils in a way that offers them a more far-reaching skill than the games which most of us play. Before she can do this, she must recognize it and have it herself, and she is unlikely to be in this position unless her teacher had it, and her teacher's teacher had it . . . and so on, back into history. In some European countries, the heritage of dressage riding makes this approach far more likely, and there are so many more skilled riders and trained horses that the quality of the work the pupil sees in the average riding school down the road is often in a different class. The riders and teachers who are the pupil's models imbue her with far higher expectations, and she is offered horses to ride whose basic way of going makes their fulfillment far more likely. I have heard judges at horse shows say, "Oh my God, I'm glad I don't have to ride *that*," as they watch some competitor struggling to ride a horse whose apparent woodenness makes the movement impossible for the average rider. Very often, in our riding schools, the main problem is that the blind are leading the blind, and the pupil is often caught in a frustrating catch-22 situation: until she has learned to ride the "bad" horses, she will not be given the chance to ride the "good" ones; but until she gets a decent feel on the "good" ones, she will not develop the expertise to ride the "bad" ones.

Some riders never discover the transformative possibilities which exist in the rider-horse relationship, and they limit themselves to less satisfying games. But others catch rare glimpses of the pleasure we each feel as we move closer toward our potential; and most of us find, I think, that very little in life is as challenging, exciting, and satisfying as stretching ourselves to new limits. Most of us occasionally experience one of those exceptional rides which leaves us elated and clamoring for more, wanting to repeat this different, more fulfilled, feeling. When someone helps you play the "inner game" it is as if they are offering you a path to follow, helping you find your way toward your own buried abilities. When you follow it for a while and experience its delights, other paths lose whatever appeal they might have had. I have found other games a poor substitute for the "inner game," despite its elusiveness.

Awareness Questions and Imagery

• What initially drew you to horses, or caused you to begin riding?
• How do you remember those early days, and how have your attitudes toward riding and your expectations changed since then?

Most of us start riding because we are drawn to horses—attracted by their beauty, power, and gentleness. We want to have fun, to be active and outdoors, but when we set impossible standards of excellence for ourselves, our enjoyment diminishes.

• How do you measure yourself and define "good"? Do you want to ride well and pursue excellence (to measure yourself against an ideal), or to measure yourself against others?
• Is it more important for you to look good, or to get results?

Riding is also a social occupation, which we use to make and keep friends. Do you like to be seen "in the right places," to gain prestige through your riding, or are you more "one of the gang" (who does not like to stand out)?

• Do you over- or underestimate your ability?

Inevitably, we all play games around our riding, and there is nothing inherently wrong or bad about that. But if you can recognize your own games, you can achieve a degree of liberation from them, and perhaps discover others which are more worth playing and which make riding more fun.

• What kind of riders would you ideally like to emulate, and what is it about their attitudes that you value so highly?

So how can the teacher best help the novice pupil? My belief is that the most useful thing to do is to create situations which help her develop her right-brain ability, encouraging her to perceive the feedback which will enhance her perceptions, and increase her store of useful feelages. Imprinting feelages on the right brain is rather like imprinting images on the film of a camera: in order to get the images you need you first have to point the camera in the right direction, then adjust the lens to bring them into exactly the right focus. Since the pupil does not automatically know in which direction she should point her "camera," she needs some assistance from the teacher. (It is fairly obvious that tennis players need to point theirs at the ball—but what should the rider be "watching"?) Her ability to focus is similar to her ability to concentrate, and, as we have seen, this is a skill which few people retain, and which the teacher will again need to help her with. When the focus is too broad, a wide range of information is perceived as a blur and the rider rides in the unconscious mode. When it is too fine there is also loss of clarity, and the rider loses focus through overfocusing and trying too hard. The ideal, of course, lies in the sharpened focus of the awareness mode.

Too many riders in riding schools spend their time riding in the unconscious, the trying, or the panicking modes, and as a result their learning is limited. Out on the trail the rider learns to cope with a variety of situations, developing trust both in herself and in the horse, and making the best of whatever ability she has. But the purpose of lessons is *not* to make the best of a bad job; instead, it is to develop the tools to do a good one, so the rider learns for herself the cause-and-effect rules which underlie riding, and which will eventually make her independent of her teacher. When this process begins, it is as if she begins to look through more and more powerful lenses in a microscope, discovering depth, color, and structure in something that originally looked one-dimensional and monochrome. I can remember my shock at this stage when I heard that a prospective student at the Spanish Riding School had, in his assessment lesson, spent an hour on the lunge learning to ride circles. I thought that I knew all about circles, that they were relatively easy, and that one was much like another; it was apparent to me that these people were teaching and learning something I knew nothing about, but at that time I had no idea what it was. Good riders seemed to me like magical beings from another planet, and without a cause-and-effect understanding of riding, I was at a complete loss even to imagine how they might achieve such beautiful work.

When the rider learns through working in the awareness mode she begins to recognize the origins both of her limitations and of her abilities, and in one fell swoop this banishes both her arrogance (in my case the assumption that I knew "all about circles") and the mystique which surrounds good riders. If we return to the analogy with the camera, the beginner has the advantage that all new information is imprinted, as it were, on blank film. Very soon, however, she tends to lose clarity, because any new input is filtered through her conviction that she "knows all about that now," and interpreted through the light of her old ideas. The result for the rider is that different feelages become an indistinguishable, jumbled mass, and she has no idea how she is positioned, or what she is doing.

The teacher can best help the pupil sort this out by ensuring that she works mostly in her stretch zone, with some respite in her comfort zone. (Working horses and riders continually in their stretch zones tends to overstretch them!) Awareness is greatest in the comfort zone, so it is a good place to refine skills, but new breakthroughs usually happen in the stretch zone. By challenging the pupil to become more focused and aware than she has been previously, the teacher makes it impossible for her to fall into the casualness and tedium of the unconscious mode; by asking only for work which she has a good chance of being able to do well, the teacher minimizes the pupil's chances of falling into the trying or panicking modes.

Initially the focus has to be on body parts, unraveling the rider's "knotted" way of sitting, and bringing each part into its right alignment. Instead of obeying the teacher's commands and trying to become what she is not, the pupil's first task is to find out what she already is. This is the equivalent of saying that she can only find her way to a specific destination once she has found out where she is starting from—and this is the point that foxes most teachers and pupils. A new pupil came to me recently saying, "All my teachers tell me how tense my arms are. I have tried and tried, and it seems that there's nothing I can do about them." All of them had made the assumption that this was where the problem lay, and none of them had looked in sufficient detail at the coordinations she was using in the rest of her body. Because they had been unable to distinguish causes from symptoms, and had glossed over the real problems, none of them had identified her real starting point, and this meant that change was impossible. After watching her working for a very short time, it was obvious that her seat was so out of place that her arms were making up for her lack of security, and were clutching at the reins, just in case ... After doing some basic repositioning and imagery work with her pelvis, she gained the security of feeling that she was taking the horse, and the tension in her arms released easily. Freed from the need to keep fighting her old bad habit, she was then able to focus on other parts that were ready to change, and to view her position as a means through which she could develop a more wholesome interaction with the horse.

As well as focusing on body parts, we can use more generalized ways of amplifying feedback which tells the rider how her body is at a certain moment. One of the best ways to do this is by using the numbering exercise (which we also used to evaluate fear). The rider chooses a body part she needs to know more about, or a quality she needs more of—perhaps how firm and steady she feels in her lower leg, or how much she is bumped around at sitting trot. She then rates this on a scale from zero to ten, beginning perhaps by calling her normal way of riding a five. Every few strides, the teacher asks her for the number that corresponds to the way she feels, and as the pupil replies, she notices and labels the changes. So she might ride along saying "five, five, it's four now, five again, six, six, five," and so on. The exercise is most successful when the pupil offers the numbers off the top of her head, without worrying about them, and if she finds this difficult, it is a sure sign that she is judging herself as she is riding (using left-brain interference to paralyze her right-brain perception). But with gentle encouragement, most pupils soon find that they can distinguish far more subtle changes than they have noticed before, and this automatically increases their body control. Instead of internally criticizing her performance and telling herself what to do, the rider is purely *noticing*, in a nonjudgmental way, and this enables the right brain to learn and perform to its maximum.

Another way of amplifying feedback, and focusing on the rider-horse interaction, is by noticing differences that the rider feels in herself and the horse in different parts of the school. Horses are very helpful in that they almost always choose the same parts of the school for the same evasions: they speed up going toward home, and slow down going away from it; they fall in on one corner, and fall out on another. Most novices sit and wait for the worst to happen, instead of realizing that they could be acting to stop it— and they need to discover the importance of prevention rather than cure. In fact, this is not just limited to novice riders. Participants in my workshops, even experienced riders, have said, "It's almost as if I'm watching a movie of me riding. Someone else has written the screenplay . . . and it's all going by so fast that I can't step in and change it!" I find this an extremely graphic description of how it feels to be reactive rather than causal, and I encourage riders to "step in" before it is too late. So I suggest that the time to give an aid is when they feel the horse contemplating slowing down—when his impulsion slows from a ten to a nine, not from a ten to a three—and this little beginning is usually a quarter of a circle before the worst actually happens. When the pupil begins to respond to these more subtle changes (perhaps at first by catching the horse when his impulsion drops to a five, and then when it drops to a seven), she changes from being a passenger to being a far more active, effective rider. As the rider develops the ability to know what is about to happen in any new situation, she becomes able to nip the horse's evasion in the bud, and in the ideal state, the onlooker sees neither her aids nor the horse's attempts to evade her.

Instead of helping the pupil to discover more about what *is*, most teachers insist on telling her what *should be*. "You should be leaning back more; your hands should be still." Oh, no, thinks the pupil, I've heard all this before. Without a right-brain understanding, however, she still cannot make the required changes. Very often, they both have differing perceptions of the same situation: the pupil "knows" that she is vertical, and the teacher "knows" that she is leaning forward. The teacher's vision is obviously more objective, but at the same time the pupil's body is playing tricks on her: because of her distorted kinesthesia, she feels that any position—however contorted—is "home" if she has held it long enough.

Faced with the conflicting feedback from her teacher and her bodily sense, the pupil has to decide which to believe, and she will instinctively bet on her body. Even if she goes so far as to try out the teacher's suggestion (which few pupils do), it is bound to feel so grotesquely wrong that she cannot wait to get back to the old familiar feeling she knows and loves. The teacher, then, when she has suggested a position correction, and gently coaxed a pupil away from "home," must ask, "How does that feel?" Very often the pupil replies, "It's awful; I hate it!" Riders whom I have asked to lean back more have said to me, "I feel as if I'm about to somersault backward over the horse's tail"—and this is before they have even reached the vertical! They need me to validate their feeling before they are prepared to go along with my proposals. So I say to them, "Yes, I'm sure this does feel horrible. When your body is used to being forward all the time, this position is going to feel way out of balance. Are you willing to trust me for a while, and to stay here however strange it feels? In fact, now you know, when you feel weird you are indeed in the new place." Once they have been listened to and understood, most riders become willing to trust their teacher's perceptions, and, as their new position begins to feel normal, they become prepared to take some more risks. When a teacher refuses to take their objections seriously, however, she puts herself in a position in which she and her pupil are fighting each other. (I shall never forget one of my university lecturers who, having failed to get us to understand one of the finer points of physics, threw up his hands and said, "I'm stumped! All I've got left now is proof by repetition, and proof by intimidation. Which one would you like?") Although repetition and intimidation are the stock-in-trade of the riding teacher, they rarely work, because the pupil's internal perceptions are far more real to her than the teacher's words. Many potentially good riders are written off as "stupid" or "inattentive" simply because their teachers have never managed to meet them on their own ground and gain their trust.

Asymmetry is one particular area in which pupil and teacher can have very different perceptions. From the pupil's earliest days on the lunge, it is obvious that riding on one rein is more secure and comfortable than riding on the other. Changing this imbalance requires such apparent contortions that few riders ever completely counteract their own asymmetry, or discover how to position the horse into any turn. Unfortunately, it is instinctive logic to riders that the horse ought to turn when they pull on the appropriate rein. However, the horse considers all pulling on the rein an injustice, and he responds either by pulling back himself (so that he stoically refuses to turn) or by turning his head and neck, breaking at the withers, and jackknifing, so that his body continues going straight on! All of us have seen the anguish of novice riders struggling to make turns. Instead of issuing them a host of directions about what to do with their arms and legs (which they probably cannot do anyway, and which has the danger of paralysis by analysis), I simply show them the "opening rein," where the rider's inside hand moves away from the horse's neck without pulling back. I also make sure that they realize that *a turn begins before it happens;* it needs advance preparation, which includes both the use of their peripheral vision to look where they want to go, and the necessity of having the intention to get there. I suggest too that their inside thigh—while staying against the saddle—point in the direction of motion, as if it could lead them around the turn. In doing this it becomes an "aikido leg," with the same subtle strength as the "aikido arm" described in the exercise in Chapter 3, and this enables it to indicate direction to the horse in a far more powerful way than any rein aid could.

Moreover, it is generally helpful, along with these positionings, to think of steering the horse's shoulders rather than his nose. His nose will go where his shoulders put it, but the reverse is not true —in attempting to steer the nose, control of the shoulders is lost. In effect, steering a horse is rather like steering a wheelbarrow: if you grab one handle and try to pull it round a corner you are liable to find its contents strewn all over the yard—so instead you get behind it and push. Beginning a circle or turn by imagining that you want to push the horse's shoulder away from the wall is a very different experience from beginning it by trying to pull his nose away. If your body is well positioned, the first will work easily, and

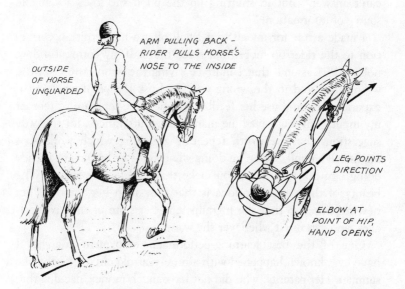

17. Pulling on the inside rein encourages the horse to break at the withers, or to pull back against you. Think instead of your inside thigh pointing out the direction of the turn. It is then far easier to use the hand as an opening rein.

his forehand will come round in front of you as if it were a wheel-barrow. Pulling on the inside rein, on the other hand, is likely to put your body into a position from which the turning aid cannot work. (We will look at this in more detail in Chapter 8.)

Improved performance is dependent on a subtle balance be-tween learning and enjoyment: together, all three have a triangular relationship, which collapses as soon as one is missing. Observa-tion of athletes in training has shown that performance suffers four to six weeks after loss of enjoyment, so when riding school riders stop enjoying their lessons their performance will suffer, and when they stop learning their enjoyment will suffer. Even in class lessons the learning process is far more enjoyable and effective when the teacher takes the time to communicate with each pupil, as one human being to another, so that she listens to their feedback, rather than talking *at* them like a sergeant major. A friend of mine recently met one such teacher when they were both candidates in a teaching examination, and she asked her if she always taught like that. "Yes," she said, "I do. It stops people asking me questions I can't answer." But in shutting up the pupil she loses a valuable source of information.

I made a rule for myself that I will offer a new position correc-tion to the rider no more than three times. If my correction does not work, I assume that I must be saying the wrong thing, at the wrong time and in the wrong way. So I ask the pupil what she is experiencing, and use her feedback to help me rephrase or reorder my input. This has saved me many wasted utterances, for the only suggestions that are worth repeating are those which work; so I might tell a pupil, "Keep on doing whatever it is that you're already doing," or ask her, "Can you make that ' x ' feeling again?" The beauty of these interventions is that they help her "groove" her new response, so that she ingrains it in her store of effective feel-ages, and can use it whenever she wants.

One of the best learning-performance-enjoyment triangles I have ever known happened with a nine-year-old child I taught one summer. Her parents, who did not have much money, decided that now was the time to invest in her riding; she had become compe-tent enough to be safe, and neither of them knew where she should go from there. The child became my teacher—I would send her away each week with homework, asking her to find out what happened at home when she was riding her pony. She would come back and tell me in the minutest detail, showing such astounding insight that I began to believe in the old saying that "out of the mouths of babes and sucklings" comes great wisdom. Her reports went something like this: "As I came down the side toward the gate, he speeds up, and sometimes I can feel myself tipping forward. Then on the corner he falls out, and goes even faster, so it's very difficult not to pull on the inside rein. The next corner I can't do at all well, but then he slows down again going away from the gate, and I can find my seat again and feel that I'm taking him. The next corner is easy, and I can keep both seatbones in place. On the next one he falls in, and I can feel how my outside rein goes into a loop, but I don't know what to do about it. . . ." At this stage, her ability to feel what was happening was far greater than her ability to do anything about it; but a good grounding in this first stage makes the next relatively easy, and she and many others have proved to me that beginners and young people can, very early on, develop a perceptual framework through which to understand the skill of riding.

One of the reasons why her learning was so exciting was that we kept alive her beginner's mind. She was never able to say, "I know all about that now," because I continually asked her questions and set her tasks that she could only answer and put into practice by increasing her awareness, although I would help her by making suggestions about how and where she should "look" for the answers. It became a game, in which she had to take responsibility for her own learning, rather than being fed by my knowledge. Most people's experience of learning—after learning to walk and talk as a young child—is of being "done to"; so they sit and wait for the teacher to provide the answers. There are rare individuals who retain their childlike ability to learn—the people who almost immediately pick up a posting trot and say, "Well, I saw the others going up and down so I did it too." Often their learning seems so effortless that other riders find them extremely annoying: their own struggle involves so much longing, determination, blood, sweat, and tears that it seems grossly unfair that *these* riders should improve so much when they seem to care so little. The paradox is that within this apparent carelessness they actually utilize the natural learning abilities of the right brain, and take responsibility for their own progress.

It took me a long time to discover this. For years I treated myself rather like a patient who was sick—I saw myself as the victim of all the things my teachers said were wrong with me, and I expected them to put me right. A turning point came one day when one of my teachers yelled at me in exasperation, "Can't you control your body?" What immediately went through my head was, Of course I can't; if I could I wouldn't be here. A while later it began to dawn on me that neither she nor anybody else was ever going to control it for me, and with this realization, I began to transform myself into a pupil who was able to get far more benefit from her riding lessons.

Awareness Questions and Imagery

- Do you tend to ride in the unconscious, the trying, the panicking, or the awareness mode?
- What kind of internal obstacles make it difficult for you to focus your attention? Where does it tend to go while you are riding?
- If you were to be the kind of rider you would ideally like to be, how would you have to be different?
- Through how fine a "microscopic lens" do you look at riding? If your perceptions are rather bland, it is likely that good riders seem very mysterious to you, and that changes in yourself and your horse "just happen." Can you identify any cause-and-effect rules which underlie these interactions?

Uncovering these requires you to discover which body parts are dependent on which, so that you can identify causes and symptoms. This is one of the most difficult parts of learning, and a teacher who can help you with this will open the door to dramatic changes. It is important to remember that problems in the extremities of the body are usually symptomatic of difficulties far nearer the center. Whenever you feel stuck, return to the floor exercises of Chapter 3, and use these to help you bring your working muscles under more conscious control. Also use mental rehearsal to help you identify the discrepancies between this and your actual riding posture.

The numbering exercise can be used to refine your awareness of many body parts and coordinations—how good you feel (as a generalization); how much you feel in control of your body, or how much the horse bumps you about; how still you can keep your lower leg, or your hand; how much impulsion you have, and so on. Be inventive in the way you use it, and notice the difficulties you have. Is it hard for you to give numbers off the top of your head, and are you so critical of your work that you tend to use only very low numbers, and not to register improvements?

- How aware are you of differences in yourself and the horse in different parts of the school? Can you give a running commentary while riding, or recall afterward what happened at each point? How much does the horse take you by surprise when he deviates from his ideal passage? Can you notice these changes earlier, and give your corrective aids earlier?

For instance, after working with circles or even just going along the rail, see if you can answer the following questions:

- Where is the easiest part of the circle—at what point does it begin, and how long does it last?
- How do you know that it is easy? What do you like about it? How would you describe the feeling in your seat and body, the rein contact, and the horse?
- How does this contrast with the most difficult part, and the feelings you have there?
- How do you know when you have lost the good feeling, and how far in advance do you sense that it is about to go wrong?
- What would have to change in you and/or the horse, for you to be able to hold the good feeling longer?
- How much say do you have in precisely where the horse goes (whether he falls in or out) and how he goes (his speed, outline, and the regularity of his steps)? Are you causal or reactive?
- What goes through your mind when you know that the difficult part is approaching?
- Can you pinpoint any changes in your body positioning which

correspond to changes in the horse? If not, can you at least identify how you are tempted to react with your hand?

Both the times in the school when you "get it" and those when you "lose it" are the points which offer the most valuable feedback, because once you know exactly what happens in each case you gain far more control over yourself and the horse. "Getting it" is usually a sudden and dramatic change which you can easily feel (even if you do not yet know exactly how you did it). "Losing it" is usually a more subtle, gradual process, which is much harder to identify.

• To what extent do you take responsibility for your own learning? Are you waiting for your teachers to "cure" you, or are you looking for your own answers? The pupils who learn most easily are fairly autonomous, but they also listen to the teacher, and are willing to explore with her the discrepancies between her input and their own kinesthetic sensation.

I often find that the work I see in riding schools depresses me, and it obviously depresses horses too. One of my teachers once said to me, as he watched me struggling to find enough impulsion on one of his school horses, "The problem here is not that he's physically tired, it's that he's morally tired." The horse has often had such a hard time dealing with incompetent riders that he protects himself by going dead, and who can blame him? He is not a machine, and he is not stupid. The way he saves his energy and takes advantage of the rider's inability makes him very hard to ride. (What injustice this is for the novice rider, who needs all the help she can get!) Instead of the rider being the brains of the rider-horse alliance, with the horse being the brawn, the horse becomes the brains and the rider becomes the brawn. She uses all her physical resources to try to make the horse go, but the more she kicks him, the more her efforts become like background music which he hardly notices. So she adopts more desperate measures; her concern is with the end she wants to achieve, and not with the means. She is barely aware of the tension through her body, and the conflicting signal she is probably giving the horse with her hand. In the rider's face you see gritted teeth and a furrowed, sweating brow.

In the horse's face you see total unconcern. What should be a conversation between horse and rider has turned into a monologue: the horse refuses to participate, and in doing this he becomes far more intelligent than the rider.

Horses—and riders—very often do not play fair, and in lessons the teacher plays a large part in determining whether the rider is sacrificed to the horse, or the horse is sacrificed to the rider; she allows the horse to be bone-idle, or the rider to be stick-happy; or she encourages them into a relationship which is based on mutual respect. All too often teachers view the horse as something on which the pupil is carried as she goes round and round and practices her position. This requires minimum involvement from the horse, who is all too happy to ignore the rider and economize on effort. When I get on a riding school horse I am usually shocked at his deadness, woodenness, and lack of willingness to cooperate with me; and I may have to hit him quite hard to reawaken his spirit, so that he is willing to take an active part in my work. Pupils (and teachers) usually believe the horse when he insists that his contribution to the lessons should be minimal, and their expectations are so low that they do not even realize how different he could be. Thus, as pupil and horse negotiate their work contract, the pupil will come off worse, unless the teacher intervenes on her behalf. When I meet a rider who is rather passive, and who feels defeated before she starts, I often have to psyche her up, until she finds the faith in herself to insist to the horse that she is right. I encourage her to ride as if she were a more competent rider, or as if she believed in herself, because only then might the horse believe in her too. I learned the importance of this when I was a junior teacher on the staff of a large riding school. There was one horse in particular whom I often rode in my lessons, and I found her extremely difficult; but sometimes I taught other students on her, and when I got on to demonstrate I could produce some quite nice work with far less sweat. At the time I could not understand this discrepancy, but later I realized how different my attitude was in each case. In one I rode as if I did not know what I was doing, and in the other I rode as if I did, and the change in my expectations (and possibly hers) was sufficient to have an enormous impact on us both.

The rider's effectiveness is in part a matter of faith, and in part one of technique. The average riding school horse will sell out on the pupil whenever he gets the chance, but she needs to have faith in his respect and attentiveness if she is to learn useful driving aids, and to believe in her own efficacy. This faith is vital, because the aids lose their meaning if they are held over a prolonged period of time, and this is exactly what the rider is tempted to do if she does not believe they will work. Many riders use their leg in a lengthy and intense squeeze, as if they are trying to squeeze the horse's internal sausage meat to somewhere else in the sausage—and this never works. As well as deadening the horse, it always leads to unwanted repercussions in their seat. Instead, their intention should be to touch the horse's skin with the quality of a light slap, or, if necessary, a sharper one, and the quickness of the aid makes it far more effective.

When I'm explaining the driving aids to children, I use the following analogy to define a good working relationship in which the horse has respect for the rider's leg. When you give an aid to the horse, it is like ringing a doorbell. You do not do that by taking a running jump at it and pressing with all your might. Neither do you keep pressing for so long that you might annoy the people inside. Instead you put your finger on it, then release. If there is no answer you do it again, and if there is still no answer you know that either the people are out, or the doorbell is not working. Since the horse is definitely in his body, it must be the communication system that is broken. To repair it, you use your stick, and you do it well enough that you do not have to keep nagging.

In reality, effective driving aids are far more sophisticated than this, and the way the rider places her body and uses her back determines how necessary and effective her leg is. Misconceptions about using the back, though, are so rife that few teachers dare even mention it. Some believe that the rider should shuffle her seat around in the saddle, others that she should shove it—as hard as she can—into the horse's back. Müseler, a famous German rider, compares bracing the back to pushing a swing, and this is, I think, a very good description of the aid. (Compare it with the floor exercises in Chapter 3.) But the horse only responds to it on the *release*, that is, as the swing begins to fly upward. Without the release, the rider pushes forever, clamping the horse between her seat and leg, actually preventing him from going forward. When her aid does not work, the assumption she makes is that her seat and/or back are not strong enough, so she pushes with them even harder until they *are* strong enough. The mere fact that she believes that the answer must lie in more strength renders her efforts abortive: good aids are marked by their lightness and their short duration, but very few riders have the skill and faith to trust that the power of the aid lies in its release, and not in the force that is put into it.

This is yet another example of the way in which skilled riding contradicts all your instincts, and whether you want to turn, or start, or stop, your natural way of doing it is almost bound to be wrong. But even when you do discover the right way, your body still has to adapt to it. Although new coordinations can become grooved surprisingly quickly, it takes time for the muscles to strengthen in response to the new demands. Research has shown that the beginner in any activity needs to do it at least twice a week if the necessary physical changes are to take place, and the physical demands of riding are so strange that I think it takes the body an abnormally long time to adapt. Until it does, the novice rider finds herself in the dilemma which we noted in Chapter 3: when she tucks her seat under her and brings it sufficiently far forward, her leg comes up (into the armchair seat), and when she brings her leg into the right place, her back hollows and her seat slides back (into the fork seat). Generally, teachers begin by sculpting the rider's leg in the hope that her seat will follow. But in my experience it does not, and unless we start with the seat, we create riders who look passable but who feel ineffective.

Another aspect of this dilemma concerns the difficulty the rider has with staying vertical while she takes up a rein contact. "Shorten your reins!" shouts the teacher, and as she does so, the pupil tips forward. "Lean back!" shouts the teacher—so the pupil lengthens her reins. She feels as if she has no other choice, and indeed she does not until she can resolve her dilemma by influencing the horse's carriage. Teachers are often unsympathetic to her plight, and while they do realize that both horns of the dilemma are relatively powerless positions, they do not realize that the only solution is to find yet another alternative. The rider needs to re-form her way of sitting, so that she can bring her seat bones forward and her leg down *both at the same time*. This will completely change the way she uses her musculature (see the floor exercises in Chapter 3), and will have such a profound effect on the horse that he too will reform himself. As his outline changes, he carries himself far more proudly, and comes on to the bit, resolving the rider's predicament by making it easier for her to keep her seat, her leg, and her contact all at the same time.

Until the rider discovers how to do this she is better off with the rein slightly long, because then she is not pulled forward off her seat, and she does not interfere with the horse's mouth. A friend of mine whose riding I respect tremendously runs a center offering riding holidays, and he is always complaining, "These riders who've come from riding schools! All they've ever done is to go round and round in circles, being told by their teachers to keep a contact. The result is that they're not safe to ride out across coun-try—they hang on to the horse's mouth so much and have such unstable seats that they could bring a horse down in uneven going."

In helping pupils to solve the dilemmas, paradoxes, and mys-teries of riding, I have found it immensely useful to recognize both how subtle the skill of riding is and how immensely capable human beings are at learning. Starting from the premise that the oak al-ready exists inside the acorn changes my approach both to the novice rider and to the riding school horse. When I look at them, I see them as they are now and as they could be; my intention is to help them fulfill their potential. So, rather than leaving them to battle it out, and to ingrain their bad habits even more, I intervene to offer them new ways of being. The rider is likely to get bored of endless repetitive circles, or to get stuck and frustrated fighting her own bad habits. If we give her the tools to do a good circle, it becomes interesting, and what was once a meaningless geometrical exercise becomes an absorbing, satisfying task. Without even real-izing it, the rider develops a taste for dressage, and balancing this with outdoor work will mold her into a good all-round rider, who will make an easy transition into the next stage of her work.

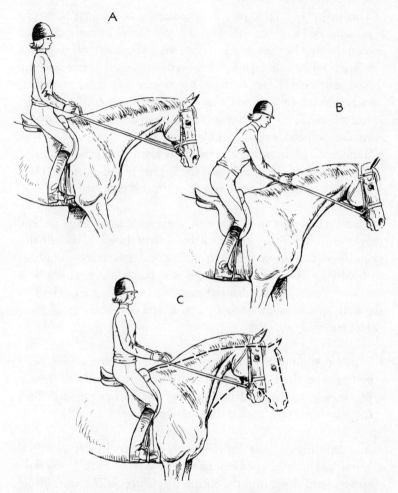

18. The learning rider's dilemma: she either sits upright with a rather long rein (A), or she tips forward as she shortens it. Only when the horse's carriage changes can she sit upright with a shorter rein.

Awareness Questions and Imagery

- In your rider-horse relationship, who is the brains and who is the brawn?
- To what extent do you expect the horse to take notice of you?

This will play a large part in determining how much notice he actually takes of you. (Riding school riders, in particular, are often limited by their low expectations.) You may have to psyche yourself up or ride as if you believed in yourself before you will have much effect. Try riding as if you were a far more confident, elegant rider, or as if you were your own teacher, or some rider you admire. This exercise will be most potent if you choose to emulate somebody with your own body type.

• Riding school horses are difficult to learn on because they so often ignore all the rider's aids, forcing her to use more and more desperate tactics. What do you do when this happens?

Many riders start to shove with their seat, using large forceful movements. Then they nag at the horse with their leg. Usually this gives the walk a heavy, dragging quality, and it is far more effective to hold your seat still so that your seat bones move within your backside. Then you can demand impulsion with your leg. Think of the walk having intention and purpose, and of it being crisp rather than lumbering and slow.

• It is important only to use your legs with the express purpose of getting a result. Do you use them out of habit, without the expectation that they will be effective? Are you prepared to back them up using your stick if they are not?

You can only use your leg effectively if it initially lies in a good alignment, and is independent of the rest of your body. If you push your legs hard down into the stirrup this is impossible; instead, let them make a V shape which reaches out around the horse's barrel so that they rest lightly in the stirrup. Think of wrapping your whole leg around the horse, rather like a napkin ring around a napkin.

If you have trouble keeping your lower leg still, feel for the contact which the top of your boot makes with the lower part of the saddle flap, and aim to hold your boot continually in the same place. You can also imagine that your stirrups are tied together beneath the horse's belly.

To hold your legs in the correct alignment, imagine a rod connecting your backside and your heel. Then keep this rod vertical.

- Establish these images in walk and rising trot before you work with them in sitting trot and canter. During which paces and movements do you lose them most easily?
- Notice the quality of your own leg aids. Are they sharp or prolonged? Are they like a squeeze or a slap? Does your toe turn out, your heel come up, or your whole leg move back? How do these movements affect the muscles below and behind your knee? Does your aid affect your leg above your knee, or your belly, or the way your backside contacts the saddle?

Ideally, the lower leg moves inward (not backward) without there being any repercussions in your knee, thigh, belly, or seat. It makes a quick sharp movement, so that a light aid is like tapping the horse's side, and a more impressive one is like slapping it. In each case the leg rebounds immediately. Does yours rebound or stay glued onto the horse's side? If you use your leg in a prolonged squeeze there are bound to be repercussions in your seat and thigh. It has to make a short, sharp movement.

- If you find the sharper aid difficult, which many people do, imagine that you want to hit the horse's belly with the inside of the stirrup iron. Think of using the whole of your lower leg, as if it were a wooden boot tree within your boot. How does this change the way you use the muscles just below and behind your knee?

Allow yourself to be rather crude with this at first, and it will be easy to learn subtlety later.

- Which horn of the learning rider's dilemma do you habitually choose? Do you position your seat at the expense of your leg, or your leg at the expense of your seat? Do you lean forward and keep a contact, or sit vertical and ride with a longer rein?

Such problems are inevitable at this stage, and to help you develop your muscular use keep returning to the floor exercises in Chapter 3, and to the previous Awareness Questions and Imagery sections. It is worth taking time to ingrain these basic building blocks, because they are foundations which will enable you to progress further.

6 On the Bit:
The Mental Problem

Ideally, the rider would gradually pass from being a kind passenger to being an active, effective rider, able to influence horses, so that they worked on the bit. This would happen as a by-product of her increasing awareness and skill which, over time, transform her body into a far more effective tool for molding the horse into shape. Seemingly of their own will, her horses would happily cooperate, rearranging their carriage and movement to become the beautiful "dressage horses" most riders so envy.

In practice horses don't make it that easy for their riders. But I have seen many horses begin to offer their learning riders exceptionally good work, without the riders' having to struggle and fight to achieve it, or having set it up as a glorious—and probably unattainable—goal.

However, this certainly was not my experience, or that of most riders I know. My days of innocence and enjoyment came to a sudden end when the teacher announced one day that we were going to learn to get the horses on the bit. There was a sudden change in emphasis: I had previously seen my position as being completely separate from the horse: I was now supposed to be actively engaged in getting a certain result from the horse, and this seemed unrelated to my position. I had no cause-and-effect framework for linking the two ways of riding, and consequently I was stumped. Faced with this demand for a specific result, I contorted my body more and more, as I tried various permutations of driving with my seat, squeezing with my legs, and vibrating my fingers around the rein. I began desperately wanting to get my horses on the bit, and the more desperate I became, the more the horses resisted me.

This is the stage at which many riders became disillusioned. They are active riders, using strong tactics that do not work, and they do not perceive themselves as having any other choice. Their desperation, determination, and misunderstandings lead them into all sorts of problems—and this syndrome is worst among those who want to be professionals, and who want, at all costs, to be good. From my observations of students in training I am not surprised. I once watched a lesson in a renowned riding center, when a staff member was teaching a group of trainees. The principal of the school was due to come in and take over, and all the riders seemed anxious. Each time the ride came past, one of the students whispered to the teacher, "Please get me off this thing," "You've got to let us walk soon," "Please, can we stop?" When the new teacher finally appeared, I realized the reason for this pupil's panic. She announced her arrival with the demand, "Get these horses ON THE BIT!" Momentarily horses and riders all froze. Then there was a shortening of reins; hands began to jerk and saw; legs to bang or cling; the horses' evasions increased.

Despite their good intentions, riders at this stage often do a lot of damage to horses. A rider who thinks she knows more than she does, and who is determined to get results, is far more dangerous than a more ignorant rider who makes fewer demands. Supposedly knowledgeable riders look down their noses at riders who get their results through resorting to ironmongery, but they themselves, with their greater pretensions, can be equally destructive. When any rider substitutes strength for skill, her horses have to find ways of protecting themselves. Typically, they become scared to put their power into forward movement, because they know that the only reward they will get when they do is a thump on the back or a sock in the teeth. Instead their movement becomes more up-and-down, tensions increase, and they contort their bodies. Eventually the most sensitive horses become nervous wrecks or nappy.

I call this syndrome "the spiral of increasing tension," and it is the instinctive protective mechanism of a horse who feels that his back, sides, and mouth are being exposed to harsh, insensitive treatment. He hollows his back in an attempt to take it away from beneath the rider's seat. He draws in his belly and rib cage in an attempt to take them away from the rider's leg. As he holds them tensely, he clamps his tail between his legs, and he also restricts his breathing—to the extent that he may even hold his breath. As a natural counterpart to hollowing his back, he raises his head, and takes his mouth up and away from the pull of the rein. This posture stimulates the adrenal glands, and as his adrenaline flow increases, the horse reacts with his fight-or-flight reflexes. The cramping of his back muscles reduces his ability to coordinate the back and front halves of his body, and under the more generalized effects of tension, his joints no longer act as shock absorbers. The net result is that his back becomes extremely uncomfortable to sit on.

Individual horses show variations on this theme. As we have seen, many riding school horses respond less dramatically, and cope with their situation by anesthetizing themselves to the rider. In their evasive movement, horses protect themselves reflexively by tensing up to produce the pattern described above, and/or by deadening themselves to kinesthetic input. With their individual variations, different horses look and feel very different. Some feel as if they thrust a ramrod up the rider's spine at every step. Some wobble about, so the rider feels as if she is riding an enormous hunk of jelly; some bounce, as if they are moving on pogo sticks; some feel like a plank of wood; and some become what I call "mushy in the middle," so the rider feels as if she is sitting on a deep, soft featherbed which has no bottom. The horse's response (whatever it is) makes it harder for the rider, who resorts to brute force or the fetal crouch; and this in turn makes it harder for the horse. Gradually, they become locked into a spiral, and when it is wound to its fullest extent, both horse and rider lose conscious choice about their actions, and become caught in the grip of the adrenaline which runs their fight-or-flight reflexes.

Horses rarely, if ever, change the direction of the spiral, so it has to be the rider who unwinds it, changing her way of sitting so that her seat, hand, and leg exert a far more positive influence. Only then is she able to evoke the exact opposite set of reflexes, which I call the "seeking" reflexes. Instead of taking his back, sides, and mouth away from the rider's seat, legs, and hands, the horse seeks contact with them. He lifts his back up underneath the rider's seat,

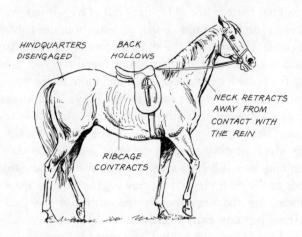

HINDQUARTERS
DISENGAGED

BACK
HOLLOWS

NECK RETRACTS
AWAY FROM
CONTACT WITH
THE REIN

RIBCAGE
CONTRACTS

19. The horse's response in the spiral of tension.

filling it out so that his back feels higher and broader—the effect is rather like sitting on a tabletop. His rib cage and belly release, so that his sides seek contact with the rider's legs. At the same time his breathing becomes deep and regular, following the rhythm of his step, and often he snorts gently as he exhales. Once the horse has released his back muscles, his tail and his neck can also release, and his neck stretches and arches to seek a light contact with the rider's hand.

As the horse moves into these seeking reflexes his whole top line lengthens, stretching the ligament which runs from his tail to his poll. Instead of being loose, like an unstrung bow, or a hammock, it takes on the shape of a strung bow, or a suspension bridge. Through being raised and arched it becomes far more resilient, changing the feel given to the rider on top. The ligament is drawn up in the middle by being pulled down and out at each end; its attachment at the end of the spine moves when the horse's pelvis rotates, bringing his croup and tail closer to the ground. He then carries his tail, and it swings freely from side to side with each step. The joints of his hind legs bend more, which gives better shock absorption and allows him to take longer and/or higher steps underneath. The attachment of the ligament at the poll moves as the horse extends the top line of his neck out of his withers, so that it stretches and arches to produce that majestic, rounded curve which we all crave. The withers, the thoracic part of the spine (see Fig. 21), and the loin area are then quite literally pulled upward— making the horse look and feel bigger and more impressive. As his rib cage fills out, it becomes easier for the rider's leg to contact the "magic spot" area near the girth (so called by Molly Sivewright in her book, *Thinking Riding*). A touch in this area stimulates nerve endings which lie close beneath the skin, and connect directly to the loin muscles just behind the saddle. So the horse automatically responds to the rider's leg aid by drawing his spine up even more, thus increasing the suspension-bridge quality of the back. The horse's hind legs now carry slightly more of his weight; his forelegs thud less heavily onto the ground, and instead of trying to pull him along, they merely support the (reduced) weight of his forehand. This allows his head and neck to be used as a much more subtle and efficient balancing aid. All these changes make the horse's movement far easier to sit on, and this helps the rider, who in turn helps the horse. As they each make it easier for the other, they gradually move into what I call "the spiral of increasing ease."

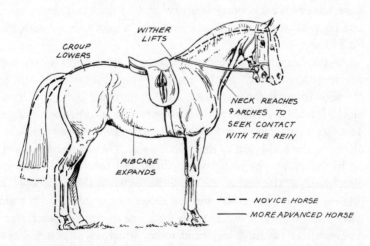

20. The horse's response in the spiral of ease, showing the carriages both of a novice and of a more advanced horse.

The seeking reflexes underlie all correct work, regardless of whether the horse is at a novice or an advanced stage of training. Throughout this progression, his quarters lower and his forehand lightens, so instead of moving in a longer, stretched outline, he gradually adopts the upright carriage of collection. As his balance and agility improve, and his body becomes compressed, it is as if he "sits himself down," flexing the joints of his hind legs, but still seeking contact with the rider's seat, leg, and hand. Traditionally, we tend to think of these changes in his carriage as beginning with the increased stepping of his hind legs. If it is indeed possible to identify a starting point for this interwoven set of responses (which I doubt), I would place it farther forward, in the area of the horse's back, withers, and shoulder blades. This echoes the words of the Baron Von Blixen Finecke, a leading trainer and Olympic medalist, who says: "We all want lightness of the forehand. In order to achieve it we work on more engagement of the hind legs. I invite people to think the other way round: work on lightness and submission of the forehand; the hind legs will engage as soon as there is room for them."*

Unlike man, the horse has no collarbone—his rib cage is suspended between his shoulder blades, held in place only by ligaments and muscles, and this means that the back and withers can be raised or lowered between the shoulder blades. In the seeking reflexes the back and withers are pulled upward, so his croup is relatively lowered. Regardless of the exact anatomical facts, however, I find this a very useful piece of imagery for the rider, who can influence the horse's hind legs by focusing *not* on his head position, or solely on his quarters, *but on his back, his shoulders, and the base of his neck.*

Perhaps more important than the detailed mechanism of these changes in the horse's carriage is the general rule that *horses give up the uniqueness of their evasive movements when they display the seeking reflexes.* This is a vital clue to the puzzle of riding; if it did not happen, the rider would have no way of knowing what a good movement was, and there would be no way out of the confusion most riders experience. As it is, all horses surrender much of their

*Horse and Driving, January–February 1984

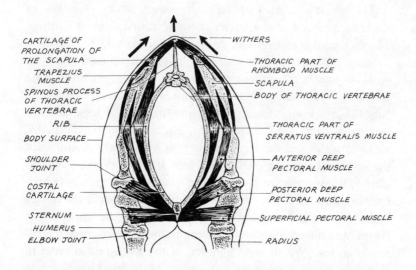

CARTILAGE OF
PROLONGATION OF
THE SCAPULA
TRAPEZIUS
MUSCLE
SPINOUS PROCESS
OF THORACIC
VERTEBRAE
RIB
BODY SURFACE
SHOULDER
JOINT
COSTAL
CARTILAGE
STERNUM
HUMERUS
ELBOW JOINT

WITHERS
THORACIC PART OF
RHOMBOID MUSCLE
SCAPULA
BODY OF THORACIC VERTEBRAE
THORACIC PART OF
SERRATUS VENTRALIS MUSCLE
ANTERIOR DEEP
PECTORAL MUSCLE
POSTERIOR DEEP
PECTORAL MUSCLE
SUPERFICIAL PECTORAL MUSCLE
RADIUS

21. A cross section of the horse's body, showing his rib cage and shoulder blades. Since they have no bony connection, the rib cage can be raised or lowered between the shoulder blades.

individuality and begin not only to look very similar, but also to *feel* very similar, when they move well. The rider who has felt and seen this enough times begins to know what she is searching for, but without this knowledge the work can be very perplexing. I often hear riders complaining: "Yesterday when I rode X I couldn't sit at all, but today, on Y, I was really good. I don't understand how I can be so different." "My legs are being really useless. I can't get them anywhere near this horse's sides, and I thought I'd learned to do that." "The last horse I rode responded really well when I did *x*, but this one just becomes more and more resistant." And to their teacher they say, "Why are you telling me to do *x*, when yesterday you told me to do just the opposite?" To get some perspective on this problem, imagine that each horse, in his evasive movement, resembles one entrance to a maze, which has at its center the good movement we are seeking. With every horse we go on a unique journey, and initially, in particular, the feelings he gives us and the difficulties he poses may be strikingly different. The knowledge we

glean from one journey may only serve to confuse us on the next
—at times we may even have to do the exact opposite of something we previously experienced as being a surefire way of getting
us to the center. The rider has to have a tremendous amount of
experience on a lot of horses before she can store enough quality
right-brain feelages to know how to persuade each horse she rides
to give up the individuality of his evasive movement, and to produce really good work. When she is particularly skillful she will
then be able to do this in a matter of a few minutes.

Once the rider can change the direction of the spiral, she is
instantly rewarded for her efforts, because the horse immediately
becomes far more comfortable to sit on, and far more maneuverable and pleasant to ride. We often expect change to be slow—a
gradual wearing away of stiffness—but in my experience the most
useful breakthroughs are sudden alterations of the mechanism used
by the rider and/or the horse, which have immediate effects on the
way they feel and look. If we think of the rider's seat as being fifty
percent the horse's back (how comfortable it is to sit on) and fifty
percent the rider (how capable she is of sitting well) then we realize that the rider will remain stuck until she can get over the hurdle of persuading the horse to rearrange his body, and make himself
possible to sit on. At this point she is caught in a devastating
catch-22 situation: until the horse goes well, the rider will not be
able to sit well; but until the rider can sit well, she will not be able
to persuade the horse to go well.

So many riders are caught in this dilemma that it is our traditional, expected norm. Often the rider is so limited in her ability
to influence the horse that he remains stuck in his own particular
brand of evasive movement, and she is conned by his insistence
into believing that this is all he has to offer. Many, many riders
imagine that they have no choice but to ride horses which are
contorted and uncomfortable, but that is not true. When I was
training with a teacher in France, I walked into the riding school
one day to see her lungeing a new young horse in side reins. While
he had potentially excellent movement, his back was very hollow.
My teacher said to me, "I work theese horse on zee lunge because
eet ees not amusing for me to ride 'eem like thees." She had decided to use lunge work as the first step toward making his back

easier to sit on, and to save them both from the agony of what might have been a difficult encounter.

Awareness Questions and Imagery

• Think of different horses you have ridden: how would you describe the various feelings they give you in their evasive movement? How are they all different, and how does each horse make it difficult for you to sit well?
• Can you recognize the feeling of good movement?

Imagine that the horse is like a stuffed toy. The horse who slops along without impulsion feels as if he has hardly any stuffing in him. Others, who give the feeling of an unexploded bomb, have so much stuffing in them that they might burst. Stuffing is analogous to muscle tone, and it is the rider's job to determine just how much tone the horse has, and where in his body it is distributed. Imagine how it might feel if you were sitting on a stuffed toy horse which was rather limp. Then imagine someone pushing more stuffing into the horse from the back of his quarters. The toy horse's rib cage and belly would expand, feeling broader, higher, and firmer, giving you something far more solid to sit on. Its neck, which was previously limp, and possibly heavy in your hand, would now be more solidly attached to the body, and would hold itself erect, without any intervention from you. The toy horse would now feel very different.

When a horse moves into the seeking reflexes, he literally feels half a hand higher, and broader underneath you, enabling you to make a far closer contact with his back and sides. These changes have the effect of lifting his withers toward your navel, so that they come back and up at a forty-five-degree angle, thus allowing more "stuffing" to pass through into his neck, and lifting his withers relative to his croup. Think of sitting behind this huge bulge of stuffing, but in front of the dip in the horse's back.

In good work the horse's back forms such an effective bridge that it is very comfortable to sit on, and his back end and his front end no longer feel like two separate pieces. Think of him moving in

STUFFING

UNSTRUNG BOW

STRUNG BOW

22.   The stuffed toy horse is like an unstrung bow, while the horse which is more full of "stuffing" is like a strung bow. Your aim is to keep the "stuffing" passing into the horse's neck, while he will probably want to try to pass it back again, underneath the front of the saddle. The imaginary connection from your solar plexus to his neck is a great help in holding you both in place.

one piece underneath you, so that you feel as if you are being carried along on a conveyor belt.

As you ride, your task is to hold the horse in this shape underneath you, doing nothing which would inhibit this forward flow of "stuffing." As soon as your seat and thighs squash the horse, the "stuffing" will be pushed down and back, so he will hollow. If you pull back on the rein you will scrunch up his neck and stop the "stuffing" from passing right through to his ears.

• The horse may, of his own volition, try to remove the "stuffing" from his rib cage and neck. Hold yourself so that it is difficult for him to collapse underneath you, or to push the "stuffing" back under the front arch of the saddle.

Imagine that you want to hold yourself in an on-horse position without having a horse to support you. This means that you have to sit as if you wanted to levitate, hanging in space with your legs apart.

- Schooled horses carry themselves underneath you in a different balance from green horses, although on both your intention is to hold yourself so that your body acts like a framework around the horse and holds him in shape, rather than being a load on top of him which he would naturally hollow away from.

Imagine a pole which begins just below your rib cage and goes about two-thirds of the way along the horse's crest. This pole connects your stomach to his neck: imagine that you can push his neck down and away from you by lengthening it. Whenever you have the feeling of this connection, and can keep the horse moving in one piece, you are well on the way to producing correct basic work.

I believe that a lot of the problems riders experience in attempting to ride their horses on the bit stem from their *attitudes* to the horse and his training, and these often contain misconceptions which influence their own physical behavior. First, they make some rather wild assumptions about how the horse learns; and second, they believe—as I did for many years—that all they need to do in order to bring their horse on to the bit is to make his nose lie on the vertical. But the horse whose nose has been pulled inward has been restrained from displaying the seeking reflexes—and these are the real determinant of whether he is correctly on the bit. The difference between the two approaches is rather like that between squeezing a tube of toothpaste from the bottom, so that it fills out toward the top, and squeezing it backward from the top, so that it is compressed at the bottom. Many, many horses who are supposedly on the bit look to me as if their heads have been scrunched back into their necks, and their necks have been scrunched back into their withers; this syndrome (known commonly as riding the horse from front to back) produces horses whose outline is as unattractive as the badly squeezed tube of toothpaste.

The whole point about the seeking reflexes is that they are not *conditioned* reflexes, like the response of Pavlov's famous dogs (who, after a few trials with real food, began to salivate whenever they heard a bell ring). Instead, they are *instinctive* reflexes—as salivation is an instinctive response to the sight, smell, and thought of food. The horse's response to voice commands (apart from his instinctive response to the tone of your voice) is a conditioned re-

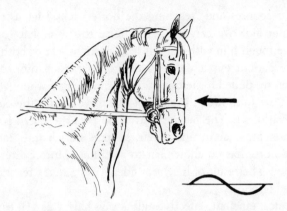

23. The horse's neck is raised and arched, but his head has been pulled in. The bow is not correctly strung: it has been pulled into two curves instead of one.

flex, and so is his response to the rider's leg as it asks him to move forward or sideways. But his response to a well-placed body is instinctive. This means that the correct use of the seat, leg, and hand as shaping aids produces an instinctive response which is inescapable—*it cannot not happen.* The best riders cooperate with these reflexes: they shape the horse and make him malleable by positioning themselves so that he inevitably responds in the way that they want—seeking contact with their seat, leg, and hand to produce that majestic outline. Less knowledgeable riders do not realize that these interchanges are happening, and instead of cooperating with them, they overlay them with attempts to teach the horse to come on to the bit, or to perform the various school movements—an approach which I often call "teaching the horse tricks." Although most of us are blissfully unaware of them, the reflex interactions which lead the horse and rider into the spiral of ease or the spiral of tension underlie everything we do, and it is these changes which determine the quality of the work we produce. Thus, while you may be convinced that you are teaching your horse all sorts of valuable things, something quite different is happening underneath—and this "something" actually controls just how successful you will be.

To illustrate the difference between cooperating with the horse's natural responses and "teaching the horse tricks," let us consider the canter aid. We can teach the horse to canter left (or right) when we touch him with our left leg, our right leg, or both legs. If we were patient enough, we could probably teach him to canter left when we pulled his left ear, and to canter right when we pulled his right ear (although I would not like to vouch for the quality of the transitions!). The most effective aid puts the *rider's body* into the canter movement, and when she puts herself into canter on top, the horse has no choice but to put himself into canter underneath her. The result of her "gear change" is a reflex reaction, not a learned response.

The most efficient, effective aids always have this as a basis, and although we often hear that a system of aids should be *logical,* it is really far more important that they be *reflexive.* When used well, aids are communicated to the horse without his even being aware of them—and he certainly does not decide his response by means of a reasoned, thought-out process equivalent to "If the rider does this, then I must do that." The many riders who think they are appealing to their horse's rational mind have enormously high expectations; they are assuming that the horse has a degree of choice about his movement patterns which they—despite their superior intelligence—do not have about their own. But even when the horse *can* be taught to give the response to an aid, and he has a conscience, and he does what he knows he should, he will do it in a carriage which is determined not by how well he has learned his lessons, but by how much he is protecting himself—through his own unconscious mechanisms—from the rider's indelicacies.

Instead of taking it upon themselves to create conditions under which the horse will reflexively move as they want him to, most riders resort to the more left-brain approach of reward and punishment. But this assumes that the horse can be made to look beautiful by being subdued, manipulated, and made to be obedient; that he can learn, by domination and reason, to hold his body in a certain way. Training methods based on the stick and the carrot are only partially successful, because they overestimate the horse's reasoning power and ignore the myriad exchanges that are happening somewhere outside the rider's awareness. A client of mine discovered the limitations of this approach when someone advised her to teach her horse not to pull on the rein—by hitting him every time he did. The outcome was that he kept pulling at the rein, and then learned to run away from the stick immediately afterward! She was rather slow to realize that her tactics were never going to get her the result she wanted; it would have been far more appropriate for her to eliminate the horse's need to pull on the rein by discovering how she could change the mechanism of his motion—primarily by changing the way that she was sitting on his back and hanging on to the rein herself. (It would also have helped to check his teeth.) On other occasions, when horses evolve some remarkably intelligent responses, they are not too good at discriminating between when and when not to use them. I was given a very amusing example of this by a newly arrived riding school horse, who surprised me by suddenly stopping dead as my novice client lost her stirrups in canter. (My pupil, needless to say, was even more surprised!) I later discovered that the horse's previous owner had fallen off a lot, and the horse had learned to stop and wait for her. Perhaps he even caused a few more falls.

That is an example of a conditioned response, but the vast majority of the horse's responses are instinctive, and this means that he does not always behave in the ways our rationalistic minds expect. This is particularly true as regards his outline. The sad truth is that the rider's attempts to "teach" him the correct posture inevitably provoke resisitance, until she discovers the part she unwittingly plays in perpetuating the cramping and deadening reflexes: the ways in which horses actually respond—seeking or retracting from the rider's seat, hand, and leg—are far, far more complex than mere obedience to a system of signals which she, in her infinite wisdom, deigns to teach them.

Until they learn to perceive these multilayered communications, many riders find themselves becoming horribly frustrated, and most like to find reasons which explain why their work is not going as well as they think it should. Some find justification for their difficulties in the horse's conformation, so they say, "He'll never look right because he's got such a long neck" (or such a short one), or, "With movement like that, he can't come properly on to the bit." Some conformation traits do indeed make it more difficult for the horse, but rarely to the extent that the rider believes. I particularly enjoy seeing the look of pleasure and astonishment on a rider's face when she first sees or feels her horse moving in a way that she had not thought possible. This often requires her to review just who has been responsible for what aspects of the problem. Other riders ease their frustration by allowing their horses to have pervasive opinions about the work, and because "Tootsie doesn't like dressage," Tootsie, along with his owner, is let off the hook. Some horses are "still only a baby, you know," years after they have reached maturity, and others "will never be able to do it properly." Less benevolent owners are often heard exclaiming, "This horse is such a brute!" or "My horse just won't obey me." What all these riders share is a reluctance to admit that they themselves do not have the skill needed to activate the seeking reflexes and therefore the horse's own best movement. They perceive the problems they experience as stemming from the horse, and not as having anything to do with them, and at times they punish the horse for his cussedness.

More skillful riders realize that they have played a part in creating and perpetuating evasions which can seem, at first sight, to belong only to the horse. But this does not in itself provide the solution, or stop them from hitting the horse in exasperation. I make a distinction between getting angry—a conscious, deliberate choice through which you tell a horse that he is overstepping the mark—and losing your temper, when you act out of brute instinct, and pay the price through your inevitable entry into the spiral of tension. As a rider becomes more perceptive and gains "requisite variety" over the horse, her enlarged repertoire of effective responses enables her to nip his evasions in the bud, and this gives her so much more power that she is under far less emotional pressure. But the very best riders are in a better position still: they ride the horse so skillfully (and set their goals so realistically) that he naturally, reflexively, offers just what they want, and the difficulties other riders experience just do not appear.

Meanwhile, the "other riders" are still complaining about their horses' disobedience, or their lack of ability—and to overcome these problems, they resort to more heavy-handed tactics. It is inevitable that horses pay for their riders' ignorance, but at times the price becomes too high. One of the most renowned trainers in my country once said to me, "I think one of the biggest problems in England is sour, resentful horses." These poor creatures are seething at the indignity and discomfort of the riders' attempts to force them into a certain shape of movement. As they become more and more uncomfortable, a new set of evasions are built on top of the original fight-or-flight defenses; they become progressively more difficult to ride in a way that encourages them to come from behind into the seeking reflexes. Typically, in this second level of evasions, the horse becomes overbent, or breaks in the neck in front of the fourth vertebra (showing a swan neck, in which the poll is no longer the highest point). He may also tilt his muzzle and/or move in short, tense steps, with his quarters deviating from the line of his forehand. Because of the rider's preoccupation with the idea of making his nose vertical, his body will look as if it has been compressed backward from the front and, although his head may be raised, his rib cage will have dropped between his shoulder blades (see Fig. 23), which leads to a cramping of his movement. This may convey the impression that both he and the rider are treading on the brake and the accelerator at the same time.

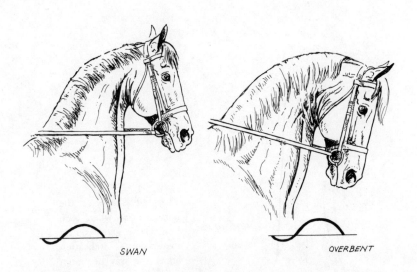

24. The horse with a swan neck, and the overbent horse. Again, the bow is incorrectly strung, making two curves instead of one (see also Fig. 23).

Over a period of time, this kind of work has a considerable effect on the horse's muscular development, leading to lean quarters and a neck which is overdeveloped on the underside. In particular, the muscles waste away at the base of the neck, where it has been compressed back into the horse's withers, and from a narrow base the neck broadens toward the poll. (If you look down at the neck when mounted and see this, it is a sure sign that the horse you are riding has been incorrectly worked.) This means that he does not have the strong muscles needed to support the weight of his own head and neck—so he will probably ask you to do it for him, by leaning on your hands.

The horse's muscle structure can tell us an enormous amount about how he has been worked, and conversely, working him differently can change a lot about how he looks. With sustained good work (done in moderation, of course, because untrained muscles are being brought into play), a ewe neck and lean quarters give way to a far more beefy and beautiful top line. Muscle develops to fill in the hollow of the weak neck, strengthening and widening its base so that it tapers from there up toward the poll. Although the skeletal structure cannot change, the head no longer seems too big and the neck too short, as they do when the horse has been worked

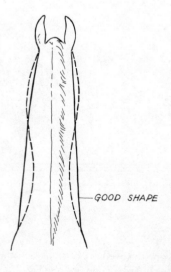

GOOD SHAPE

25. The shape of the horse's neck when seen from above gives you an immediate indication about the way he's been worked.

from front to back. So, as the muscle structure changes in response to his new carriage, the horse becomes (whatever his conformation) a far more impressive, beautiful creature.

I often ask riders, "To what extent are the horse and rider each responsible for the quality of the work they produce together?" Most riders say, "About fifty-fifty"; some say, "Well, the horse is just how he is, really, and you can't do much about that"; and a few say, "It must be about eighty or ninety percent determined by the rider." These few are usually the more skillful riders, or at least the ones who have been around a bit, and who have had the experience of seeing a far more skillful rider than themselves get on their horse and transform him before their very eyes from an ugly duckling into a swan. Or perhaps, they have ridden other people's advanced horses, so they know that it is not just a question of pushing button B and waiting for the result.

I also ask riders, "To what extent must the horse and rider each learn the other's language?" Here I also get varying responses, but the most common is, "He must learn mine, of course." To me it is not this obvious. Through their resistance, or in the ease and willingness of their paces, I believe that horses are trying to tell us something. Very often we are so busy saying things to them (and teaching them to be obedient) that we do not sit still long enough to hear—or feel—what they are saying to us. Much of the miscommunication between horse and rider occurs because *riders* do not listen—not because horses do not listen—and by overriding their horses' cries (literally as well as metaphorically), riders actually put themselves into a position in which they become reactive, not causal. Paradoxically, the ability to receive and decipher the horse's messages empowers the rider; the horse tells her exactly what is appropriate, and in a sense he becomes her teacher. But she becomes a rider who is capable of making much finer distinctions, and she can respond to the nuances of each moment from this new standpoint in her relationship with the horse. When Denise McCluggage writes, in *The Centered Skier*, of the skier's body movement and her relationship with the mountain, she makes a point which is equally applicable to the rider's body position, and her relationship with the horse which she is bringing into the seeking reflexes: "Through appropriate actions you are creating a condition under which *it* will happen—the physics of movement demand it. And then you *let* it happen."

Until they have seen it with their own eyes (or preferably felt it in their own backside), few riders believe just how much influence the rider actually has. In his book *Fundamentals of Riding*, Charles Harris goes so far as to say, "Horses have poise just like their riders —efficient or inefficient—the end result depends *entirely upon the rider* [my italics]." Can this really be? Is it really true that old Dobbin, or that funny-looking horse with the scraggy neck and the big head, could really move with the catlike poise and agility which we would normally only attribute to "dressage horses"? Unless you have ever seen an exceptionally good rider on Dobbin you will probably say no, but if you have, you will know that putting him —or any other horse—into the seeking reflexes enables him to produce his own miniature dressage show, and to look just like a "real" dressage horse. Although he may not have award-winning conformation and paces, he does have his own best movement, and that majestic outline is not the prerogative of a few special horses. Somewhere inside each and every horse—be he cob or thoroughbred—lies the potential for poised and beautiful movement, and the rider can either help or hinder. If you feel that extracting this kind of elegance from your horse is rather like trying to get blood out of a stone, it may be that your presence on his back is having an inhibiting effect.

Awareness Questions and Imagery

- To what extent do the horses you ride confound you with evasions? How much can you tell about their previous way of working through looking at them from the ground, and when mounted?
- How much do you attribute the difficulties you have with your work to the horse?
- What do you tend to say about him?

It can be a very pertinent exercise to take things you say about your horse, or attitudes that you attribute to him, and to try saying them about yourself. Thus, "My horse is such a brute" becomes "I'm such a brute," and "My horse doesn't like dressage" becomes "I don't like dressage." There is often more than a grain of truth in these statements; find some that are appropriate for you. How does it feel to say them like this?

- To what extent do you believe that the rider and horse are each responsible for the quality of the work they produce together? Express these as percentages adding up to 100 percent.
- To what extent do the rider and horse each need to learn the other's language? Again, express these as percentages.
- Is your work primarily based on "teaching the horse tricks," or can you decipher his language well enough to utilize the underlying rider-horse reflexes to your advantage?
- How does your version of "on the bit" compare with the shape and movement generated by the seeking reflexes? Does it include some riding of the horse from front to back (so that you "scrunch up the toothpaste tube")? Think of your hand as being like the lid on the end of the toothpaste tube: it does not pull backward, but neither does it allow the toothpaste to leak out.
- Do you believe that your horse (or horses you ride) has within him the ability to show the carriage and movement of a "real" dressage horse? You may have an enormous amount of evidence to the contrary; if this is so, are you still willing to believe that it might be possible?

In contrast to many, the most skilled riders are often very humble. In their search for more skill they have had to answer the questions, What do I do to the horse? What does the horse do to me? and How do we each contribute, in our separate ways, to this ongoing situation? Usually they discover that they have contributed far more than they would ever have imagined—that they have given as much or more than they got. As well as humility, this gives them exceptional clarity, which enables them to see the horse exactly as he is, without inventing scenarios about how he is a "pig," a "brute," "out to get them," or "such a lovely baby who tries so hard for his Mommy."

We all have ingrained attitudes toward the horse which color our whole approach to riding, and often they go so deep that we do not even realize their effects. Some, for instance, see him as a monster, who is either a threat to their safety or a threat to their competence, and this means that they are always on the defensive. When a rider has a great investment in being good, and she believes (consciously or unconsciously) that the horse is out to shatter her image, he becomes a threat—rather than a challenge—and this triggers the fight-or-flight reflexes, thus ensuring that her worst fears become reality. Riding is one of the few sports where there is no outlet for your frustration; smashing a ball out of court does no one any harm, but smashing the horse does, and all too often he becomes the scapegoat—punished—when really the rider is angry with herself. So at one end of the scale are riders who punish the horse unjustly; but at the other are riders who never confront or punish him at all. They are the nice, polite riders, who defer to the horse and let him choose how and where he goes. One rider I know found her horse so much more comfortable on one rein that she soon stopped riding on the difficult rein altogether. Having successfully organized this, the horse may go on to decide that he does not like cantering, or does not like leaving his fellows. When the rider colludes with the horse, she encourages him to become nappy, until he finally decides that he does not even want to go out of the yard.

Other riders surrender their power in far more subtle ways. Some treat the horse like Dresden china; they are in awe of him, and afraid they might ruin or hurt him. I treated the first advanced dressage horse I ever rode like this, but when I was not even able to steer him around the edge of the riding school, I realized that he was taking me for an idiot, and that my reverent attitude was not likely to prove productive! While more established riders are evolving theories to explain exactly how and why the horse cannot do x, novices are often perplexed by the intricacies of their relationship with him. At times they have said to me, "I'm just not sure how tough I should be on my horse. Is he pulling my leg, or can he genuinely not do it? Should I be patient with him, or should I hit him?" More often than not the horse is indeed pulling their leg, and I for one have often had some important breakthroughs when I have summoned my faith in myself, and changed my attitude from, "Oh dear, neither of us can do it" to "Right, horse, it's time you paid some attention to me." The horse does sometimes need a reminder of his role as the brawn and not the brains of the partnership, but he also needs the rider to appreciate his efforts. Primarily, however, her job is to eliminate his need to protect himself from her, so that she can cultivate his willingness to work in the seeking posture.

It is impossible not to have an attitude toward the horse and his work; the problem arises when our attitudes cause a lack of clarity, and a loss of form. I know some well-established professional riders, for instance, who can work very well with someone else's horse, but when it comes to their own—one they love dearly and have special ambitions for—they get into trouble. Suddenly they become (as one of my friends put it) a soft touch, or, alternatively, their ambition and determination drive them to push the horse to the point where they create resistance. With someone else's horse, they know that his evasions are not meant personally, so instead of blaming themselves or blaming the horse (and making themselves under- or overaggressive), they get on with the job of riding through them. With this clarity they are able to see what they do to the horse and what the horse does to them, and this enables them to work within the confines of their combined stretch zones, and to draw on the full extent of their individual and interrelating skills.

The difficulties that accompany our attitude and lack of skill can often seem insurmountable; they actually become far easier to deal with once we discover which of them really belong to the horse and which belong to us. Riders who attribute all their problems to themselves tend to let their horses take advantage of them, and those who attribute them to the horse are often tempted to go and buy another one! Horses who go along with their noses in the air, or who will not do lateral work, are supposedly replaceable with ones who will perform properly, and there are many riders who tell themselves, If only I had a real dressage horse, then everything would be fine. But the search for a "real" dressage horse, who automatically looks beautiful and does everything right, is like the search for a red herring—neither exists. It can be very disappointing when a rider pays a high price for a horse which looks superb under a good trainer and then finds, when she gets him home, that everything begins to go wrong. The horse soon uncovers the rider's weaknesses and begins to play on them; he also receives the kind of treatment which discourages him from exposing his back, sides, and mouth to the rider's indelicacies. Very soon she finds herself with a horse who poses similar difficulties as her last one, and until she accepts the problems as her own rather than disowning them, and solves them for herself, the search continues.

In riding, there is a great dividing line between riders who can and riders who cannot successfully put the horse into the seeking reflexes. Sometimes I think that educated riding resembles one of those board games where you have to throw a six before you can start—so while some riders shoot ahead, others wait uncomfortably on the sidelines. A large percentage of all our horse talk reflects this preoccupation with whether or not we managed to "get the horse going." (Inevitably this means different things to different people, but the implication is that the successful rider had the horse on the bit—in whatever way she understands the term.) For many riders, this is the end product of the work, and the result of so much trial and error that their feelings of having "made it" are very apt! But the best riders know that this is only the beginning of the work—once you have got the horse really on the bit, you have "thrown a six," or put your foot on the bottom rung of the ladder —and nothing that has happened up to that point can be classed as work.

Getting to this stage is probably the crux of riding. Riders who are struggling with it often feel as if they are chasing a will-o'-the-wisp, and they are not sure what it will be like if they ever find it. Pupils who finally *have* found it have responded by saying things like, "But this feels so weird, is it really what I've been looking for all this time?" and "I imagined that once I got it, it would feel lovely, but this *hurts*." What shocks them most is the realization that their seat, and not their hand, is holding the horse's head and neck in place—and this often requires more muscle tone than they thought they were capable of producing! Other riders have said, "But surely that couldn't have been right because it went away again. I thought once I got it, it would stay that way." Having the horse truly on the bit and working *in* the seeking reflexes is rarely how they had expected it would be, and there are so many misconceptions in popular teaching and terminology that I am not surprised.

I have very clear memories of a time when I too was struggling with this. I remember how frustrating it was when good feels would come and go so fast that I never knew what I had done to get or lose them. There was never enough time for me to get the feedback I needed in order to recognize them again, and mostly I was bewildered. Often I would think that I had got it when I had not, and only when I did finally get it did I realize how inaccurate my original perceptions had been; and once I had got it, I did not know what I should do with it. My instinct was to sit as still as possible, hold my breath, and pray, but as soon as I did this I stopped riding the horse forward; my own tension and restriction communicated itself to him, and he would drop back out of shape. Often, I did not even have time to congratulate myself on "getting it" before it had all gone wrong again. The horse and I seemed to change from being in the spiral of ease to the spiral of tension so fast that I never knew which of us had initiated the change, and how it had happened.

I watch this process happening with pupil after pupil. They get the horse on the bit and then, whether they pause to congratulate themselves or are overcome with surprise, they stop reshaping him at every step. Without this positive influence he loses his good carriage, and they have to begin once more at the beginning. Even when the rider does sustain her influence beyond this initial stage, it only takes some tiny thing to go wrong for her to panic, lose her seat, and react with her hand; the horse, who is probably very tentative about the seeking reflexes, immediately hollows again, and reverts to his evasive movement. This hand reaction is often so ingrained and instinctive that it is beyond the rider's awareness, so she has no idea what she has done. If (like most riders) she has her attention far more on the position of the horse's head and neck than she has on the feel of his back, there is no way that she can use her body position to hold him in the seeking reflexes. Instead she tries (knowingly or unknowingly) to correct any deviation with her hand, and this produces just the kind of evasion she was dreading.

Riders who have spent many years struggling to bring their

horses onto the bit often find this change in focus extremely difficult to make. Their attention becomes riveted onto the horse's head—held there by the strength of their determination and anxiety—and until they are able to let go, they cannot sense any other input. Ironically, this means that it is often far easier for novices to learn to shape the horse, becaue they are less thwarted by their left-brain interference, and far more able to focus on useful feedback. For many years in my own learning I would change from a right- to a left-brain mode every time the horse hollowed, and I would scold myself as I struggled to bring his head back down again. Only when I became willing to look in detail at my mistake (instead of trying to erase it as fast as possible) did I realize that it actually contained vital information, which I had consistently failed to notice. Only then was I able to intensify my concentration, become far more consistent, and experience bodily feelings which cleared the fog of confusion, giving me a cause-and-effect framework to answer the question, What do I do to the horse? and What does the horse do to me?

Awareness Questions and Imagery

- Do you feel satisfied with your ability to ride horses on the bit, or are you still struggling with this? Is it the end point or the beginning point of your work? How much do you know about what you do to the horse and what the horse does to you? How do you deal with your own frustration? How does this differ when you are working alone and when other people are watching you?
- Do you tend to use the horse as a scapegoat, or defer to him? Do you blame him, or blame yourself?
- Are you threatened by the horse, or challenged by him?
- Are you in awe of him, or do you despise him?
- Between the pair of you, you have 100 percent of the power inherent in your situation. What percentage of this do you take, and what percentage does the horse take? (The first numbers that come into your head will probably be the most accurate.) How do you surrender your power to him? How does he use the power he is given?

- To what extent is your focus of attention on your hand and the horse's head, and to what extent is it on your seat, leg, and belly, and on the horse's back? Again, express these two as percentages adding up to 100 percent. It can also be useful to do this when you are riding, rather in the way that you would use the numbering exercise.
- As you work to bring your horse onto the bit, how much information do you have about how you "get it" and how you "lose it"? To what do you normally attribute these changes? Once you have "got it," what do you do with it? Can you keep re-creating it in each successive stride?
- How easily can the horse disturb your state of relaxed concentration?

Very often, riders who are struggling to shape the horse look intently at his head to see if it is in position. This disturbs their ability to feel, because as soon as they focus their gaze, they lose touch with their kinesthetic sensation. It is most important to keep your peripheral vision—even when the horse suddenly brings his head up—and to ignore anything he does which might take your attention away from your bodily feelings.

- Use mental rehearsal to remember times when you have ridden well, and times when everything has gone wrong. How does your kinesthetic recall differ in each case? Do you only have a visual recollection of the difficult times; does your internal replay skip some bits? If it is necessary, use slow motion to help you find the missing pieces.

When you have access to an accurate kinesthetic recall of what happened, you will be well on the way to making change.

7 Completing the Circuit: The Physical Solution

At one time, when my riding was fraught with difficulty, it seemed to me that conflict between horse and rider was inevitable. Either my horse was bullying me or I was bullying him, and I could not find a way out of our battles. (Since it has often been said that the horse's temperament will soon begin to mirror that of his rider, this does not say much for my mental/emotional state at the time!) But I finally realized that the only way out of our conflict was to *transcend* it, and this change in my attitude opened the door to dramatic physical changes. Transcending conflict with the horse is the process of putting him "in front of you." (Theoretically, putting the horse on the bit implies the same thing, but this term has been so misunderstood that I prefer not to use it here.) When the rider puts the horse in front of her it is as if she tunes the horse's will to hers, rather as one would tune a musical instrument before playing it. Like people, horses are usually reluctant to start work, and they begin with an attitude of "Don't bother me with all this, I'm not in the right mood today." The horse's work is never of high quality until he wholeheartedly puts himself at the rider's disposal; once he reaches the seeking-reflexes mode he becomes physically and mentally far more malleable, and he offers her his body in what Erik Herbermann, in his book *The Dressage Formula*, calls "the blank check state."

I often liken the relationship of the horse and rider to that of the child and teacher in the classroom. When the child wants to look out of the window and the teacher tries to force her to pay attention, all she gets is an unwilling pupil who, even though she may feign attentiveness, takes in very little of the lesson. The highest-quality learning takes place when the teacher becomes more interesting to the pupil than the distraction, so the child (and the horse) forgets her interest in what is happening outside, forgets about her tiredness or lethargy, and forgets to wonder how long it will be until lunchtime. Instead, the lesson itself becomes so fascinating that it focuses her into a state of relaxed concentration.

The very best teachers are so interested in their pupils and the lesson that they too are in a state of relaxed concentration. But this is rarely true of riders: those who motivate themselves using willpower and determination tend to overstress their horses— imagining, perhaps, that they too shared the same kind of fervor; those who allow their mind to wander lack the focused attention which gives meaning to their work. The truth is that neither approach will successfully put and hold the horse in front of you, because you can only bring him into the "blank check state" when you have learned to hold *yourself* in that elusive state of right-brain concentration.

When riders transcend their conflict with the horse they begin to experience those magical rides which are rare events for most of us, and which provide a striking contrast to those based on the peace treaties, power struggles, and compromises which underlie most of our work. But once the rider has put the horse in front of her, she has to tread a very fine line, for if she over- or understesses him, he will fall back behind her again. She has to aim her work at the balance point where she neither colludes with the horse nor pushes him beyond the limits of what he can do. She minimizes his desire to evade her as she develops "equestrian tact," and even if he does oppose her, she knows when his opposition is based on genuine difficulty or panic, and when he is pulling her leg. She knows when to calm him and when to confront him, and she chooses just the right moments to ease him into new heights in his work . . . so he surpasses himself without even realizing that he has just done something difficult. She always respects his generosity, and she never picks fights which plummet them both into the spiral of increasing tension.

On occasions when I have been unable to put and hold the horse in front of me, it was usually because I was being plagued by my anxieties, and by notions about how it *should* be, and these ("I wonder if I'll be able to do it today"; "This is the kind of horse I always find difficult") took my attention away from each present moment. When I ride well I forget all about them, and my interest and fascination provide fuel for my right-brain concentration. With practice, I have learned to maintain this state (regardless of any distractions the horse may throw at me), and to glean the sensory information which tells me how to respond. In *The Dressage Formula*, Erik Herbermann talks of this basic rider influence as "completing the circuit": the rider motivates the action of the horse, so that the impulse from his step passes from his hindquarters through his back, neck, poll, and jaw to the bit. It is then received into the rein, through the rider's hand, her elbows, shoulder, and back to the horse's back, so the cycle can begin again. There are many places where the impulse can become blocked: the horse may not allow it to pass through his back muscles, or through his neck, or he may withdraw from the bit so that it cannot pass through into the rein. He then loses the efficient, beautiful movement in which the minimum number of muscles are used to the maximum advantage—the hallmark of all successful athletic performance. The rider has to intervene at this point—making adjustments which unblock his energy flow and recomplete the circuit. But she too can cause a break in it, losing her centered posture, tensing or becoming too flaccid in her hand, arm, back, legs, or belly. Riders who pull back on the rein, squash the horse with their seat, or show other aspects of the fetal crouch reactions are never in a position to complete it in the first place; once achieved, however, the circuit is vulnerable to the minutest mistakes, especially when there is insufficient impulsion (or energy) to keep it well fueled.

To hold the circuit complete continuously requires constant surveillance and frequent adjustment, using subtleties which go way beyond the system of aids described in most books. By making minute changes to her own position the rider continually intervenes to "make it feel right" and *to keep the net result the same*. Once she can hold the circuit complete she has little else to do. One of my teachers often shows me this—and annoys me extremely—by getting on a horse with which I have just been struggling, and saying, "Look, it's so easy, can't you understand?"

26. The complete circuit, showing the positions of the possible breaking points.

Immediately after he mounts he has completed the circuit, put the horse in front of him, and established the seeking reflexes. Trying to ride the same horse when either he or I have broken the circuit is a different experience altogether—and something my teacher cannot seem to understand! The most absurd thing about riding is that the two apparently contradictory statements used to describe it—"It's so easy" and "It's so difficult"—are both in fact true. When the rider has completed the circuit the horse is automatically on the bit, his body is malleable, and he is easy to ride. But when the rider or the horse has broken it, each finds the other extremely difficult.

Another way of looking at this is to consider the relative positions of the rider's and the horse's centers of gravity. A person's center of gravity is about an inch below her navel (slightly higher when she is sitting down), and about halfway between her back and her front—in much the same position as her center of energy and control. A horse's center of gravity is just behind his withers, and about halfway down his belly—much farther forward than his center of energy and control, which lies, with his pushing-power, deep within his pelvis. The exact position of his center of gravity depends on how high he carries his head and neck, and on whether his rib cage is raised or lowered between his shoulder blades; the center of gravity of a galloping racehorse, therefore, is farther forward and lower down than that of a horse performing dressage movements. When horse and rider together are in motion, the rider can only stay in place *by balance alone* as she brings her center of gravity into optimum alignment with the horse's. At faster paces it needs to come slightly in front of the horse's, so jockeys advance theirs by riding with a short stirrup and crouching forward, while dressage riders adopt a more upright seat. The danger for the dressage rider is that she lets her center of gravity slip *too far back.* Instinctively she realizes that something is wrong, and the physics of the situation demand that she compensate, usually by "water skiing"—bracing on the stirrups and pulling on the reins to support herself. The horse feels (understandably) as if he is dragging her along: instead of pulling her hand back toward her belly, the solution lies in advancing her *belly,* and bringing her center of gravity forward toward her hand.

Practically all the exercises and images used in this book are designed to help you find the muscle power which will draw your center of gravity into the optimum balance point. Anatomically, this poses the problem of how to bring both your knee down and your seat bone forward at the same time; and as we have discovered, this requires a rather strange muscular use. It is here that one of the biggest confusions of riding lies. Many riders imagine that staying in place "by balance alone" implies that they should be as relaxed as possible, without actively doing anything to stay in place. But when the rider becomes this passive, she cannot take responsibility for her own weight, and she slips toward the back of the saddle; once here she is reactive rather than causal; her seat becomes relatively useless; and she has to grip onto the saddle and pull on the rein to hold herself in place. Riding at high muscle tone is not the same as gripping—in fact, it eliminates your need to grip and, instead of clasping the saddle with your legs (and squeezing yourself up off the top of it), you can wrap yourself around the horse's barrel, feeling as if you are being sucked down around it. The current preoccupation with relaxation means that many riders have gone to the extreme of becoming floppy; but used well, muscle tone provides muscular forces which reposition your center of gravity and enable you to ride—without any superfluous effort—at the optimum balance point.

Many years after I had started riding, at a stage when I was supposed to be quite accomplished, I was still having trouble with this. When I rode on the lunge, I would let go of the saddle and suffer the embarrassment of feeling completely helpless, as my backside gradually bumped out from underneath me. It seemed that there was nothing I could do to hold it in place; I would feel it slip away, and think, Oh no, not again. Of course, this was happening in my normal riding too, but until I experienced sitting well on the lunge (using my hands to hold the saddle), I had not realized just how far out of place my seat was. Although I had not felt good, I sustained the illusion that really everything was all right. I argued that it did not even matter that much if the rider sat rather to the back of the saddle. I was prepared to defy even this most definitive statement made by all the great masters in my determination to believe I was doing well.

I received very little useful help from my teacher, who was himself an exceptionally skilled rider. His talent was largely based on the fact that his muscle structure had naturally developed with sufficient tone to stabilize his center of gravity. Like most talented riders, he assumed that mine would be the same, and of course it was *not*. It took another five years of experimentation and searching for me to discover the contortions apparently necessary to create enough tone in my muscles. Only then did I work on the lunge again, and when I let go of the saddle my backside stayed firmly in place. My muscles had learned to supply the force which would stop me from sliding back—the force I had previously had to supply with my hand. I had solved my biggest problem.

Inevitably, beginners are thrown about by the horse's movement, and as they improve, this involuntary movement decreases, until they are slightly bumped about, and later just slightly wobbled about. But here the learning process often stops. If they manage the next stage they eliminate all unnecessary movement, reducing it to a minimal, voluntary, precise, localized movement of their seat bones. They begin to look and feel glued onto the horse or, better still, sucked onto the horse. But even this is not enough: the best riders look as if they have *sucked the horse up underneath them*—like one rider I know, who was so skillful that he was nicknamed "the vacuum cleaner." His exceptional way of sitting provided muscular forces which not only held his center of gravity in place, but also drew the horse's back and rib cage up underneath him into the shape of the seeking reflexes.

The rider solves the central riddle of riding once she can bring her center of gravity into the one point where it lies in perfect relation to the horse's. In riding, no two moments are ever the same, and this balance point will change with the slightest change in the horse's carriage, and with changes in direction or gait—so the rider must be able to adapt instantly. The optimum balance point also changes with different horses, whose conformation and way of going make different demands on her. The static entity which most riders regard as "the correct position" does not really exist; instead, the rider is continually making adjustments, passing through an infinite number of minutely differing positions. In the state where "it's so easy" she remains causal, and determines where and how the horse goes by making subtle changes to her own center of gravity. Instinctively, he responds to these changes by adjusting his. In the state where "it's so difficult," the horse defines where and how he wants to go through adjusting *his* center of gravity, and the rider becomes reactive, responding to the changes as best she can. Either the horse takes the rider or the rider takes the horse, and whichever of them controls the positioning of his/her own center of gravity controls the positioning of the center of gravity of the combined rider-horse system—and has the ultimate power.

Awareness Questions and Imagery

• At which points do you and your horse normally break the circuit?

- Where would you put yourself on the sitting scale? Are you thrown about by the horse, bumped about, wobbled about, glued on, sucked on, or sucking the horse up underneath you?
- When you ride, are you aware of the degree to which you bring your hand toward your belly, or your belly toward your hand?

Advancing your belly toward your hand requires so much work from the thigh muscles that most people experience pain here. Depending on the particular situation, this pain can be on the inside of the thigh, on the front of it (particularly at the point where the leg meets the body), and even on the outside and underneath the thigh. Treat this pain as feedback that you are on the right track. Riding on the edge of pain can actually be quite pleasant, as long as you do not overdo it and you rest when you need to. Make friends with the pain, and learn how to produce it at will. Like any athlete, the rider is always aiming to ease her body toward new limits, and to do this you must frequently work on the edge of pain. Do not expect it to go away once you are reasonably skilled; on the contrary, use it to help you become even more effective. *But note:* Pain in the lower back is contraindicated, and dangerous. In my view, the thigh and abdominal muscles should take most of the strain in riding, and in doing this they protect the muscles of the lower back. If you are exposing your lower back so much that it hurts, your muscular use could lead to injury.

Many riders who do not develop enough muscle tone to sit really well compensate for their lack of depth by excessive movement in the small of the back, so they develop a "wobble." This can be a way to sit reasonably comfortably, but in my experience it limits the rider's effectiveness, because her center of gravity is not far enough forward, and she sits so loosely that she cannot feel and influence the horse's back precisely enough.

- In sitting trot, can you feel the individual movement of each side of the horse's back? If not, keep referring back to the chapter on dismounted work, and to the earlier Awareness Questions and Imagery sections.

Add to those basic ideas the following:

- Imagine making your thigh as narrow as possible from side to side. Also imagine a line joining the back part of your thigh where it meets your buttock, to the inner part of your thigh near your crotch. Then make that line as short as possible.
- Imagine a wafer-thin arm and hand, made out of some very strong material which comes from the ring of the bit, and which passes between your thigh and the saddle, with fingers that curl beneath and around the back of your seat bone. With one arm on each side, imagine your two seat bones being pulled forward in the palm of each hand.
- When your center of gravity comes into the right place, the horse feels as if he is moving underneath you in one piece. Think of drawing him up together by bringing the back of your body toward the front of your body, and the front of your body toward the pommel. To do this, it may help to imagine that you want to make your body two-dimensional, with no thickness.

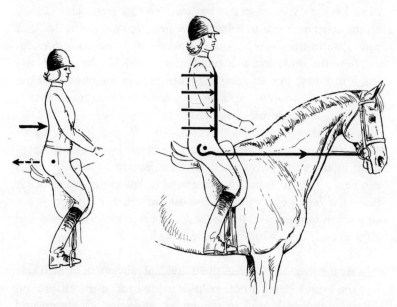

27. If your back "wobbles" in the middle, your seat bones are likely to slide out from underneath you. To stabilize your back and seat, first reorient your pelvis, and then imagine being two-dimensional and having a wafer-thin arm which curls around each of your seat bones and pulls them forward.

• On a young or green horse who feels wobbly and difficult to steer (rather like riding a piece of india rubber), or on a horse who overbends, breaks at the fourth vertebra, and/or does not reach into the rein from the withers, imagine a pole which begins just beneath the back of the saddle. It then passes under the saddle to the horse's withers, and along the crest of his neck to his ears. Are any parts of this pole missing? Riders often lose the part of it just in front of the withers, or just before the ears, and this means that there are breaks in the circuit. How do you have to sit in order to complete and maintain this connection?

With a more advanced horse, think of his crest reaching away from you while his withers come up toward your navel—as if you could hoist his withers up on a winch.

Armed with the concepts of seeking, cramping, and deadening reflexes, and a knowledge about centers of gravity, we are now in a

28.   The imaginary pole which passes from beneath your coccyx to the horse's ears, showing the positions of the most likely breaks—when the horse over-bends, breaks at the fourth vertebra, and/or does not reach into the rein from the withers.

position to understand more about the dynamic interaction of the horse and rider. To simplify our arguments, I am going to consider the case of the horse who abandons the seeking reflexes, either by nose-diving and falling on his forehand, or by hollowing his back, which brings his mouth up and away from the end of the rein. So, having had the circuit complete, you, as the rider, are faced with an evasion which breaks it—and with the challenge of mending it again.

As ever, your instinctive reactions will only tend to make the break worse. When your horse begins to fall on his forehead and pull on the rein he pulls your arms and shoulders forward, and as a counterbalance, your backside will tend to slide *backward*, folding you into a slightly fetal-crouch position. As you begin to pull back on the rein, the act of pulling will draw your pelvis *even farther back*, and the net result (since your pelvis is so much bulkier) is that your center of gravity will move backward as well. The changes in the horse's carriage also encourage this to happen: as his forehead drops and his quarters splay out behind him, his back hollows and his rib cage collapses (as if it were a balloon, and someone has let some air out). With absolutely no effort from you —and even without the added effect of the pulling—your backside will tend to slip backward into the dip he has just created for it, and once there, its only effect will be to squash his back and encourage more hollowing. (The changes we are talking about may literally only be millimeters—but the subtlety of this art is such that millimeters count.) From this new position you are reactive rather than causal: your seat is no longer an effective anchor, and you can retaliate only with the strength of your arms. Since the horse can pull longer and harder than you can, he has rendered you virtually powerless.

To you as a rider, it can seem as if the horse has trapped you into pulling back, and when your teacher starts yelling, "Surrender your hand, it takes two to pull!" you will find that seemingly you have no choice but to *keep on pulling!* However well you may understand her intellectually—and even agree with her prognosis—it feels impossible to surrender the rein. The pulling, however, is only a symptom of the problem: the cause lies in the fact that, unbeknown to you, you have tipped forward and slid backward, closing the angle between your leg and your body, and rotating your pelvis so that your back hollows. To complement the hollowing back, the front of your abdomen has pulled in and lengthened, restricting your breathing, and creating the ring of tension we discussed in Chapter 3. As we have also seen (in Chapter 4), *whenever a rider pulls on the rein, she also (unknowingly) pulls in her belly;* so only when you release your belly muscles and return to the feeling of bearing down can you surrender your hand and stop pulling.

This has enormous implications for riders. Feedback from the hand (i.e., the feeling of the horse pulling) is far more obvious than feedback from your back and belly, so if you do not feel your pelvis rotate and your belly pull in—as the vast majority of riders do not—you have no choice but to keep pulling. Every time you react with your hand you have already thwarted yourself, and since it is far, far easier to bring your hand back toward your belly and pull than it is to advance (or at least stabilize) the huge and relatively insensitive muscle bulk of your torso, this is everyone's instinctive choice.

The other choice becomes possible once you are no longer consumed by the feeling that the horse is pulling on the rein. Then you can begin to feel the narrowing and dropping of his back: in the early stages, you will feel it sink but not be quick enough to confirm your own alignment—so you will automatically accommodate the change. Gradually, as you become able to preempt the sliding back, your refusal to accommodate the alterations in the horse's carriage *makes it impossible for those changes to happen.* If your body is positioned solidly enough (which takes some considerable awareness, determination, and muscle tone), you will even find that you are holding his back so securely in place that you can momentarily advance one hand—usually the inside hand, especially if you are on a circle—and surrender the contact *without* the horse nose-diving more. In fact, this will prove an effective antidote to his pulling, because he will suddenly find himself with nothing to pull against. So every time the horse tries to pull, you reinforce your pelvic positioning (encouraging his back to stay lifted underneath you) and surrender your hand (so that you refuse to take part in the pulling match). The net result is that the horse gradually has to reform himself, drawing his withers up between

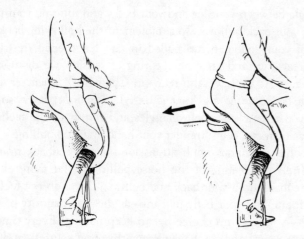

29. Changes in the horse's carriage invite you to close your front leg-body angle, and slide down the slope of the saddle into the hollow of his back; as soon as you reach this position, you have become reactive rather than causal.

your legs, filling his back out underneath your seat, engaging his quarters, and arching his neck—all according to the stage of his training—so that he makes a lighter contact into a shorter rein, and moves in self-carriage.

My hope is that this discussion may have reminded you of the last dismounted exercise which we did in Chapter 3, where you positioned yourself in a riding-type balance, and your partner tried to pull or push you out of place. (If you can find a willing partner, it would be very helpful for you to repeat the exercise now.) If your partner succeeds, it is because she has managed to destroy the integrity of your body alignment in much the same way that the horse does, so if she pulls your shoulders forward, your backside will inevitably start to protrude out behind you. Through this exercise, you may begin to discover a concrete body position where you refuse to be pulled forward, and refuse to pull back, and this gives you the centered, causal alternative to the (oh-so-devastating) battles in which you are one-of-the-two-who-pulls. If you succeed in this, you will no doubt become far more aware of your pelvis as your center of control, of your grounding, of your muscle tone, and of your concentration—and perhaps you will discover just what it takes to become a rider who can position her center of gravity so precisely that the horse's evasions cannot displace it and render her powerless.

All of us are well aware that the horse often tries to *pull* us forward, but few riders realize that he often tries to *push* them backward as well. The opposite of the nose dive is a situation in which the horse brings his head up and away from the end of the rein, so that he hollows his back and comes "above the bit." Less obvious evasions are also based on his attempts to contract his head back into his neck, and his neck back into his withers; and as he scrunches his body up like a concertina, it is as if he pushes back on the rider. Sometimes I see the rider's upper body suddenly tip back, and at other times the force seems to act on her knee—as if someone were pushing her thigh bone into her hip socket, which in turn pushes her pelvis back in the saddle. The rider may well compound the situation by suddenly pulling on the rein in a desperate attempt to bring the horse's head back down again. Of course, as soon as she does this, she tips forward and slips back-

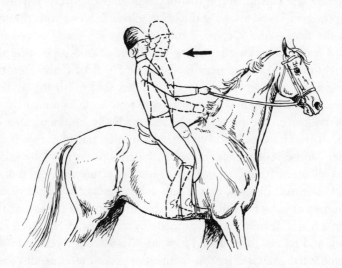

30. As the horse comes "above the bit" he effectively pushes back at you, often with these consequences.

ward. Either way, therefore, she is rendered reactive rather than causal, and her seat, in its new position within the hollow of the horse's back, serves only to perpetuate his evasion.

As before, the answer lies in becoming aware of the way in which changes in the horse's carriage tend to affect your body posture. Then, as you refuse to be pulled forward or pushed backward, and to slide into the hollow of his back, you become causal—able to influence the horse so that he brings his back *back up again*, filling out the space you have left for it and coming once more into the seeking reflexes. As you become even more skillful, you will sense when the evasion is about to happen, so you will exert a little more effort to hold yourself in front of the dip in his back, and by doing this you will prevent it. Once you are a good enough rider to come into the "vacuum cleaner" category, you will constantly hold the horse's back in place underneath you so efficiently that he will never even try to hollow or nose-dive in the first place.

Beginners, however, and even experienced riders are very easily caught by these evasions, and I must have spent hours of my life feeling powerless as my backside gave way, and my arms ached, and the horse I was riding pulled his way around the arena. Like most riders, I was caught in the traditional dilemma between lengthening the rein—and allowing the horse to shuffle along with his nose on the floor—and keeping a contact, in which case I tipped forward and slid backward, pulling on the rein, and supporting the weight of his head and neck for him (see Fig. 18). Only when the ache in my arms was finally replaced by an ache in my thighs did I become causal, finding enough muscle tone to hold myself out of the hollow of the horse's back, and gradually becoming so well placed that he couldn't even wheedle himself out of shape. If the rider can be resilient enough when he tries to do this, she gets a very different feeling in her hand: instead of immediately pulling back, she feels him jerk on the rein as he attempts to nose-dive and she does not react. I call this "meeting the horse on the end of the rein"; it is a definite statement made by a rider who refuses to pull back and refuses to be pulled forward—just like the person in the dismounted exercise. In this momentary jerk, the horse discovers that his rider is immovable, and he has no choice but to reposition himself underneath her. Once the rider reaches the "vacuum cleaner" stage, the horse tends to accept his good carriage much more and is less likely to fall on his forehand; if he begins to, the rider need only *reaffirm her seat positioning in order to reaffirm his back positioning,* and through this aid (the half halt), she is able to maintain him consistently in shape. By using it as a preventive measure she can improve his balance before a corner or any new movement, and bring him into the best possible position from which to carry it out.

The half halt must be *the* enigma of riding. It has puzzled riders for centuries: countless authors have tried to explain it, and equestrian arguments have raged about it, while some riders (particularly the British) have sworn blind that it does not exist. Just as it is a prime candidate for "paralysis by analysis," so its muscular detail must, ultimately, be unknowable, and, because of the limitations of language, it is far easier to say what it *does* than to say what it *is*. Once felt, however, its effect on the horse is so striking that it is never forgotten. When a half halt works, or "goes through" (i.e., goes right around the circuit), the horse's response is instantaneous: his back comes up to fill out the rider's seat, his quarters lower, and his forehand lightens. No pulling on the rein is involved—instead, the rider "meets the horse on the end of the rein," and any increased pressure on the bit is momentary. In that moment, the horse seems almost to pause in midair, and to sit himself down. The circuit is recompleted, and its direction (down at the back, up at the front) is reinforced. The horse continues with a lighter step, in a carriage which is more powerful and more elevated.

In *The Dressage Formula*, Erik Herbermann proposes the idea that the bit is like "neutral territory," on which neither horse nor rider is allowed to pull. But this does not mean that the rider should forever follow the horse's head just where it wants to go, always keeping the contact the same. Riders who have grown up being rather accommodating are often shocked at my insistence that they sometimes have to confront the horse and say, "No." But to be effective, this "No" must have its origins in their body positioning. The hand has the function of receiving and directing power which is generated and stored by the rider's body. To use Erik Herbermann's image, it acts rather like the nozzle on a hose. When the rein is slack, water (or energy) just flows out, but a sensitive hand can regulate the water flow, causing either a complete halt, or the kind of mist or jet that might correspond to collected or extended work. But the hand is secondary to the power source: without an effective pump (seat, driving aids), there is nothing to regulate, and no pressure (muscle tone, energy) can build up in the horse.

I never set out to teach riders the half halt; instead, I wait until it happens one day in the moment when they are making a position correction. Often, when a rider has ridden quite a few, I tell her what she has just been doing, and I get an amazed response: "That? . . . You mean that's a half halt? I thought it was something to do with restraining the horse . . ." When she had tried to ride one previously, she had stopped taking the horse, and had let her body sag backward and lose tone. In doing this, she drew in her belly and pulled back on the rein—much the same scenario as an incorrect attempt at a full halt (which we will discuss later). This change in posture breaks the circuit, and ensures that the horse will pull back against her. Whereas a correct half halt happens in an instant, the moment the rider drops back, or pulls in her belly, or rams her seat bones into the horse's back, she creates resistance which leaves her pulling on the reins for the next few strides. Not only does her aid not work, but she is worse off at the end of it than she was at the beginning.

Usually riders have to ride a lot of unintentional half halts before they can learn to make intentional ones. (The whole process is, I think, far too subtle to be learned through the medium of the conscious mind.) Often, riders do not know exactly how they do it, but that does not matter. The important thing is that they have an adequate and appropriate response system through which they can make ongoing adjustments to the positioning of their own and the horse's centers of gravity, tactfully thwarting any attempts he might make to break the circuit. By using their body position continually to monitor his carriage and his balance, they employ the most powerful and subtle tool—and they reap the most delightful rewards.

One of the skills of a rider who has become causal is her ability to ride the horse so that he makes a light and constant contact with the end of the rein. I particularly enjoy feeling the way the bit rests solidly yet easily on the bars of the horse's mouth, but it is all too easy for this feeling to disappear. You can be riding along gaily, congratulating yourself on how light the horse is in your hand, only to find—sometime later—that he has been working slightly over-bent. Even your best friends may be reluctant to dispel your illu-sion, and you have to be a particularly discriminating rider to realize for yourself. The second-level evasions, where the horse retracts from the end of the rein by overbending, tightening in the poll or gullet, or showing a swan neck, are particularly subtle breaks in the circuit, which originate—as always—from misde-meanors with your hands (riding the horse from front to back), a faulty body position, and a lack of impulsion (see Figs. 23 and 24).

Although some very experienced trainers deliberately ride their horses overbent during some stages of their training, this is not a good idea for the average rider. When done deliberately by a rider who knows how to bring the horse back onto the end of the rein, it may have some value, but few riders have this degree of choice, and without it they are on dangerous ground. Raising the hand can provide a temporary solution to the problem, but the horse will

31. As you unknowingly allow the horse to overbend, you tend to tip slightly onto your fork, so that your body comes forward and your thigh moves too much toward the vertical.

always overbend again unless the rider can adjust her body position, use this to recomplete the circuit, and maintain enough impulsion to keep it well fueled. The break in this case is just in front of the withers, and when a horse has conned me by overbending, I usually find that he has persuaded me to tilt my pelvis to that I'm sitting rather on my fork. As I reposition myself and my horse, I often feel some strain in the tendons at the front of my thigh in the angle where it meets my body. But when I can hold my position here I can "meet the horse on the end of the rein," and I no longer have to try to lift his nose with my hand.

When a horse breaks the circuit by tightening in the poll and gullet, it is possibly more difficult to persuade him that he can trust your hand enough to let that tension go. He needs you to ride him in a longer, lower, freer outline, so he can build up confidence in your ability not to draw in his front end; the evasion is, after all, really a case of him saying, "I'll retreat before you hurt me," and he needs to believe that you will not hurt him. When he breaks in his neck in front of the fourth vertebra, you have to use similar tactics to those for overbending, and it can be extremely difficult to convince him that instead he can come truly into the rein without fear. As with all these evasions, a rider with the skill to ride out of them is usually a rider who has the skill not to get into them in the first place; although this is not much help to the learning rider, it does at least emphasize the importance of having a guide on the ground (and sometimes on the horse) who can keep you on the straight and narrow, and help to shine light on these pitfalls. Even the greatest riders admit that they learned their art through making mistakes—that they had some failures along with their successes —and from these they learned what *not* to do, finding ways to avoid the many traps which beset the unwary.

Awareness Questions and Imagery

- When the horse falls on his forehand or comes above the bit, can you feel changes in your body and his back, or are you only aware of the change in his head and neck and your rein contact? Do you work primarily from your kinesthetic sense or your visual sense?

Whenever his back hollows and you slide back down the dip, your seat bones will no longer be so distinctly beneath the level of your pubic bone. At the same time your belly may pull in and your back may hollow. Use the numbering exercise to become more aware of these small changes.

Monitor also the front angle between your leg and your body because as you tip forward this will close. Think of leaving enough room between your leg and your body for the horse's neck to arch out in front of you. Hold yourself behind this bulge of "stuffing," and in front of the dip in the horse's back. It will help to imagine making yourself two-dimensional, as if you had no thickness.

- Whenever the circuit is complete, the horse will feel as if his nose is out on the end of a pair of wooden shafts which cannot contract backward. Imagine them attached to the bit rings and coming from your solar plexus, pelvis, seat bones, thighs, or calves. Think of them as originating higher if the horse tends to overbend, and lower if he tends to hollow. Can the horse lull you into a false sense of security and disappear from the end of the shafts without your noticing? If you do not monitor them constantly, your horse could con you by overbending, or showing some other second-level evasion.

- When the horse retracts from the end of the shafts, and pulls his neck back into his withers, are you aware of the way in which you are pushed backward? Does this seem to affect your body or your knee?

When it affects your body, you may tip back, or begin to sag in the middle. To help you hold your alignment, imagine a big piece of hardboard nailed on to the front of your body. Your aim is to keep it vertical and advanced forward. Also aim to keep the connection from your solar plexus to the horse's neck. (See Fig. 22.) Whenever the horse tries to break the connection and shrink away from it, think of pushing his neck back out.

The horse's retracting force may also act on your knee, and have the effect of ramming the top of your thigh bone hard back into your hip socket. Imagine a slight gap between the two, as if they were joined by a piece of string. This means that your leg can reach out of your hip socket, and feel separate from your body. If you can keep your thigh reaching out of your hip joint, you will be able to keep the horse's neck reaching out of his withers so that he seeks contact with the end of the rein.

To help you, think of your thigh bones as iron bars, which cannot be bent backward. These can then form a framework, joined by a bar which passes through the horse's belly between your knees, and one which passes through your pelvis to give you the pinch feeling. Which parts of this framework do you lose most easily?

• When the horse falls onto his forehand and makes a pull on the rein, how do you respond? Do you pull back, let the reins slip through your fingers, or accommodate this move by advancing your elbow and shoulder? Do you feel any accompanying changes in his back, or in your pelvis and belly? Are you familiar with the experience of "meeting the horse on the end of the rein"?

• In a situation where the horse is tending to pull in the rein, where does your attention go? Can you keep it primarily on your seat and the horse's back? Use the numbering exercise to help

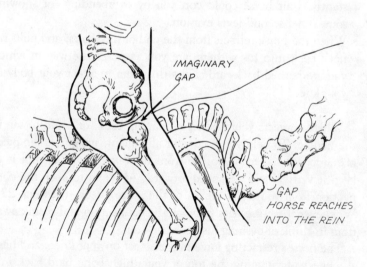

IMAGINARY GAP

GAP HORSE REACHES INTO THE REIN

32. Imagine your thigh reaching out of your hip joint, pointing forward toward the horse's shoulder, and encouraging his neck to reach out of his withers.

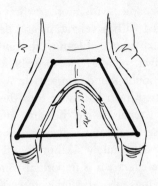

33. To help stabilize your seat, imagine a framework of iron bars passing through your backside, down along each thigh and through the horse's belly.

you monitor changes in your pelvic orientation and your contact with him. Do you feel the moment when your body first starts to accommodate changes in the horse's carriage? The more sensitive you become to this, the easier your preventive measures will become.

• How often do you feel that it would be safe or it is not possible for you to advance your hand and ride with a lighter contact? A negative answer is a sure sign of tension in your belly, and a signal that the horse is taking you. This means that you have already been accommodating changes in his carriage. What images and attitudes best help you to become causal again?

• How correctly can you ride a half halt? Do you clearly feel the horse "sit himself down"? Can you do this deliberately, or does it only happen unintentionally? How clearly can you "meet the horse on the end of the rein"? Do you find yourself in a pulling match instead? Are your half halts instantaneous, or do they take a long time? If you still have difficulty with them, be patient with yourself, and instead of *trying* to do them turn your attention to the more basic factors in your body alignment and muscle tone, because these will ultimately give you the answer.

One could be forgiven for feeling that the postural interactions between the horse and rider are in themselves enough to cope with. But they are coupled with another whole range of difficulties, which are associated with acceleration and deceleration. Perhaps you have had the experience of leaning forward in the back seat of a car when the driver suddenly has to brake and, if you were unprepared, you no doubt found yourself thrown forward. Possibly you have also been thrown backward into the seat when he suddenly accelerated. I regularly see the same effect with riders, not only when the horse accelerates or decelerates of his own volition, but also when they deliberately ask him to alter his pace. In order to understand these effects, it is important to realize that on some occasions, the driving aids are simply intended to maintain the feeling of liveliness—especially when going from an easy to a more taxing movement. At other moments the desired outcome of the aid is more miles per hour. This increase—or any intended decrease in speed—should occur within the same tempo, so that the horse takes either longer, more powerful steps, or shorter, more elevated steps, but at the same rate. The danger, however, is that either he hurries on (taking short, quick little steps) or he "winds down" (taking slower, more dragging steps) until, like a clockwork toy, he may finally run out of impulsion.

Riders who are causal are able to regulate their own body movement so precisely and pervasively that the horse has no choice but to move in this constant tempo underneath them, regardless of any changes in his speed. It is as if they have set a metronome, which never varies its beat. These riders have the ability not only to control the tempo, but also to stay with the horse whenever he accelerates or decelerates. Less skillful riders ask the horse to go faster, and are then not ready to stay with him when he does; they do not provide the requisite extra muscle power which will hold their center of gravity in place as he accelerates. Similarly, they do not stabilize themselves well as he decelerates, and their center of gravity again deviates from its ideal balance point.

Think back to the dismounted exercise where your partner tries to push or pull you out of alignment, and now add another dimension. Imagine that someone can suddenly pull the rug out from underneath your feet, so as well as dealing with the pushes or pulls which your partner or the horse exert on your upper body, you also have to keep your balance on an unpredictable support. (In reality,

34. Although these are rather extreme reactions, most riders show some slight loss of stability either when the horse accelerates or decelerates.

the horse's response is often predictable, but the fact that the rider is supposedly expecting it does not seem to stop many from losing their balance!) Pulling the rug forward mirrors the effects of acceleration; pulling it back mirrors the effects of deceleration. Although an attitude of relaxed concentration is required, complete physical relaxation is *not* the answer. Holding your center unmoved requires even more muscle tone and an even more grounded posture than the original exercise, and if you can find (on the rug and on the horse) the muscle control and concentration which enables you to maintain the integrity of your body alignment, none of the problems which beset less stable riders will ever materialize.

The effects of acceleration and deceleration are not quite so predictable in riding as they are for the person sitting in the car or standing on the rug, and riders at different levels react in different ways. Novices, for instance, are likely to be sucked forward into the fetal crouch in response to *any* change. More confident riders, especially those who rely primarily on brute force and ignorance, respond to most situations by tipping back. In an unexpected acceleration, for instance, a novice or nervous rider will tip forward and grab at the rein, while a more confident, experienced rider is more likely simply to be "left behind." When they *ask* for an acceleration, novices again tip forward; it is as if they are saying to the horse, "I'm going, will you come too?" but more confident riders, whose attitude demands and expects that the horse will respond to their aid, are not always ready to go with him when he does. While one group tends to overcompensate, the other tends to undercompensate.

The same is true when they ask for decelerations, and while novice riders lean forward and pull on the rein, more experienced riders lean back and pull on it: neither remain in the optimum balance point. Unexpected decelerations, however, take all of them by surprise; although novices soon learn to prevent those unpleasant landings on the front of the saddle, they still experience something of the same effect even years later, and usually this is so subtle that they do not even realize what has happened. All they know is that they have somehow broken the circuit, and it often takes quite a lot of trial-and-error groping for them to discover just how they can mend it again.

It is easy to understand why acceleration and deceleration cause so many problems, especially when the change is unexpected or rather extreme—when asking for a lengthened trot or canter, for instance. But few riders can make the required adjustments when asking the horse for a more active walk! Here, the majority fall back, making no adjustment rather than too much, and if they learned to ride on extremely lazy horses, one can perhaps appreciate why they are not expecting their aid to have an effect. But many lazy horses who insist on jogging rather than walking on do so because their riders have been "left behind" after they have given the aid. Then, if the rider half expects the jog and tries to prevent it by pulling on the rein, she of course only succeeds in making matters worse; regardless of whether she leans back more or tips forward, she makes the prophecy self-fulfilling. The only way she can preempt the jog is to stay with the horse as he accelerates, holding herself in a causal position, so that she keeps taking him and holding the circuit complete.

As a novice pupil, I can remember how tempted I was to tip forward in upward transitions, and at different times I have both over- and undercompensated. In particular, I can recall a time when being told by my teacher to ride medium trot across the next diagonal was practically equivalent to a command to hold my breath, pull in my belly, and hang on for dear life! I would prepare for the movement thinking, Here goes . . . , and whether I tipped forward or fell back, I would suffer all the inevitable consequences of not staying with the horse. Later, I discovered the advantages of breathing in rhythm with the horse's gait, checking my body balance, and providing more (rather than less) muscle tone to hold my center of gravity in place. Sally Swift offers a very nice image for this in *Centered Riding,* when she suggests that you "feel that your center is going to fly from between your hands," or that "your belt buckle is being pulled away from you. . . ." This feeling is easiest to achieve on slight—but definite—lengthenings, which last for only a short time. These give both you and the horse more chance of being able to hold the circuit complete, so that you can maintain tempo and a good balance; and they also give you the opportunity to confirm your half halts. As I practiced with these, I gradually found that I could hold my seat on more spectacular lengthenings, still maintaining the lightness of the horse's forehand and the engagement of his quarters, so that he was free to move in powerful, regular strides. Some of the first times that I experienced this I felt as if I was on board an aircraft, accelerating along the runway toward takeoff—the power I had unleashed from the horse's quarters and let through into my hand made for a far smoother and more exhilarating ride than I had ever imagined possible.

Of course, this can only happen if you have the circuit complete in the first place. But the fear that the horse *might* accelerate causes many riders to ride "with the hand brake permanently on," and to spend all their time in a slight fetal crouch. Other riders inhibit the horse by using the rein as a counterbalance—"water skiing"— so that they are permanently tipping backward. Speed exaggerates these reactions, so in canter, the vast majority of riders are tipped either too far forward or too far back, with pulled-in bellies and bumping backsides. An unexpected acceleration then knocks them for a loop, and they also have no stable base from which to initiate a transition. In particular, the downward transition to trot becomes an enormous bugbear, and often the trot-walk and walk-halt transitions are plagued by similar problems. Downward transitions are often regarded as the ultimate test of a rider, and many people ride for years without discovering how to do them well. Finding the optimum balance point, however, completely changes the rider-horse interaction, and the transitions suddenly become deceptively simple.

I remember when I used to dread riding all downward transitions, including halts. When the horse finally stopped, it was usually the result of a pulling match, during which we showed the "winding down" effect. As I knew that I was going to experience this, I concluded that I had to begin my halt aid early enough for it to happen before we reached the designated marker. I would start a counting-down process—3, 2, 1, stop (or so I hoped). But as I did this, I stopped taking the horse and motivating his forward movement. It is very tempting for the rider to do this; the opposite is rather like running (on your feet) at full speed toward a brick wall, and trusting that you can stop in the instant before you hit it. It is far more comfortable to begin decelerating well before you get there, and as a rider, I used to do the equivalent by losing muscle tone and sagging backward in a way which encouraged the horse to wind down. As this kind of preparation only makes things worse, I often suggest to new pupils that they *surprise themselves* with the halt—keeping the horse marching forward as if they had no intention of stopping. Then, when they suddenly change their minds, they are in a far better position actually to stop. In a correct transition, the horse halts directly and distinctly from a marching walk rather than fighting or ambling his way to a stop. One of my old teachers used to liken the quality of a good halt to that of an axe falling, or a knife cutting through butter, and this requires the rider to hold her center of gravity exactly on the optimum balance point.

The horse who wants to break the circuit himself makes this even more difficult for the rider, and she can unwittingly find herself cooperating with his intention of a winding-down, back-hollowing, on-the-forehand halt. Riders who fall into the hollow of his back, and who find themselves caught in a pulling match, usually have all their attention focused on their hand; they are unaware of how their belly pulls in, and their back hollows, and their thighs clasp onto the saddle. The only solution is for them to bring their attention back to their body and, in particular, to make sure that they keep the feeling of bearing down. To begin with, this is easier if you halt as you exhale, and if you hold your body absolutely straight and vertical (with no tipping forward or back). Then you are holding yourself in a causal alignment, and you are refusing to play the horse's game. He has no choice but to reshape himself underneath you, bringing his back into the shape of the seeking reflex, and lowering his quarters so that he halts by "sitting down" slightly. Then, instead of pulling, you momentarily "meet the horse on the end of the rein," and, as he becomes progressively more and more willing to halt in good form, so your hand has less and less to do. In the ideal case, when you stop your seat bones from going *with* the walk movement, the horse has no choice but to stop walking underneath you; similarly, if you change your seat-bone movement from canter to trot, the horse has no choice but to make the same transition underneath you.

I shall never forget the delight of one new pupil when he rode his first correct halt. From our work earlier in the lesson he had figured out how he thought it ought to work, so he said, "No, don't explain it to me, I want to have a go." So he went ahead and, because the horse he was riding was quite well schooled, he halted beautifully in the instant when he stopped his seat bone movement. The rider was flabbergasted; his only previous experience of halts was of those rather fuzzy non-halts, where the only thing he had been aware of was that the horse was not responding to his pulling, but now he had an experience which he could generalize into other situations. For although no two downward transitions are ever exactly the same, they all demand the same kind of awareness, and absolute accuracy in the placing of your center of gravity.

A similar problem underlies that age-old dilemma between balance and impulsion. When the rider generates more power from the horse, she cannot direct it into a more athletic step, so instead he just runs on faster and nose-dives into her hand. Conversely, if she wants to keep him light into her hand, she can only do it by sacrificing power, so that he moves in a rather short and dragging step. For years, I would watch a better rider than me get on a horse I had just been riding, and wonder what she could possibly be doing to cause him to move in far slower tempo, with more power and spring in each step, and his body in a far rounder, more upright carriage. Gradually, as I too have learned to stabilize my body and become more securely causal, I have also become more powerful; but I still find it difficult to work a horse which has just been ridden by someone who is better than I am. Any rider in this situation has the awesome task of containing the power that the other has just generated, and while she may have a useful learning experience, she is often overwhelmed.

The primary key to this dilemma lies in your pelvic positioning and muscle tone—in the way that you do (or do not) draw your seat bones underneath you and seemingly closer together. Another important one lies, once more, in the driving aids. I regularly watch supposedly skilled riders fly higher and faster out of the saddle as they give aids at a posting trot, and as they do this the horse has no choice but to move his legs faster underneath them—so of course he falls onto his forehand. The problem is that as soon as a rider thinks about using her leg, she forgets completely about holding the tempo, and in her enthusiasm she speeds up her rise and fall. It is important to set the tempo in your mind—like setting an internal metronome—and to stay aware of this, counting to yourself if necessary, while you use your leg. In the sitting trot and canter the rider's change in tempo is less easy to see, but very often her use of her leg includes some unwanted repercussions in her seat—perhaps pulling in her belly, springing her seat bones apart, or loosening her position generally—which disturbs the horse's carriage and causes him to fall on his nose. Horses very soon realize that a successful way to flummox most riders is to make it necessary for them to give a lot of driving aids, because with each one, they have the ideal opportunity to lose their carriage and come back behind her.

Popular theory emphasizes how much you have to drive and push the horse to bring him onto the bit, and this often results in a lot of overdriving, either in the form of a forceful pushing of your seat into the saddle, which merely encourages the horse to hollow, or through an overuse of the leg, which includes all the accompanying contortions. These driving aids can have a variety of effects. The horse may lose his balance and carriage and go rushing off; this will, typically, loosen the rider's seat and leave her hanging on to the rein for support. Alternatively, he may cramp his movement and use this to protect himself—so, in fact, he tends to withhold more. This leads to a very painful vicious circle: the more strongly the rider drives the horse, the more strongly he holds back, and both of them utilize so many extra muscles that their bodies practically knot up! All the rider's instincts tell her that more strength is necessary, but in fact the reverse is true. She is only liberated from the sweat and anguish involved once she puts *less* muscle power into the driving aids themselves, and *more* into stabilizing her seat (particularly into holding the pinch feeling). Then, instead of practically digging holes in the horse's back and sides, she sits in a way which allows him to flow on more freely underneath her, and she makes sure that she can maintain herself in balance as he does. Very soon she discovers just how light her aids can be, and how easily the horse can respond.

This all boils down to the fact that when the horse has too little muscle tone (so that he runs on in rather loose steps, or trundles along in rather soggy ones), the rider instinctively tends to match him, losing tone as she too becomes too loose (flying up out of the saddle) or too soggy (sagging down on his back). This only worsens the situation, and she can only improve his movement by *increasing* her own body tone, becoming causal so that the horse matches her and increases his. Only then will she stabilize her seat and his back so effectively that the muscles of his quarters will generate a much crisper, springier, more controlled movement. When the horse's muscle tone is too high (so that he is nappy and resistant), the rider is always tempted to use too much tone herself, forcefully pushing herself into the sadddle in her attempts to drive him forward. Both of them are effectively treading on the brake and the accelerator at the same time, and she can only improve his move-

35. A "soggy" horse and rider and a tense pair: unintentionally, you will automatically tend to match the horse's tonal quality. Only when you become causal can you influence him so that he matches yours.

ment by decreasing *her own* body tone, holding herself in a more appropriate balance, so that he too can take his brakes off and flow on more freely underneath her.

Obviously, there are an infinite number of ways in which the rider's body can deviate from the ideal balance point, and an infinite number of causes for the problem. For me, however, the fundamental point lies in realizing that your primary battle is with yourself—not your horse—because once you have fine control of your body it becomes an effective tool, and the horse becomes like putty in your hands. Your need is to keep monitoring the positioning of your own center of gravity, adjusting it as necessary, so you can counter the horse's evasions, cope with acceleration and deceleration, and maneuver him precisely into and within new movements. Through these slight adjustments in your body you keep your basic feelings the same, holding yourself in a causal alignment and completing the circuit; in this way, whatever the horse does, you counter his moves, and (in theory anyway) make it impossible for him to break it.

Awareness Questions and Imagery

- How easily are you left behind as the horse accelerates, or tipped forward when he decelerates?
- When you ask for an acceleration or a deceleration, do you tend to tip forward or back? Does your preparation for the transition actually help or hinder? What would you need to do in each case in order to maintain the integrity of your body alignment?
- As you ride a transition (either between gaits or within a gait), where do you focus your attention? How much is it centered on your pelvis and the horse's back, or your hand and the rein contact? (Express these as percentages adding up to 100 percent.)
- Do your difficulties lie in the quality of the original gait, or in the transition aid itself? How does your leg aid affect your seat, the horse's tempo, and his carriage? Do you leave enough spare attention to monitor the changes you must make in your body in order to stay in balance with him?

Make sure that you think of adding the transition aid onto the end of everything else that you were doing beforehand. If you forget about the "everything else" and replace it with the transition aid, you are likely to lose your basic positioning and the horse's carriage.

- Are you able to hold the horse's carriage in your upward and downward transition aids? What precautions do you take to ensure that you do not fall into the hollow of the horse's back? Are you aware of changes in your seat bone–pubic bone placement, and so on?
- In upward transitions, think of holding your body so that you keep up with the horse as he accelerates. Can you keep taking

him? Is his movement still in one piece? Think of staying two-dimensional (as if you had no thickness), and pushing the front of your body forward as he takes his first few steps in the more powerful gait. If you tend to slouch forward, imagining yourself as being two-dimensional—particularly in the area of your upper back and chest—will be more effective than trying to think of sitting up straight.

• In downward transitions, do you pull in your belly? Do you tip forward, tip back, or sag in the middle? To help yourself stay in exactly the right alignment, imagine a piece of hardboard fixed on to the front of your body; this will stop you sagging in the middle or pulling in your belly. Timing the halt as you exhale will also help you to keep bearing down rather than pulling up and in. Your aim is to hold the hardboard exactly vertical. Extremely small deviations from this alignment have a noticeable effect on the halt: monitoring the front angle between your leg and your body is a good way to fine-tune your perceptions of these deviations. Can you feel and hold the tendons which lie in this angle (see Chapter 4)? Many riders who tend to tip back find that holding their body in exactly the right alignment gives them some pain here. Absence of this pain tells them they have let go of these front tendons and will fall backward.

Work with these ideas in the halt-walk, walk-halt transitions, because these will give you a basis from which to understand all the other transition aids.

Once you can ride downward transitions without pulling in your belly, it is possible to become far more aware of the way your seat contacts the horse's back. Then you can influence him by changing your seat-bone movement.

• As you go from walk to halt, which seat bone do you tend to bring up last? Which hind leg does the horse normally leave behind?

• Can you make a canter-trot transition by changing your seat-bone movement, or do you just find yourself caught in a pulling match?

• How does your seat-bone movement change as you go from trot to canter? Which seat bone do you tend to lose as you prepare for the transition? Which seat bone initiates it?

- How do you cope with the dilemma between balance and impulsion? Do you try to make life easier for yourself by sacrificing impulsion, or do you ride your horses more powerfully, and find that they run on into your hand?
- Can you hold the horse in tempo and balance as you generate power? This requires an extremely stable seat, with very high muscle tone in your working muscles. It is also vitally important that you can use your lower leg without there being repercussions in your seat.
- At a walk and sitting trot, can you control the speed of movement of each seat bone, or are they so loose that the horse can jiggle them about?
- At a posting trot, can you control the height and speed of the rise, or does the horse throw you up and down at his own chosen speed?
- At a canter, can you control the tempo by sitting for the whole canter stride, or does the horse displace your seat and hurry on underneath you?
- Does using your leg weaken your seat, or can you direct the horse's energy to exactly where you want it?

It is impossible to control the horse's tempo with your seat if it lacks depth, so to remedy the situation, go back to the images which will help you with this basic positioning.

8 Asymmetry

Asymmetry must be the most complex facet of riding. It is far easier to shape the horse from back to front and bring him onto the bit than it is to shape him from side to side and create a lateral bend; this is at least partially because his base of support is so much narrower here. Horses have their own inherent asymmetry and so do riders, so both find it easier to turn in one direction than in the other. But horses, at least, are surprisingly versatile, and they can change their asymmetrical holding within moments for a new rider. They also sometimes flummox their normal riders by changing their asymmetry during different stages of their training. So whenever we look at a horse and rider we have to ask, Who initiated the problem of their combined asymmetry? Did the horse adapt to the rider, adopting an asymmetry which makes use of her weaknesses, or did the rider adapt to the horse, falling into whatever position the horse has chosen for her so that he can perpetuate his own evasions? Often the answer is not clear, but either way, the rider has become reactive rather than casual, and her attempts to bend and turn the horse are fraught with difficulty—in one direction at least.

To simplify the situation, let us look first of all at the rider's asymmetry. From the very beginning, riding on one rein seems easier than riding on the other, and the problems of the difficult rein are compounded when working on a circle. Here, the rider's backside tends to slip outward, because the centrifugal force (the same force that sends the laundry to the outside of the dryer) is acting on it, and she does not have the natural ability to counteract. The more her backside slips out, the more she leans in to compensate, and the more precarious she feels. Meanwhile, her inside leg rides up, clinging onto the saddle and making a desperate effort to hold her in place, so she tends to lose her stirrup. Her inside seat bone makes the firmer contact with the saddle, and her outer seat bone "floats," barely touching it at all. While the whole of the inside of her body is contracted, the outside of it is lengthened; her outer shoulder is raised, and her leg (which has difficulty contacting the horse's side) stretches down into the stirrup, sometimes with an over-lowered heel, sometimes pressing into it on tiptoe.

As the rider leans in and presses more onto her inside seat bone, her outside seat bone lifts and twists. (Test this for yourself while sitting in a chair.) The more her inside seat bone presses down, the more her outside seat bone and thigh lift away from the saddle, also twisting her outside shoulder, and tipping her body even more forward and over to the inside. We then have a situation in which both her seat bones and her shoulders face *into* the circle. When watching the rider from the inside on this rein you can see far more of her chest than you can see on the outer rein, where her seat bones and shoulders will naturally face outward. The twist also carries through to her legs, so on the "good" side her thigh lies clearly against the saddle, while on the "bad" side it dangles away from it, and becomes much looser. Thus if the rider is sliding out so

36. The collapse—seen from the back. Notice that the rider's inside leg-body angle closes, while the outer angle opens.

badly that she has to cling on with that leg, she clings on with just one part of her inside thigh—and her knee still points outward. (These all provide very useful guides for teachers, especially when working with a pupil on the lunge.) The rider usually feels much less stable, secure, and effective on the rein where the pelvis points inward than she does on the other one: she also finds it far more difficult to turn the horse and create a lateral bend. However well-intentioned she may be, her attempts to position the horse all too often degenerate into pulling matches. It is not that she is stupid, stubborn, or not listening (as so many teachers believe). It is simply that she has become reactive rather than causal: her hand *has to* make up for what her pelvis cannot do, and until she can realign herself and maintain a causal position, she has no conscious choice in the matter.

Most riders are very quick to define one of their sides as "good" and the other as "bad," but the truth is that neither side is perfect, and each has something to teach the other. Riders also sometimes meet horses and circumstances where their "bad" side seems to become "good," and their "good" side seems to become "bad," so it is folly to get too dogmatic. Many riders become confused because there are so many theories about the turning aids and the lateral bend which, even though they agree that the rider's inside leg should be on the girth and her outside leg behind it, contradict

37. The rider's "good" and "bad" sides—seen from the center of a circle. As the rider collapses you see more of her chest, and the twist carries through to her thigh, so that it hangs away from the saddle and she clings on with just one part of it.

each other when it comes to the intricacies of her pelvic position-ing. They also agree that her inside hand should never pull back-ward, but they argue about the positioning of her shoulders relative to her own pelvis and the horse's shoulders. This is the kind of confusion, however, which dissolves when you discover that one of the choices works better. But the answers are by no means straight-forward, and the two sides of the body can be so different that corrections which are appropriate on one side are not useful on the other, and we have to judge each individual case on its merits. Inappropriate generalizations contribute enormously to the prob-lem, and send many riders barking up the wrong tree. In order to avoid this possibility I like to look at asymmetry (as well as the whole of riding) through the light of one of Albert Einstein's be-liefs—that everything should be made as simple as possible, *but no simpler.*

The most useful generalization is that riders will always tend to ride so that their whole torso points slightly to one direction. (My osteopath assures me that at least eighty percent of the population have their pelvis twisted slightly to one side.) On the rein where her inside shoulder, point of hip, and seat bone lie in advance, she will have little problem, and her inside leg will naturally lie on the girth while her outside leg comes behind it. Her outside shoulder is also naturally farther back; but many teachers believe that the rider is in optimum alignment when her hips lie parallel to the horse's hips, and her shoulders lie parallel to his shoulders. Thus, while they are content with her pelvic positioning, they ask her to ad-vance her outside shoulder and make a twist in her body. Usually, the easier rein is the *left* rein, but on the right rein, the picture changes. Here, the rider has a tendency to collapse; her outer (left) seat bone and shoulder *already lie in front of* their counterparts on the inside. So if she advances her outside shoulder even more, she will exaggerate this difference; her outside seat bone and thigh will lift even farther off the saddle, and the collapse will almost cer-tainly get worse as a result. (Test this out again sitting on a chair.)

Recently, many trainers have suggested that the rider is better placed when her hips and shoulders are both parallel, and she sits parallel to her horse's hips. She then faces slightly *out* of the circle on both reins, and even though one would instinctively imagine that the rider should face into the circle, my observations suggest that facing outward proves much more effective: you can always look to the inside. To leave the outside shoulder behind (if this is indeed a fault) has far less devastating consequences than advancing it too much.

Another area of confusion concerns the weight aid. Most riders learn to bring their inside seat bone forward and *down*, believing that this brings their center of gravity to the inside, thus facilitating the horse's bend and/or movement in this direction. On the right rein, however, where the rider tends to collapse, her inside seat bone is already somewhat lower than her outer (left) one, which tends to float. So, if she lowers her inside seat bone even more, her outside (left) seat bone will naturally tend to come *up* even more—and this exaggerates the collapse. On the left rein, however, she may need to lower her inside seat bone, since it will probably still float slightly while her outer (right) one makes the clearer contact. As we shall see, this lighter inside seat bone is actually very helpful, and the difference between the two seat

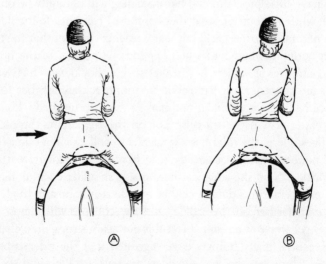

Ⓐ   Ⓑ

38. Effective weight changes require you to move your whole pelvis across the saddle (A), not merely to press harder on your inside seat bone (B); doing this will cause your knee to rise, which encourages a collapse.

bones is usually much less exaggerated on this rein than it is on the other.

There is yet a third area of confusion, and this concerns the workings of the hip joint itself. It does not follow that a seat bone which is drawn forward automatically comes down—in fact, the reverse is true. As we saw in Chapter 3, the hip and knee work as reciprocal joints, and as the rider draws her seat bone forward it comes *up*—into her buttock—opening her hip joint and enabling her to lower her knee. If she pushes it down, it goes farther *back*, and at the same time as her hip joint closes, her knee comes up. This means that lowering the inside seat bone does *not* lower the inside knee—as many people believe—and looking at any rider with a noticeable asymmetry will show you that on the "good" rein her pelvis is well forward while her knee is well down, while on the "bad" rein her backside folds backward as her knee comes up. If you ask her, she will no doubt tell you that her inside seat bone then presses firmly (down and back) into the saddle, while her outer seat bone is farther forward, and less clear.

It is also important to realize that even though it is instinctive logic to expect the rider to sit deeper on the rein where her inside seat bone presses more clearly into the saddle, this is not actually so. The problem arises because the seat bone is both angled and placed *farther back*, digging into the horse's back and closing the angle of her hip joint, so that her leg and her shoulders both come forward. When the rider brings it forward and *up*, she creates a hard pad of muscle which lies just in front of the seat bone, and this enables her to straighten out her posture. A lot of confusion arises because many riders mistake this pad for the seat bone itself, but by sitting on the muscle pad, the rider develops a much stiller, softer, firmer seat, which protects the horse's back and encourages him to raise it underneath her. This in turn lightens the contact into her inside rein, helping her to create the bend or positioning that she wants.

These changes to the inside of the body are far easier to make if you first stabilize the outside of it, and few people who are aware that they have a "bad" rein realize that their outside (usually left) seat bone is continually floating. Recently I was working with somebody whose asymmetry was so marked that the corrections she made on her stretched (left) side made her feel as if she was riding like a jockey (with her heel lifted up and her body squashed down), while to my onlooker's eye, of course, she looked beautifully aligned. She made the change by deliberately raising her heel, which had been braced well down, and imagining that she would like to bring her hip down to *the level of her knee,* as if she could make her thigh horizontal. (Of course, this is impossible in practice, but it is nonetheless a useful image.) This reorganization brought her left seat bone, thigh, and buttock into a much clearer contact with the saddle, and now that they were available to take her weight, she could take it off the offending right seat bone. On the inside of her body she had to make a correction which would bring her pelvis forward and her knee down both at the same time, since she had looked, initially, so folded up that she might have been punched in the stomach! She made the correction by imagining a pivot point lying about one-third of the way down her thigh. From here, her lower leg and thigh came backward, making a much clearer contact into the stirrup, while her upper thigh and pelvis came forward. (If your leg tends to come forward and up, it is much more effective to think of correcting it from this pivot point than it is to try to bring your whole leg back from your hip.) To start with she found this lighter seat somewhat strange (and taxing), but she soon realized that she was—for the first time— actually with the horse. By pinning the outside of her body back and drawing the inside of it forward, she brought herself into a causal position, which made her far more effective, and far more elegant.

When your body has developed lopsidedly, however, it is no easy matter to maintain it in this new alignment. As we noted in Chapter 3, the rider's thigh muscles work in one of two ways: either they pull her knees up toward her pelvis (which is known as "gripping up"); or they pull her pelvis forward toward her knees (which is known at "sitting deep"). The rider can only stabilize her pelvis when she can first stabilize her *knees,* and when these act as two fixed points her thighs become like a framework around the horse, which pulls her pelvis into place (see Fig. 33). Few riders realize that their thighs do not point out at the same angle, but that the twist in their pelvis is such that the one on the collapsed

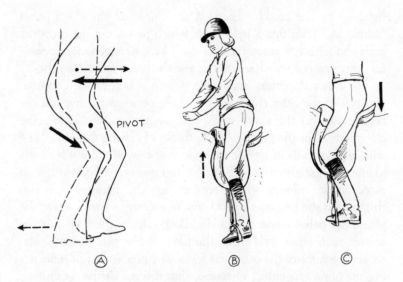

PIVOT

Ⓐ   Ⓑ   Ⓒ

39. The "bad" side of the body is folded too much (A). As you straighten it, think of drawing the point of your hip forward and your lower leg backward, as if you had a pivot point one third of the way down your thigh. The "good" side of the body (as seen on the outside of the curve) is often still too stretched-out (B), so that your seat does not make clear contact with the saddle. Correcting this (C) will make you feel as if you have much bigger bends in your hip, knee, and ankle joints, and will bring your foot into a light but stable contact with the stirrup.

side always falls away from the saddle. By bringing this thigh inward and matching it with the other one, they suddenly find that it no longer seems to have a will of its own: instead of gripping up or wobbling about, it stays where they put it. It also pulls their whole pelvis *across* the saddle, angling it so that their inside seat bone lies in advance of their outer one. This naturally brings the rider's center of gravity to the inside in a way which does not allow the collapse. Her outside seat bone comes toward the inside of the saddle, and she supports herself here (where the horse's back is more able to take her weight), rather than sitting predominantly on her inside one. She can exaggerate the pulling effect of her inside thigh by placing it so that she feels the whole length of her inner thigh muscle lying against the saddle, particularly the part right up by her crotch. Then, if she thinks of the thigh as an "aikido leg" (emitting a light beam which points out her proposed path and leads her around it), its effect becomes even more powerful, affecting not only her seat but also the horse underneath her.

The other important stabilizing influence is the pinch feeling. As soon as the rider collapses, the angle between her leg and her body closes on the inside and opens on the outside, where she effectively loses the pinch. As she thinks of closing this angle, she will automatically bring her backside over toward the inside of the saddle and straighten herself up; she also makes her body into a far more stable column which remains upright between her two thighs, and she becomes able to choose exactly how and where she places her pelvis across the saddle. Both sides of the body push in toward each other, and when the force of one side slightly overcomes the force of the other she has a very precise way of influencing the horse (assuming, of course, that this is a deliberate choice, and not just a part of her natural asymmetry). Instead of leaning, and sliding, and twisting across the saddle, she becomes causal, making subtle adjustments in response to the nuances of each moment, and balancing out her own and the horse's asymmetries, rather than being the victim of them. In some very magical moments, I have found that making these corrections has had an immediate effect on a horse who had seemed (to me) to be impossibly stiff: when I put myself into the correct position on top, he willingly put himself into the correct position beneath me, dissolving evasions which had flawed me for a long, long time.

Awareness Questions and Imagery

Dismounted checks

- Becoming aware of your asymmetry while you are off the horse can be a significant help in correcting it when mounted.
- Sitting in a chair, collapse your body to one side. Which side did you choose? When you collapse to the other side, does it feel equally familiar?

Preferably while standing in front of a mirror, place your thumb on your bottom rib, and your first finger on the point of your hip. Then compare the distances you are measuring on both sides. Are they equal? Make a similar comparison by measuring the distances on each side between the point of your hip and the projecting bone on the outside of your thigh. If your measurements are unequal, how do you have to stand in order to equalize them?

- Standing with your feet apart, bend one knee so that you drop your hip. Which side did you choose? When you do it on the other side, does it feel equally familiar?
- When you walk, does each foot take an equal amount of weight?
- How do all your findings relate to each other? With some people the correlation is much more obvious than with others, and in its different segments, the body can be contracted on different sides (one leg is more contracted than the other, but the rib cage is more contracted on the opposite side, for example). More often, it is apparent that one side of the body is contracted relative to the other, and of course, the rider will have a tendency to collapse to that side.
- Sit cross-legged on the floor, and feel the contact that each seat bone makes with the floor. Probably one (on the side of the leg which lies closer to your body) feels more pointed and farther back, while the other feels rounder and farther forward. How does this compare with the way you feel your seat bones as you ride? Now cross your legs the other way. Does this feel unfamiliar? How does it change your seat bones?
- Sit on the floor with your legs out in front of you. Now slide your feet toward your backside until you can hug your knees. Compare the feeling of each seat bone as it touches the floor. Does one feel sharper and clearer than the other, and/or is one farther back? Can you rearrange yourself to bring up the seat bone which is behind, and get the same feeling on each? To do this you may have to lift up your buttock and put it down again, shifting your flesh. Does it have to come more in front of your seat bone, or more behind it?
- Run through the floor exercises again which we did in Chapter 3, paying particular attention to asymmetry. Are the tendons at the

front of your thigh stronger on one side than on the other? Are your hamstring muscles (on the underside of your thigh) stronger on one side? They may well be weaker on the side to which you tend to collapse, where your seat bone will naturally lie farther back.

Armed with this information, you can choose to strengthen your weaker muscles, by repeatedly contracting them, using both short and prolonged contractions. You can also pay attention to how you sit and walk, seeking out ways of becoming more symmetrical. This may take some time, but it will give you more clarity when it comes to your riding.

Mounted work

- Do you ride with your stirrups level? Check this before you mount, because your normal feelings of "rightness" are not to be trusted!
- On walk, ride straight lines and circles on both reins. Does one of your seat bones feel clearer on the saddle? Is one farther forward than the other? How does it affect you when the less clear, floating seat bone lies on the inside or on the outside of a circle?
- Imagine carrying an old-fashioned milkmaid's yoke on your shoulders. In what directions would its two arms point? Is one always farther forward than the other, regardless of which rein you are on? How does it affect you when the arm which points farther forward lies on the inside of the circle, and how does it affect you when it is on the outside of a circle?
- Imagine that the horse's head points toward twelve o'clock. Relative to this, where do your thighs point? Does one lie against the saddle while the other falls more away from it? How does it affect you when the firmer thigh lies on the inside of the circle? What about when it lies on the outside of the circle?
- Do your two feet rest in the stirrups with an equal pressure, or does one make a firmer contact than the other? Is one heel lowered more than the other? Does one foot contact the stirrup on tiptoe? What difference does it make to you when the foot that makes the firmer contact lies on the inside or on the outside of a circle?

You may or may not notice obvious differences in each of these cases. The likelihood is that they will fit together in a pattern, so that when your outside seat bone floats slightly, your inner shoulder will point back, and your inner thigh will be looser. You will probably then make the clearer contact with the outer stirrup. This will be your "bad" rein, where you feel less secure, and have more difficulty turning the horse.

• What adjustments do you have to make to make your "bad" rein more like a mirror image of your "good" rein?

If you manage this successfully, you will feel extremely contorted!

When we think of the rider collapsing to the inside, we normally assume that her backside slips too far outward. But I have found that this is not always the case. If the rider is pulling on the inside rein in her attempt to turn the horse, the act of pulling pulls her backside *back over again,* so that it may end up too far to the inside. The horse's evasions can also change her positioning across the saddle. Imagine a rider working at a posting trot, when her horse suddenly dives onto his inside shoulder. Unless she immediately compensates, she will then come down into the saddle too far over to the outside; similarly, if he suddenly dives onto his outside shoulder, she will come down too far to the inside. (Imagine how this would look if seen from above and slightly behind the horse.) This can also happen in sitting trot and canter, although very few riders realize how easily they are moved across the saddle. Most think of placing themselves relative to the horse, and of sitting slightly to the inside when working on a circle. But I would like to suggest that they think of placing the horse *relative to them,* as only this power relationship will ultimately render them causal.

The horse at liberty turns by leaning onto his inside shoulder and breaking at the withers, so that his head and neck turn outward. If you have ever sat on a turn like this (and who has not!) you will know just how precarious it feels; the importance of the correct bend is that it gives the rider much greater balance, precision, and control. However, many riders intervene in ways which make their predicament worse: if they continually pull the horse about with their hand, the base of his neck becomes so rubbery that he can fall onto either shoulder at will, and career about as if he is drunk. (One of my pupils suggested that the horse in this state is rather like one of those supermarket carts which never goes in the direction you want!) This reaction is superimposed on the horse's natural asymmetry, and it is quite normal for his hind legs to track slightly to the right of his forelegs, so that his quarters are displaced slightly to the right. (When you watch a dog trotting you will often see the same effect.) With the horse, it can happen to such an extent that you find yourself unwittingly doing ten-meter circles on the left rein, while it is almost impossible to bring him off the track on the right rein, where his outside shoulder seems glued to the wall. One of the most fundamental aims of schooling is to reposition his shoulders and bring them in front of his quarters, but the ideal of symmetry is rarely, if ever, achieved. (Although we often hear about the horse's quarters falling out, this usually only happens when he is very much on his forehand, and this then needs correcting first. It is normally much more effective to straighten the horse by bringing his shoulders in front of his quarters than it is to work the other way around.)

I have very often seen a horse appear stiff to one side with one rider, and then reverse his asymmetry for a new rider. This leads me to believe that his reaction to the rider's asymmetry is *at least* as pervasive as his own natural asymmetry. It is easy to understand why the horse becomes so much more difficult on the rein on which the rider collapses. Let us suppose that she is crooked to the right, so that her inside (right) seat bone digs down into the horse's back. He hollows on that side to avoid it, and as his back drops down his neck stretches out, creating a pull on the right rein. This tempts the rider to pull back more, and the act of pulling draws her seat bone and shoulder on that side *even farther* down and back. To protect himself, the horse hollows more, so that she pulls more, making her seat bone dig in more and making him hollow more, and so the cycle goes on. If the horse already has difficulty turning to the right this is going to make him worse, but even if he does not, he will soon find correct bends extremely uncomfortable. And he may well protect himself by reversing his natural carriage.

Quite often, riders find that while one rein is more difficult in trot, the other is harder in canter, and this has often been explained in terms of the horse's asymmetry. In trot to the right, for instance, the weaker right hind leg may have difficulty dealing with the added strain of being on the inside, while in canter, the *outer* hind leg is said to take more strain because it comes down on its own. This would make canter left more difficult; but this is not always the case, especially when the horse moves at liberty. I am not convinced that our argument holds water, and it may be that the diagonal pair of legs (the second canter beat) is more important because it stabilizes the horse rather like the pivot point of a seesaw. What I *am* sure of is that many riders whose asymmetry makes them upset the horse's carriage on the right rein at trot actually *need that extra "tuck under"* to deal with the increased impulse of the canter bound, so here they sit well. On the other rein, however, where they sit well at trot, they are thrown out of the saddle in canter. Their bumping seat then encourages the horse to run on underneath them, so that he falls onto his inside shoulder and their inside hand, creating a new vicious circle which can only be solved by a dramatic reorganization of their seat.

It must be obvious from this that it is no easy matter to discover what the horse does to you and what you do to the horse; but most riders find that their horses consistently take a stronger contact into one rein (in trot anyway). This is in part, at least, a manifestation of their own asymmetry, but usually they are far more concerned with the horse than they are with themselves. The ruined "drunk" horse with a rubbery neck poses enormous problems. Think of him in the analogy of the wheelbarrow in Chapter 5; he behaves like a wheelbarrow with rubber handles and a will of its own, able to compress or extend either "handle" at will. More carefully schooled horses behave like wheelbarrows with solid but unequally weighted handles, and the rider experiences more difficulty on the rein where the heavier contact lies on the inside. (This is usually the right rein.) In teaching, my first priority is to take the pupil's attention *away* from her inside hand and bring it *onto* her torso. All too easily, she gets caught up in a pulling match where she attempts to steer the horse's nose, but as she does this she loses control of his body (as well as her own): either he will pull back against her, or he will point his nose in the required direction while his shoulders continue straight on. Both situations will probably make the rider collapse more, and only the correct pelvic positioning will render her causal, giving her control of the horse's shoulders so that she can place them in exactly the right alignment relative to his quarters.

The most important change in emphasis is to think of leaving the track by easing the horse's outside *shoulder* off the wall, rather than by pulling his *nose* off. This in itself can have a significant effect on the rider's pelvic positioning, and change the whole feel of the turn. It encourages her to keep the outside of her body wrapped around the outside of the horse; whereas if she collapses, grabs at the inside rein, and pulls herself across the saddle in an attempt to pull his nose around, she is bound to lose the contact which her outside buttock and thigh should make with the saddle. In the new way of turning, she feels far more securely wrapped around the outside of the horse, and then she no longer finds that her attention is drawn to her inside hand. Instead, she discovers that the key point which seems to initiate the turn is the angle where *the outer muscle of her outside thigh comes into her body.* When I help a rider to sense the importance of this angle, I often poke my fingers quite hard into it (and more lightly into its counterpart on the opposite side, so that she feels both sides of the pinch). Whenever she collapses, this angle will open; by emphasizing its acuteness and maintaining it she can hold herself upright, and choose exactly where she positions her pelvis across the saddle. This enables her to reposition the horse's shoulders *relative to her,* and to counteract his evasion so that his forehand comes easily off the track without him jackknifing or pulling back. Instead of attempting to control the inside front quarter of the horse—and losing control of the rest—she now sits in a way which influences the whole of his body. Her lower legs come naturally into the right placement (her inside leg on the girth and her outside leg behind it), and her inside thigh assists her by becoming an "aikido leg." But it's in her outer leg-body angle that she feels the train of turning the horse, almost as if her outside thigh can push him over, and this means that her inside hand has practically nothing to do.

There has been a lot of discussion recently about scientific research showing that there is a marked lack of flexibility in the horse's spine. This has been a surprising discovery, as horsemen for

OUTER ANGLE
BETWEEN LEG
& BODY

40. As you begin a turn or circle, think of easing the horse's outside shoulder off the wall. It is particularly important to establish and maintain the angle where the outer muscle of your outside thigh comes into your body. Think of initiating the turn from here (see also Fig. 17).

generations have believed that their prized lateral bend owed itself to his spinal flexibility. However inaccurate this model may have been, it has proved its usefulness, and we can certainly say that a horse working correctly looks and feels *as if* his spine can bend. It now seems likely that the optical illusion is created by a rotation of his rib cage, so that it bulges out more on the outside and falls away under the rider's inside leg. This means that the horse's spine actually lies to the *inside* of its imagined alignment, so that even as the rider sits slightly to the inside, her outside seat bone is still supported on his outer back muscles, which can take her weight more easily than the inner ones. If, however, she rests on her outer buttock and her inside stirrup, she spares him the agony of having to hollow away from a protruding inside seat bone. But we shall never understand the exact mechanism of the bend, and while intellectual arguments about it can be fascinating and fun, they are often self-defeating; for the truth is that the working body responds

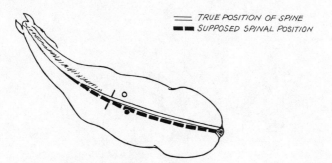

41. Recent research has changed our assumptions about the flexibility of the horse's spine. When the rider is well placed, her weight is supported primarily on his outer back muscles.

far better to "as if" than it does to any amount of left-brain knowledge.

Let us return to the analogy of the horse as a stuffed toy. If our stuffed toy horse is rather limp (i.e., not "in front of the rider"), he can easily break at the withers, and fall onto one or other shoulder. Thus the rider's first task is to ride the horse so well in the back-front plane that she puts much more "stuffing" in front of her, raising his forehand relative to his croup, and filling out his rib cage and neck so that he arches into the rein. This automatically makes his shoulders much, much more stable, and prevents him from falling about like a drunkard. She then has to rearrange the "stuffing" she had just created so that it bulges out more on the outside of the horse's body. This means that he comes round to the right, say, through the action of rotating his rib cage to the left and reaching into the left (outside) rein. This is not his natural instinct, however, and riders too find it somewhat paradoxical that a turn to the right should happen, because of this reaching, with the horse making a firmer contact into the left (outside) rein.

When the rider can "rearrange the stuffing" exactly as she wants to, she gains control of the whole of the horse's body. The ligament which lies along the crest of his neck flips over to the inside, so that the curve of his neck matches the apparent curve of his body, and his hind legs follow in the tracks made by his forelegs. When the correct positioning of the horse from back to front combines with a correct positioning from side to side, his withers are drawn upward, and his shoulder blades appear to come up and in toward the raised withers (see Fig. 21). His withers and shoulder blades then function as one unit, and to make a graceful, accurate curve they have to tilt slightly inward.

In his book, *Basic Training of the Young Horse*, Reiner Klimke compares turning the horse to turning a bicycle: in each case the rider and her mount have to compensate for the centrifugal force by leaning inward to a degree appropriate to the turn. Many people throw up their hands in horror at the thought of the horse leaning inward, but a small tilt *is* necessary. Any photograph of a horse working well on a circle will show this quite clearly, and will also show how the rider leans (without collapsing) by just the same amount. The problem is that the horse normally avoids both this lean and the consequent weighting of each hind leg. So, instead of steering the one point of his shoulder-blades-and-withers, the rider is continually facing situations in which his right shoulder drops out to the right, or his left shoulder drops out to the left. This destroys the integrity of his forehand, so that its separate bits go their separate ways. The effect is rather like trying to turn a bicycle by keeping it completely upright while pulling its handlebars and front wheel to face in the direction of the turn; if you have ever done this, you will know that you may well end up on the ground! When you lean the bicycle around its curve you barely have to turn the handlebars, and so it is with riding. But it is not always the rider who turns the "handlebars"; sometimes the horse does, by dropping onto the outside shoulder and turning only his neck. If you think back to the dismounted exercise where your partner pushes and pulls you, this is the equivalent of a situation in which she pushes against one arm while pulling at the other, and this is a powerful assault on the integrity of your body alignment. But whoever initiates the evasion, the resulting break makes the ideal tilt impossible, and the turn is fraught with difficulty. Thus the rider's task is to sit in a way which repositions the whole of the horse's forehand so that his shoulder-blades-and-withers act again as one unit, tilting inward to just the right degree, and leading his quarters around the turn.

42. When seen from behind, the horse and rider making a good turn will lean inward to exactly the same degree.

This optimum carriage is a very precise, elusive quality, and many riders have misconceptions about the feel of a correct bend —deliberately riding the horse so that his outside shoulder drops outward. The old adage that you should just be able to see the horse's inside eye on a correct turn is limited in its usefulness, because this can also be the case when he is breaking at the withers. So often while riders are congratulating themselves about how deeply they can ride into the corners, the horse is actually evading. I have found that people are often very surprised when they first get the feeling of a correct bend: surely this can't be right? They are not prepared for the way that the whole of the horse's forehand comes round in front of them, so I may suggest that they feel it coming round "like a bus." Taken to their extreme, the aids used would produce a turn on the haunches, which provides a very, very different feeling from that of the illusory bend created by a break at the withers.

"Handlebar" turns are instinctive to riders; they make logical sense, and they are inevitable to the degree that your hand will always make up for what your pelvis cannot do. Consequently, even in the face of feedback that they do not work too well, many riders continue to turn like this for years. (After all, the horse really ought to listen next time!) But although instinct tells you that the inside hand should predominate, all the great masters emphasize the outer one, saying that you should ride the horse "from your inside leg into your outside hand." This is easiest to understand if you think of "rearranging the stuffing." In a correct turn, the bend is created through the horse filling out the outside of his body and reaching into the outside rein. Some barrier is needed, though, in order to keep that bulge of "stuffing" in place, and without the outside rein contact, it just "leaks out"—usually via the break at the horse's withers. Taking up an image used by Sally Swift in *Centered Riding*, I like to think of the rider's body and the horse's skin like the walls of a curved funnel which water (which has energy equivalent to the horse's energy) passes through. Any stream of water exerts the greatest force on its outer bank—hence the need for an outer rein contact which will stop the funnel eroding, and a lighter inside rein contact which does not scrunch up the funnel and stop the water (horse, or horse's energy) from passing through. Turning aids based on a pull and a collapse often

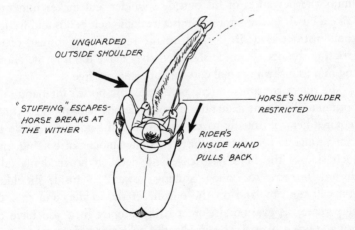

UNGUARDED
OUTSIDE SHOULDER

"STUFFING" ESCAPES-
HORSE BREAKS AT
THE WITHER

HORSE'S SHOULDER
RESTRICTED

RIDER'S
INSIDE HAND
PULLS BACK

43. An illusory bend: When you pull your inside hand backward and make a "handlebar" turn, you pull yourself to the inside of the saddle. As a result, the horse's inside shoulder is restricted while his outside shoulder is left unguarded; this allows him to break at the withers.

scrunch up the inside of the horse (as well as the rider), and they break the circuit, destroying the integrity of his forehand, limiting the freedom of his inside shoulder, and ensuring that impulsion is lost.

It takes a lot of obviously correct turns for riders to gain faith in the "inside leg into outside hand" idea, and to position themselves in the causal alignment which makes this possible. When they do, they often make comments like, "Wow! I never knew it could be this easy... and I hardly have to do anything with my hands." Their pelvis and thighs, however, do much more work, and they often feel the strain. Usually there comes a time, on a difficult horse, when they are not sure if they are going to make the corner, and so, of course, they revert to the rein and a "handlebar" turn. When riders get busy with their inside hand, they usually forget about the outer one, and like the outer handlebar, it advances; because their rein contact stays the same, they do not realize that they have unknowingly cooperated with the horse's evasion. Skilled riders are much more stubborn. They pin their outer hand, elbow, shoulder, and seat bone in place, and feel the horse's attempts to displace them as a yank on the rein which they do not react to. In effect, they make a wall with their outside aids, which limits the deviation of his outside shoulder and makes him turn "like a bus." At the same time they realign their pelvis and inhibit their instinctive desire to pull on the rein. Then, instead of restricting the horse's inside shoulder, they make room for it, allowing him to make a gradual curve and to step out freely.

The rider's continual attempts to bring the horse's forehand into optimum alignment demand some considerable fine-tuning, which requires her continually to reposition herself across the saddle so that *relative to her*, there is just the right amount of bulging into each side of the horse's rib cage and neck. If he suddenly falls inward, bringing too much "stuffing" toward his inside shoulder, you will tend to land on the outside of the saddle, and thus to perpetuate his evasion. In order to counteract this, you have to bring yourself over to the inside; this will mean that, relative to you, the "stuffing" has moved over toward his outside shoulder. Conversely, when he falls outward, you will tend to land toward the inside, and once more you will perpetuate his evasion. Again you have to counteract this by moving across the saddle, so that relative to you, the "stuffing" has moved toward the inside. This is only possible when the rider's knees act as two fixed points; this allows her continually to make adjustments to the position of her thighs and pelvis in between them. At times she has to move herself literally across the saddle, but more often she just changes the emphasis, reaching more into one or other thigh. At all times she holds herself upright, although she inevitably tends to fall off-balance: at such moments her thighs and her knees may lose their placement, resulting in the crookedness and instability which put her in a powerless position.

The vast majority of riders do not perceive their positioning with anything like this degree of subtlety. Instead they believe that their problems with the bend both begin and end in their hand, so it is here that they try to solve them. Thus I often find it helpful to ask the pupil, "What are you tempted to do with your hand?" Riders at different levels use it in different ways—novices, for instance, will try to stop a horse from falling inward by pulling on the outside rein. Eventually they realize that this does not work too

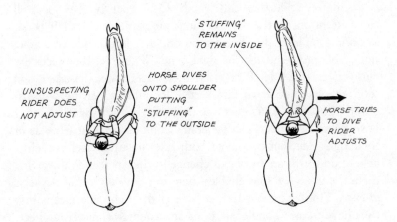

44. When the horse falls onto his outside shoulder, the unsuspecting rider is left—caught unawares—so that relative to her, the "stuffing" bulges out on the outside. If she adjusts her positioning *across* the saddle, however, she can place herself so that the "stuffing" is just where she wants it.

well, so instead they bring their inside hand *across* the neck. This is indeed a more effective antidote, and some riders make all their turns like this, stopping the horse from falling inward by making a counterbalance with their inside hand. Conversely, if the horse falls onto his outer shoulder they may find themselves tempted to bring their outside hand against—or even across—the neck, in a desperate attempt to try to turn him. Whenever one of the horse's shoulders falls from its optimum positioning, the rider becomes tempted to compensate like this, and at time she may be completely unaware of the way that she continually holds one hand higher, using a stronger contact to support the shoulder of a horse who has a permanent list to one side. As a variety of horses perform the different school movements, the possible variations for these counterbalances are almost endless; but in each case, the rider's hand is attempting to make up for the "disintegration" of the horse's forehand. Realizing this is the first step toward making the correction which her pelvis has so far failed to do.

Most riders go through phases where they are completely baffled by a certain problem with the bend. They usually perceive one rein as "good" and the other as "bad"; they do not realize that the problem is also manifested—albeit in a different and more subtle way —on the rein that they call "good." Consequently, they focus all their attention on the more obvious problem with the left bend, say, and soon after they find a solution, they begin to have a more noticeable problem with the right bend. Whenever they focus exclusively on one side of the horse they forget about the other, and soon enough they leave him with a loophole which he will discover, dive into, and use to come back "behind them" again. I have found that riders can generally think about their left side *or* their right side, but not about both sides together, and becoming able to do this is an enormous change in their perception—giving them the overview that enables them to ride *both sides of the horse at once*. Thinking about the left side *or* the right side means that they have to use "handlebar" turns and counterbalances; in effect, they lose sight of the forest for the trees. With an overview which sees the whole, they are able to put the shoulder-blades-and-withers into optimum alignment, and to steer just this unit, making graceful curves in the way that they would if they were riding a bicycle.

In helping riders to find this overview, I often suggest that they imagine how they would look if seen from behind, because from this perspective they perceive their whole body. Or I suggest that they use their legs to create a corridor, which the horse has full permission to move through, but which he is not allowed to bang against. (The inside thigh, in particular, plays a very important role in this.) However, horses are extremely clever at destroying the corridor, or manipulating it into their own chosen shape. Some thud against it, and others are more subtle: they slide against one wall of it so discreetly that the rider does not even notice, and instead of deliberately monitoring the situation and making minute corrections with her pelvis, she finds herself making even more subtle counterbalances with her hand.

Even though there are days when you seem to have solved it, asymmetry is a problem which never goes away, and at times even the most refined riders have difficulty separating their own from their horse's difficulties. Horse and rider fit together like two pieces of a jigsaw puzzle, and while it is clear that some problems are specific to the horse you are riding, there is a gray area of more subtle but general difficulties in which you are inevitably involved. The most skillful riders minimize this, stabilizing the horse's forehand by putting him well in front of them, and then they become acutely sensitive to any deviation of his shoulder-blades-and-withers from their ideal alignment and tilt. They recognize the times when it is not yet possible to straighten a young, weak horse; and when they are riding a stronger, more mature horse, they confront his areas of weakness, and nip his evasions in the bud. Their hands play a minimal role in this, and their lower legs do much less than most people imagine. They restructure the horse's movement primarily through their pelvic positioning, and subtle changes here and in their thigh can have the most astounding effects.

The delight of becoming causal is that it spares you the agony of pulling matches with these supposedly stiff, stubborn creatures. However, it does place an enormous premium on your willingness to leave "home." Initially you may feel as if you are sitting on some unknown part of the saddle, facing the wrong direction, with a pelvis which finds this alignment a great strain, and legs which complain about their new distribution of work. Surely this can't possibly be right? But the payoff (when it comes) is more security, a

deeper seat, and legs which—even though they may feel funny—
actually do what you want them to do. This has immediate effects
on the horse, who becomes far more malleable. The next challenge
is to fit all these changes together, so that you can find and maintain the overview which gives you control of the horse's forehand,
and thus of the whole of his body. It then becomes possible to work
him equally productively on both reins, choosing exercises which
strengthen both yourself and the horse to combat your mutual
weaknesses. Since practice ingrains what you are actually practicing (not what you think you are practicing, or what you ought to
be practicing), the work you do then has some value, and as the
horse becomes more supple and willing, you can invite him to
produce deeper bends and more difficult movements, so that you
once more challenge both of your inherent asymmetries.

Awareness Questions and Imagery

- When you ride the horse on turns and circles, where do you put
  your attention?
- When you begin a turn, do you think of pulling the horse's nose
  in off the track, or of pushing his shoulders off the track?
- Do you recognize the feeling of a correct bend? To what extent
  do you find yourself using "handlebar" turns, and making counterbalances with your hand?

The most important factors which will help you become causal
are the pinch feeling and well-placed thighs.

Focus on the angle where the outer muscle of your outside thigh
comes into your pelvis, and hold it so that it cannot open. Can you
get a feeling of pushing the horse around the turn from here? If
not, your pelvis has almost certainly slipped outward.

Check that your inside thigh lies clearly against the saddle, and
keeping it there, imagine that it leads you in the direction in
which you want to go (either along the track or round a curve), as
if someone were pulling on your inside knee. Think of your leg as
an "aikido leg." You can also think of the point of your hip and the
horse's inside shoulder leading the way around the curve.

- Does your lower leg stay in position as you come around the curve, or does your foot shoot forward? If it shoots forward, your pelvis has almost certainly collapsed backward.

If these corrections do not have a significant effect, you may need to use the corrections for a stretched and a contracted side (see Fig. 39). Also check that your seat bones and shoulders are clearly facing toward the outside of the circle. If the "aikido leg" image is not sufficient to hold your inside seat bone forward, think of the wafer-thin arm (see Fig. 27) curling around it and pulling it into place.

If all else fails, try the following: Hold your inside thigh close into the saddle, and imagine the line of its contact with the saddle (from your knee to your crotch) extending backward. Now imagine bringing your outside seat bone back and in so that it lies on this line. This means that you have to move the whole of your outside thigh farther back. You will almost certainly feel that you are facing far too much to the outside, and your thighs will feel very close together.

- How does this affect your ability to turn and bend the horse?
- When you become causal, you can choose exactly how you want to angle and position your pelvis across the saddle, but this is only possible when your knees act as fixed points, and your thigh muscles can pull your pelvis into place. Think of the framework we built up in Chapter 7 (see Fig. 33), where imaginary iron bars replace your thigh bones and connect the two sides of your body, passing through the horse's belly between your knees, and through your backside to give you the pinch feeling. How do you have to angle this framework on each rein in order to have the maximum effect?
- If you can find a willing friend who will allow you to sit on her back while she is on her hands and knees, experiment with these ideas. How does it feel to her if you make a turning aid by dropping your inside seat bone (be gentle!), or by realigning your pelvis so that the "push" comes from your outer leg-body angle? Think of protecting her inner back muscles and using your inside "aikido leg." Can you position your pelvis to make it equally

effective in both directions? Take a turn as the horse as well, so you get feedback from this perspective.

• Have you ever had the experience of steering the one unit of the horse's shoulder-blades-and-withers? How frequently do you lose your pelvic positioning and resort to handlebar turns? Are you aware of how the horse displaces your pelvis across the saddle? Are you the victim of his maneuvers, or can you choose where and how you sit?

As well as using the framework idea, think of positioning the horse's shoulder-blades-and-withers relative to you, so that if correcting his evasion means displacing them more toward the outside, you need to sit more toward the inside.

• Can you maintain this overview, or do you find yourself thinking either about the horse's left side or about his right side?

To help you position both your sides at once, imagine how you would look if seen from behind, or imagine using your body to make a corridor, which the horse has your full permission to move through but against which he is not allowed to bang.

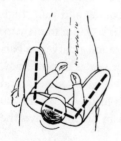  

CROOKED RIDER TO THE RIGHT IS ACTUALLY PLACED LIKE THIS

BUT SHE FEELS SYMMETRICAL

WHEN SHE IS ACTUALLY WELL PLACED SHE FEELS LIKE THIS

45. With crookedness, in particular, your subjective feelings are not to be trusted. When you counteract your natural asymmetry, you will feel as if you have brought your outside seat bone so far back that you are facing way too much to the outside.

- Holding yourself in the optimum balance point requires constant surveillance and frequent corrections. Where do you feel the physical strain of sitting like this, and how do you tend to fall from the optimum balance point? Are you aware of the ways in which you are tempted to compensate with your hand?

9 Constructive Work

It is unfortunate that so few riders are able to take their horses so constructively through the basic stages of training that they naturally ease their way into the more advanced movements, showing collected and extended gaits, shoulder-in, and half pass and clean, direct transitions (i.e., not only walk to canter and canter to walk, but also clean transitions in which the horse neither "winds up" nor "winds down"). Instead, many horses and riders get stuck at the stage where they are "just beginning lateral work." Gleefully, riders show off their six-year-old and announce that "he's just learning shoulder-in." By the time he is seven, their enthusiasm has become more muted. Often, by the time he is eight, he has become one of those horses who will never quite make it, and his rider has given up trying to work out why it seemed such a struggle to wrest such insubstantial, resistant steps from the horse.

It is in the more advanced work that the rider's mistakes and limitations really do catch up with her, and as she finds herself struggling with the horse it becomes increasingly difficult to pretend that all is well. Here, the rider pays the price for trying to run before she can walk, for trying to reap a harvest that has not been allowed to mature—when the fruit is ripe it is easy to pick, but trying to wrest it off the tree prematurely is always fraught with difficulty. In riding, as in other skills, anything done well is usually done with ease and enjoyment. When the work becomes a struggle, this is usually feedback to the rider that her timing or technique is wrong.

So, faced with the knowledge that her more advanced work is not going well, what can the rider do? To go back to basics (as most of the books suggest) is at least an attempt to heal the original wound, rather than covering it with plaster and trying to pretend that it does not exist. But even this does not always work—it can be that the basics themselves are wrong, or that the rider somehow fails to make the transition from there to the work that demands more both of herself and of her horse.

For some years my riding showed a repeating pattern. My novice horses worked quite correctly and everything proceeded well until the day I decided, That's enough of this novice stuff. Today I'm going to get some real work from this horse. I would shorten my reins, demand some more impulsion, and expect the horse to carry himself in a more advanced outline. It never worked. I did not know how to engage the horse's quarters, and lift his back and withers underneath me. Consequently, I usually only succeeded in starting a fight with him. Evasions would begin to pile up; my basic work started to disintegrate; and the advanced work I was so keen on became less—rather than more—plausible.

Faced with the demands of more advanced work, many riders seem to throw whatever skill they have out the window, and to resort to push-pull tactics. All their involuntary reflexes suddenly reemerge, summoned by the determination which substitutes brute force and ignorance for subtle, learned responses. Driven by the adrenaline of fight-or-flight, they lose any feeling of conscious choice about their actions, and so, of course, they overuse their hand. The rider in this state experiences another of the paradoxes of riding: the more concerned she becomes with getting a certain result from the horse, the less likely she is to get it; the more her attention is drawn to the process (of holding the circuit complete) rather than the product (of making the horse do the movement), however, the more likely she is to find that the movement materializes without struggle.

There is an old Zen story which illustrates the drawbacks of this excessive determination. A young man traveled across Japan to the dojo of a great judo master. When he arrived, the master granted him an audience, and the student said, "I want to become the greatest judoist in the land. How long must I study with you?" The master replied, "Ten years." The student was distraught. "Supposing I study twice as hard as all the other students?" "In that case," said the master, "It will take you twenty years." "Supposing I study three times as hard?" "In that case, it will take you thirty years." The moral of the story: he who has one eye fixed on his goal has only one eye with which to see the way.

For many riders the school movements, particularly shoulder-in and half pass, are important goals, and yardsticks by which they can and do measure themselves. But as soon as the rider's self-image or self-worth is dependent on getting a certain result from the horse, so much is at stake that she can easily fall into the trying and the panicking modes. The more determined she is to achieve her goal, the more likely she is to substitute trying for doing: trying to do lateral work requires no skill at all—it is easy for anyone—but actually *doing* lateral work is a profoundly different experience, and one that few riders manage.

It is almost inevitable that any rider who is put under sufficient pressure will finally reach a stage where her learned responses give way to panicked, anxious reactions. Some high-strung individuals meet this threshold very easily—their "home" is already a rather tense one. Others thrive on pressure—they need it to help them mobilize their energy. A rider who falls apart easily is usually someone who measures her self-worth according to her performance, and therefore she has a compelling need to do well. Her plight is made worse if she lacks the resources and confidence which she can only develop through learning and training in the awareness mode. When I first began learning lateral work, my feel was so limited that I had justifiably little faith in myself, and a limited understanding of how I was affecting the horse. I panicked whenever I was told to get the horse on to the bit, and being told to do lateral work swept me into a state in which I was no longer responsible for my actions! In desperation I would grab the inside rein and attempt to maneuver the horse into place. At the same time I could never work out why it was that we always finished up sprawled in the middle of the arena, while the rest of the riders were still moving laterally along the wall.

If I had acquired a more secure basis of useful work done in my stretch zone, this transition would never have been so traumatic. The most successful teacher creates a situation in which any new technique or school movement falls easily into the pupil's hand, just like a fruit that is ripe for picking. When I am teaching, I often do not state my goals overtly, and then I can say to the pupil, "What you just experienced is called a half halt," or "That was the feeling of having the horse *in front of you.*" Then the result or movement has never been set up as a goal, and, for a while any-way, we bypass all the difficulties that go with goal orientation. I experienced the delight of this when I was working with a teacher whose absolute insistence on correct basic work meant that I seemed to spend most of my time going round and round the edge of the arena, rarely doing any school movements. Then one day, when my horse was going well, he said, "Ride shoulder-in down the next long side." Despite my surprise, I did—and it was easy. There was no discussion of "this hand here and that leg there"; I had watched shoulder-in, and I reproduced what I had seen.

The problem, of course, arose later, when I tried to repeat what I had done, and I found myself back in all the old traps that ac-company trying. When a rider consistently practices trying (rather than doing) the more difficult work, it becomes increasingly diffi-cult for her to set it up so that she does not fall, yet again, into the old familiar pitfalls. I experienced this with a pupil who met the edge of her stretch zone very abruptly whenever I said the word "circle." On my command she changed from riding the horse well forward into a light contact, to grabbing the inside rein, tipping forward, and trying to haul the horse around. She hardly felt the change (which looked so obvious to me), although she had a vague awareness that she had somehow landed herself in the spiral of increasing tension. We spent several lessons working with the un-derstanding that whenever I said the word "circle," her task was in fact to stay on the track, to monitor her reactions as far as possible, and to find her way back from her panic into the spiral of ease. Only when she stopped reacting to my command were we in a position to ride a real circle, which then became relatively easy. One accomplished rider I know meets the edge of her stretch zone toward the end of any lateral movement. As the horse tries to dive out of half pass toward the track, or to dive out of shoulder-in toward the corner, she tries to restrain him—using tactics which contrast strongly with the subtlety she has shown earlier—and for a few strides all her good work is lost.

On such occasions I find myself asking, Who is the originator of this evasion? Did the horse begin it (as the rider usually thinks), or was it the rider herself who caused the horse to evade? Whether or not the horse deviates from his ideal positioning, the problem begins when the rider starts thinking, Oh no, here goes. . . . The Oh no in her mind goes with a mental image of the movement done badly, and this constitutes the direction that is given to her muscles, causing tightness in the body and the evasion in the horse. Whenever she says to herself, Oh no, here goes . . . she takes a quick breath (the type that lifts her up and out of the saddle) and prepares to face the worst. She mobilizes all her strength, involving her hand, arm, and jaw, and loses the ability to separate different parts of her body. By now she has caused a situation in which the horse is bound to go against her, creating resistance which plummets them both into the spiral of increasing tension. Each time it happens, the rider has even more reason for her Oh no, and she becomes caught in a vicious circle that confirms her image of herself as someone who cannot do lateral work.

In constructive learning, the rider uses her brain more like the servomechanism we discussed in Chapter 1. This always succeeds, because it forgets its past errors and only remembers and repeats its successes. In contrast, the rider who remembers, anticipates, creates, and magnifies her mistakes is doomed to fail. All of us are human, however, and at times we all experience the Oh no feeling about different movements that seem to trap us into doing them wrong. It may be canter transitions, shoulder-in, half pass, extensions, dressage tests, or flying changes. In the face of a threat approaching our weakness we tighten, lose our right-brain state, and thereby disrupt our ability to feel.

The possibility of change emerges when we realize that the problem lies not in the movement itself but in our reaction to it—in the fears and doubts of the mind. Our fear of the future destroys our ability to act in the present, thus creating a future that is just as awful as we feared it would be. The more important our riding is to us, the more we hate and fear our mistakes; and the more "special" the occasion, the stronger our reaction becomes. The only solution is for the rider to focus on her actual experience in each present moment, because then the mind no longer distorts reality. Instead of worrying about herself (how well she is doing, who is watching, and so on) she turns her attention to the task she has to perform. One of my most striking memories of this happened while I was riding a horse in a lesson in which I was being asked to ride school movements before I had brought the horse truly onto the bit, and my brain was practically spinning. Then suddenly I realized what was happening, and thought, This is ridiculous. With that, I called to mind some of the images that helped me most when I was riding well, and in the instant when I thought of them, the relationship I had with the horse changed so dramatically that I could continue with ease.

This example really brought home to me just how much I was sabotaging my own performance. Since then I have become more adept at noticing when a rider's problem lies not in her lack of *physical* skill, but in her way of blocking her own resources. Sometimes when I am teaching I trick the mind by asking pupils who are seemingly stuck in a self-fulfilling prophecy to show me how they would *like* to be able to do it. And very often they go and do just that. I once asked a client whose fresh horse was losing tempo and running with her down the long sides of the arena to come round the short side and corner as if she was not going to be run away with, and when she did this, she was not. Another trick I use to make something rather difficult seem easier is to link it with something slightly harder: the conscious mind gets sidetracked by this, leaving the unconscious mind free to get on with the original task without interference. (This technique, however, needs to be used judiciously, and preferably without communicating your intention to your pupil!) One of my teachers used to trick me into riding well by saying, "I bet you can't do that." Immediately I would think to myself, I bet I can, and I would mobilize my resources far better than I did when he was telling me how to do it, or implying that it should be easy. (My response to this, of course, was to think to myself, I bet it isn't!) When a rider is determined to show me how well she can do something, and is producing a degree of anxiety which is likely to mar her performance, I often let her off the hook by saying, "I wouldn't ask you to ride this horse really well; in fact, I don't think you should bring him *onto the bit* (or whatever)." By the time she has figured out what I mean and decided if I am really serious, she is usually far less anxious. And if, like me, she is inclined to do the opposite of whatever her teachers ask her to do, she will probably go right ahead and ride the horse really well!

My experiences with these ideas (both as teacher and pupil) have convinced me that any trick or approach which enables you to draw upon the full extent of your resources, and to ride as if you had faith in your ability, can provide instantaneous release from the limitations imposed by the mind. But it is far more advantageous to learn, for yourself, how to use your own brain to the best advantage. First, this means finding the state of relaxed concentration and tuning in to kinesthetic feedback. But the most skilled riders go one stage further than this. In the back of their mind they always hold what I call a "reference feel"—the best feeling they have to date for the kind of work they are doing. They then make a comparison between what they are *actually* getting and what they *would like to* be getting; and they do whatever they have to do to make the reality fit their ideal. This means that the aim or the ultimate aid is to "make it feel right," and this is far too subtle for the average verbal description. The ideas of completing the circuit and learning like a servomechanism both have within them the notion of a goal, and a comparison, and the best riders always set themselves realistic terms of reference, differentiating between the best feeling possible for a green horse, a schooled horse, and a particularly difficult horse. They always aim to complete the circuit—or, at least, to get as near to this as possible—and they are so well able to improvise and have such a broad repertoire of "feels" that they know exactly what adjustments will take them from where they are to where they want to be.

Most riders do not make this comparison, although even a beginner can have and *use* a reference feel. Perhaps this is the best feeling she has had to date at a posting trot; when she loses it, she has to use trial and error to grope her way back there again. But instead of making adjustments by referring to past feelages, most riders get bogged down in whatever the horse or their body is offering them at a particular moment, and they simply accept what they are given. When I realized that this was happening to me, I found that groping my way back to my ideal feelage was not always so difficult; the problem was more that it had never occurred to me to do it! To help you understand the difference it makes to have and use clear references, imagine two people going together on a walk through a wood. One is a botanist, the other has no special knowledge of plants or trees—so all she sees is a mass of foliage, while the other can distinguish different ferns and leaves and fruits. The botanist does this by making a (possibly unconscious) comparison between what she sees in front of her and information she has stored from her previous study. We are all well used to doing this with our visual sense; in fact, if you have the relevant information, it is almost impossible not to do it. But few people can do it as well with their kinesthetic sense, and you may find that getting this kind of overview in your riding—and acting on it—is, initially, like heaving yourself out of a semi-slumber and getting down to work.

The time you *do* manage to make a comparison, of course, is in those "Uh-oh" experiences, when your reference is hardly an ideal feelage. In the transitional stage between letting go of this and finding something better with which to replace it, you may find yourself passing through a few blind alleys. Eventually you will discover, however, what a useful, appropriate reference feel should be. At one stage I had a mental block about the lateral movements, which instilled in me the kind of dread that was bound to evoke all sorts of traumas. But sometimes I would ride slightly better and would come out of a work session elated, believing that I had found the key. When I rode the next day, I would inevitably find that I had lost it again, and I would feel suitably depressed. My emotions continued to seesaw until my success at the lateral movements ceased to be a yardstick by which I measured myself. When my feelings of self-worth were no longer dependent on my performance, my perception became clearer, and some real breakthroughs happened. Then, both my physical alignment and my mental state became very different: instead of feeling elated by my success, I felt humbled, as I became aware of what I had been doing to the horse in my push-pull attempts to make him do the movement. I had always felt indignant about how he was treating me, and I had been completely insensitive to the way that I was treating him. Now that my eyes were open, I felt brought down to size; and painful as this was, it had the effect of bringing me down to earth as well. My elation and despair were things of the past, and I could say that something was "good" or "bad" as a statement of fact, without making a moral judgment about myself.

Awareness Questions and Imagery

• What movements or situations throw you into a panic? How easily do you meet the edge of your stretch zone, and substitute trying for doing?

When confronted with one of your mental blocks, there are a variety of techniques you can use to help you focus your mind on your actual experience. Monitor a certain feeling or quality, and carry this over from the easier work into the area of difficulty. For instance, you could choose some important factor in your body positioning, the feeling of the seeking reflexes, or of the horse's rhythm; the numbering exercise may help you to do this more effectively. Alternatively, you can become aware of the workings of the mind itself—if you can catch yourself imagining the movement you are about to perform done wrong, you will find that you can change your internal image, and then change the way you actually ride the movement. Previewing any movement with an accurate, realistic mental rehearsal of how you want it to happen is one of the best ways to ensure that it actually happens like that. Then, as you ride it, keep making whatever adjustments are necessary to bring it into line with your ideal. Try riding as if you knew how to do it, or had faith in yourself, or with the attitude of "You bet I can." You could also try demonstrating to an imaginary audience how you would like to be able to do it!

• Our susceptibility to mental blocks and self-fulfilling prophecies depends a lot on the goals we set for ourselves, and on our attitudes and expectations. Do you work in a way that honors the boundary of your stretch zone, so that you can gradually ease it forward; or do you plummet yourself into your panic zone and expect yourself to cope? Do you set realistic goals for yourself, or do you set them so high that you continually doom yourself to failure?

• Write a series of sentences that describe your riding, each beginning with one of the following statements: I have difficulty with . . .; I hope . . .; I try . . .; I cannot . . .; I am afraid. . . . Then change each in turn to: It is a challenge for me to . . .; I trust . . .; I will . . .; I will not . . .; I'm excited. . . . How does it feel to say the new sentences?

Take some time to imagine how you might feel and look if your riding was based on these new attitudes. The old ones are an integral part of physical patterns you would probably love to break, and as you think of yourself in this new way, you may find that your mental attitude and your physical approach begin to match your new self-image.

Complete the sentence: "Because I'm not a very good rider, I . . . (look down, move my hands, etc.)." Now reverse it: "Because I . . . I'm not a very good rider." How does this change your attitude toward your difficulties?

Take some time to examine your own self-attitudes: how often do you tell yourself that you cannot ride well under pressure, that you always mess up the lateral movements, or that you must be the most uncoordinated rider in your class? Find out what you are actually thinking about yourself, and express each statement in a simple sentence; then make up a sentence which gives a full and positive statement of its opposite and points out the direction in which you would like to go. Thus, "I can't ride well under pressure" becomes "When under pressure I am increasingly able to refine my awareness and sharpen my reflexes"; "I always mess up lateral movements" becomes "In the lateral movements I improve my awareness of my seat, using subtle adjustments to improve the horse's positioning"; and "I am the most uncoordinated rider I know" becomes "My body is naturally coordinated. The more I increase my body awareness, the more I tap into my natural ability."

Although these affirmations may sound false at first, they begin to drive a wedge between your old self-image and the new one you wish to cultivate. Repeat them to yourself, or write them on a card, and put them in a place where you see them often. Back them up using mental rehearsal, and see if you can answer the question, What do I need to learn or how do I need to refine my perceptions in order to really manifest these ideals?

• Pick a quality that you feel your riding lacks (e.g., authority, sensitivity). In mental rehearsal imagine yourself riding as if you already had it. How does this change your attitude, posture, etc.? Then take this into real life.

Another useful technique is "substitution rehearsal." Choose two movements or gaits, one which you do well and one with which you have difficulty (e.g., your trot seat and your canter seat, upward transitions and downward transitions, half pass in trot, and half pass in canter). First take the one you do well; settle yourself comfortably for mental rehearsal, and imagine yourself riding. Experience the feeling of the movement from inside your body, and also imagine how you look from the outside. At this stage change to the more difficult skill, and imagine how this more competent self would do it. How does this both feel and look different from normal? What new qualities are you bringing into your performance, how are you using your body differently? Next time you ride, take these new feelings with you, and find out how they affect your performance. By alternating both actual and mental practice you can often refine these new techniques, and ingrain them into your riding.

• The negative, limiting attitudes we hold about ourselves are some of the most stubborn and destructive self-fulfilling prophecies. It is well worth taking time to discover how these are affecting your performance, and how you might ride differently if they did not.

Many of the difficulties that arise in more advanced work have their origins in the rider's doubts about her ability. Many riders when they feel the need to prove themselves tend to make inappropriate decisions about when to ride each movement. ("I'd better have a go at shoulder-in. I really ought to be able to do it by now.")

Timing this better makes the actual physical problems far easier to solve, for when a movement is well prepared and the circuit held complete, horse and rider are both placed under far less strain. In more demanding work, problems with pelvic positioning, with the driving aids, and with asymmetry become significantly harder to deal with—and as we all know, they flaw many riders. Collection, extension, and direct transitions are primarily based on the abilities we developed in Chapter 7, but the lateral movements and counter canter require some further adjustments.

My early attempts at the lateral movements were marred by an excessive use of my hand and my lower leg. Both my pelvic positioning and the horse's gait would disintegrate in the face of all this pushing and pulling, and even though I knew this was happening, it seemed that there was nothing I could do about it. Like many riders I found the lateral movements extremely difficult, and although leg-yielding is technically much more straightforward than shoulder-in or half pass, it made little difference whether I was attempting the easier or the more difficult movement—the result was still a mess. (Leg-yielding is ridden either along the wall, with the horse at about a 45-degree angle to it, or across the diagonal of the school. In each case he is held straight, or with a slight flexion away from his direction of movement, and he is not asked for collection. This makes the movement significantly less demanding than shoulder-in or half pass. Many trainers find leg-yielding a helpful way to introduce both horse and rider to the lateral movements, but then they usually discard it, because it has the unwanted effect of disengaging the horse's quarters.) In all my attempts at the lateral movements, it was apparent to me that I must be doing something wrong; in response, however, I resorted to doing *more of the same*, and that meant using more force. I became consumed by the process of literally trying to *push* the horse away from my leg; but this is rather like using a sledgehammer to crack a nut—except that in this case the sledgehammer does not work, because it is hitting the nut in the wrong place. When hit in the right place the nut yields easily to a minimal amount of force, and this provides the dividing line between riders who *just can* ride good lateral work (the ones who say that "It's so easy. . .") and those who *just cannot*.

The problem is that using prolonged and forceful aids is bound to make the rider reactive; in her effort she will lose the pinch feeling, and this means that her seat bones will spring apart and slip out from underneath her. This immediately affects the horse's carriage—instead of moving in the seeking reflexes, he hollows his back. This will probably displace her even more, and lead her to resort to her hand, so their attempt at the movement becomes a pulling match, based securely in the spiral of tension. One of two things then happens: either the horse pulls his way out of the movement, or he gives in—usually to the extent that he loses the crispness and impulsiveness of the gait, so he no longer moves in one piece. Instead he produces rather slow and lumbering steps in which his back end and his front end are not well coordinated. (This is a particularly common sight in riding schools!) Then, if the rider forgets about her seat, and times her leg aids by thinking, Now, now, now, in rhythm with his step, she will exaggerate the problem; it is as if she loses sight of the forest for the trees, so that as she succumbs to paralysis by analysis his movement winds down, rather like a clockwork toy. She will only be able to remain causal and use the lateral movement to improve the horse's gaits when she has absolute control of her pelvic positioning, of her leg, and of her hand, maintaining an overview which allows their combined influence to position the horse so that he naturally—reflexly—carries himself and steps in the way that she wants.

The connecting link which makes this possible lies, as ever, in the pinch feeling, and in the rider's positioning *across* the saddle. The pinch draws the two sides of the body in toward each other; if, however, force can be exerted by one side which is greater than that exerted by the other, the rider has created a powerful way of influencing the horse. It is this push, and not the lower leg, which is primarily responsible for his movement sideways. There are, however, two other important factors. First, her weight must come over on the side of his direction of motion, because the horse will instinctively step in this direction underneath her. (Try carrying someone piggyback and then ask her to displace her weight to either side!) Second, the rider must make this change of weight *without* collapsing. The tendency to collapse is even stronger in lateral work than it is on the circle, because the rider tends to lean in the direction of the horse's bend. In leg-yielding and shoulder-in, this means that she collapses over her more active leg, and away from her direction of motion, while in traverse and half pass (where the horse is bent toward his direction of motion), she leans in the same direction.

To help myself make this change of position in the lateral movements, I find it useful to think of aligning my thigh on the side of our direction of motion so that it lies parallel to the horse's body. This alignment then begins from behind my seat bone, and my leg becomes an "aikido leg," pointing toward and straight past the horse's head (so that, in leg-yielding and half pass, it points out our direction of motion). I recently began teaching lateral work to a pupil who had no previous experience of it, and even I was surprised by the ease with which she was able to position the horse and glide into the movement, maintaining his rhythm and impulsion. She took care to hold herself straight, monitoring the angle between her leg and her body on either side, and she described her

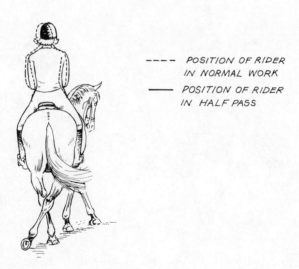

---- POSITION OF RIDER
IN NORMAL WORK

—— POSITION OF RIDER
IN HALF PASS

46. Although this horse is shown in half pass, all the lateral movements require the rider to sit more toward the horse's direction of motion. This rider has made an effective weight change. Now see Fig. 38 to compare it with the collapse that could have happened.

position change as "swooshing across the saddle." As she adopted her new "aikido leg" she said, "I can really feel the change in my energy." She could also feel how she cadenced his gait by using the movement of her seat bones—on the side away from her direction of motion the seat bone took on a forward-and-across movement, and encouraged the horse to move in this direction underneath her.

The seat bone on its own, however, will not have much effect, and the truth is that the horse will only move over when *you* move over, and stabilizing your backside in its new position requires an enormous amount of tone in the thigh muscles on the side to which you are moving. As soon as you lose this, you lose the pinch, the framework (See Fig. 33), and you begin to collapse; your hands and lower legs then take over the role of trying to make the horse move laterally underneath you, and your attempts at the movement are fraught with difficulty. Maintaining an effective pel-

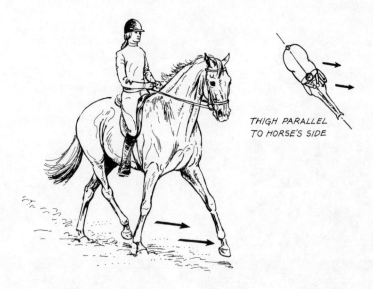

THIGH PARALLEL
TO HORSE'S SIDE

47.   This horse is leg-yielding, with a slight flexion away from his direction of motion. To initiate this movement you have to change your weight distribution while still holding yourself straight; it helps to think of making the thigh on the side of your direction of motion lie parallel to the horse's side.

vic alignment naturally brings your hands and lower legs into the right positions, and it gives them far less to do; but maintaining this alignment can be extremely taxing, especially when it requires you to stabilize your pelvis in the position you find most difficult. This is vital and unavoidable because this—and only this—will bring the horse into an alignment which he too might prefer to avoid.

All horses have a list toward one shoulder, and consequently on one rein (usually the right) they tend to move with their shoulders and quarters equidistant from the wall. This automatically makes them crooked, bringing them into a position which verges toward traverse. On the other (left) rein they are more likely to move straight, so that their shoulders (being narrower) are farther from the wall than their quarters; this puts them in a position which verges more toward shoulder-in. To exaggerate each of these positions will be relatively easy for the horse, and he may even volunteer to produce some (albeit rather poor) imitations of these movements even when the rider does not want them! The real challenge comes on the other rein when he is asked to reverse his natural carriage; because of this, it is always important to ride the lateral movements on both reins. On the more difficult rein, the rider has to "rearrange the stuffing" to such an extent that she has to be enormously skillful.

Inevitably, the same old traps await her, and on the rein where her pelvis tends to point inward, she is particularly likely to lose stability and pull on the inside rein. Many an attempt at shoulder-in, or at leg-yielding along the wall, has proved abortive because the rider has begun it by trying to *pull* the horse's nose in off the track. On the rein where his shoulder tends to stay glued to the wall, he will probably react to the rider's pulling with a refusal to move his forehand at all; on the other rein, he is more likely to bring it to the inside, but without making a correct bend. Whenever the rider uses her inside hand in an attempt to influence the horse's nose, she is bound to get into trouble, just as she does on a circle. A good shoulder-in is possible only when the rider's outside hand and inside leg are the dominant aids, while at the same time, the horse has a well-established bend to the inside, which occurs by virtue of the way that he reaches into the outside rein. But shoulder-in differs from the circle in that the rider's outside leg (on the side of her direction of motion) becomes the "aikido leg," and this requires her to change her pelvic positioning, bringing both it and her shoulders parallel to the horse's shoulders. As on a circle, she has to protect the horse's back muscles from the effects of a protruding inside seat bone, and this would be one of the dangers if she collapsed; so as she comes around the corner, and eases his shoulder away from the wall, she has to "swoosh across the saddle," holding herself straight as she makes her new "aikido leg," and this change naturally invites the horse to maintain his body position, and move laterally along the wall in shoulder-in.

In all the lateral movements, it is important that the rider ride *both sides of the horse at once*, and this is a big perceptual leap from her tendency to think about his left side *or* his right side. Only when she perceives the whole can she position the horse's shoulders in just the right alignment relative to herself and his quarters. As I do this, I find it useful to ask myself, How and where do I have to sit on the saddle so that *relative to me*, there's just the

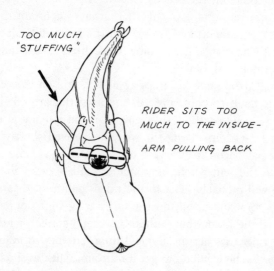

TOO MUCH "STUFFING"

RIDER SITS TOO MUCH TO THE INSIDE—

ARM PULLING BACK

48. An abortive attempt to position the horse into a circle or shoulder-in. When you pull on the inside rein you tend simultaneously to align your pelvis so that it faces inward; in this case, the horse has responded by breaking at the withers.

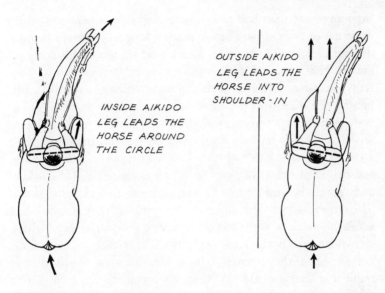

INSIDE AIKIDO
LEG LEADS THE
HORSE AROUND
THE CIRCLE

OUTSIDE AIKIDO
LEG LEADS THE
HORSE INTO
SHOULDER - IN

49. The rider's self-positioning as she "leads" the horse onto a circle or shoulder-in. As she changes her "aikido leg," she also changes her pelvic alignment, and this brings the horse into shoulder-in naturally.

right amount of "stuffing" coming into each side of the horse's rib cage and neck? How can I displace his shoulders into the right alignment, and close all the loopholes which might allow them to fall away from here? I find that this approach helps me to remain causal, so that I can make small adjustments as the movement progresses, using the pinch feeling and my "aikido leg" to prevent myself from collapsing. The forward-and-across movement of my seat bone then maintains the fluency of the gait, and by thinking like this I gain far more precision as well so that the adjustments I make can be even more minutely detailed. I can differentiate between all the different lateral movements, and can glide from one to another; in particular, I can determine the exact angle of my shoulder-in, and can hold the horse's quarters on the track so that they cannot twist out toward the wall—a common mistake which is relished by horses, as it makes the movement (done now with his body straight) far less taxing.

Similarly, leg-yielding done across the school is a much less taxing movement than half pass, where the horse is bent toward his direction of motion, and has to reach a long way forward and underneath his body to bring his active hind leg toward his center of gravity. Half pass, and its sister movement traverse (which is essentially the same, but done with the horse's nose toward the wall), present the rider with the most difficult challenge in terms of her body positioning, and many riders never manage to bring themselves sufficiently far over on the saddle. Instead, they focus their attention on trying to push the horse away from their outside leg, and this means that they end up sitting to that side of the saddle, and lagging behind him as he moves across (if indeed he does). Then they worsen the situation by bringing their inside hand across his neck as they struggle to create a bend; in fact, I have seen riders practically cross both hands over each other and the horse's neck as they attempt to move him sideways(!), with the net result that they are orienting themselves and the horse *away* from the direction they know he ought to move in. Again, half pass will only work well when the horse bends to the inside through reaching into the outside rein and, contrary to our instinctive logic, the *inside leg and outside hand* are again the dominant aids. Only when the rider sits well to the inside is her inside hand freed from the need to come across the neck, so that she can use it as an opening rein. However, sitting like this does not come easily; it only becomes possible when she has a clear pinch feeling and a strong "aikido leg" which points out her direction and stays parallel to the horse's side, bringing her seat bone well over and holding it so that, as on a circle, it is slightly in advance of her outer one. This will inevitably be more difficult on the side to which she collapses; but when both seat bones and thighs are held in their optimum positioning the movement becomes far, far easier, and the hand and lower leg have relatively little to do.

The horse's evasions are such that on one rein where he has a list toward his inside shoulder, he tends to head from the center line straight toward the wall, without bothering to move on two tracks. The rider has to "rearrange the stuffing" and create a bulge on the outside of his body, encouraging him to seek contact with the outside rein, and thus holding his shoulders back a bit so that his quarters can catch up. (Her instinctive reaction, however, will

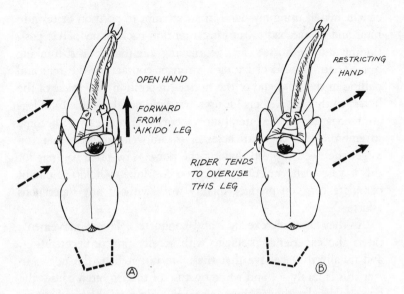

OPEN HAND

FORWARD FROM 'AIKIDO' LEG

RESTRICTING HAND

RIDER TENDS TO OVERUSE THIS LEG

Ⓐ

Ⓑ

50. Two attempts at half pass. Unless you make a deliberate effort to use the inside "aikido leg" and stabilize your pelvis (A), you are likely to slide across the saddle and collapse (B).

be to hold back the shoulders by bringing her inside hand across the neck; this has a disastrous effect both on her pelvic positioning and the fluency of the movement.) On the other rein, where the horse's inside hind leg naturally tracks farther over than his body, he is usually more than willing to move on two tracks; the problem is that he curls so much to the inside that his quarters are in advance of his shoulders, and he barely moves forward. Again the rider has to "rearrange the stuffing," limiting the bulge on the outside of his body, and encouraging him to reach more into the inside rein so that his shoulders are brought in advance of his quarters. Then, if she sends him strongly forward, his response is to carry his hind legs much farther underneath his body and to take far more genuine steps.

These problems with the lateral placing of the horse and rider are but one facet of the difficulties that arise in the lateral movements, and they place an enormous premium on the rider's ability to shape the horse. I have had many experiences when I have

caught myself using my hand in an attempt to position or restrain
him, and I have had to turn my attention back to my pelvic positioning and the horse's carriage, making sure that I was still taking
him. Then, instead of taking a stronger contact on the rein and
pulling in the *front* end of the horse, I reposition the *middle* of the
horse, so that his withers lift up toward my navel and his hind legs
are reengaged. In the lateral movements it is very easy to become
so embroiled in the intricacies of the movement itself that you
forget the need to keep shaping the horse. The price you pay for
this is very high, and only when you continue to hold the circuit
complete can you produce quality work without any superfluous
effort.

As they prepare, execute, and complete a lateral movement,
riders also experience problems with acceleration or deceleration,
and usually they believe that these are initiated by the horse. In
fact this is rarely so, and while overuse of the leg often causes the
horse to decelerate into the movement, overuse of the hand tempts
him to run out of it. A participant in one of my dismounted workshops realized this for the first time during a mental rehearsal exercise, when she felt how she came around the short side of the
school and prepared for shoulder-in by taking a stronger contact on
the rein. She believed that this would help her to maneuver the
horse into place. But as her hand became stronger she pulled in her
belly and leaned back slightly. Consequently, of course, she broke
the circuit, and as the horse pulled back against her, she tipped
back more so that he ran out from under her more. Needless to say,
her imaginary shoulder-in was not very successful. Had she been in
the actual situation she might well have interpreted these events as
confirmation of her belief that since the horse was bound to try to
run out from underneath her, a "strong" body position and a lot of
hand would be needed. As it was, she came out of the mental
rehearsal feeling rather shocked, and saying, "Do I really do that?
It all seems so unnecessary, and it's definitely me who's initiating
the problem." She was skilled enough to know that all this would
not happen if she held her body on the optimum balance point and
kept taking the horse; she would then be like the immovable rider
in the dismounted push-pull exercise, and the horse would find
himself—even if he initiated the evasion—with nothing against
which he could fight.

Canter, of course, requires the same ability, and riders who attempt to slow down the horse with their hand either find themselves battling, or—if the horse gives in—sitting to canter which no longer bounds forward as a three-beat movement. Instead, it disintegrates into four beats because the diagonal pair of legs which form the second beat of each stride come down separately, and the power of the gait is lost. Horses also evade the strain of canter work by bringing their quarters to the inside, and although this is especially likely to happen on one rein, it may happen on both. So the rider's task is to straighten the horse by bringing his shoulders over, so that they lie in front of his quarters. Of course, she is again tempted to do this by pulling on the inside rein, but she only succeeds in bringing his nose even more to the inside while his shoulders remain to the outside. In an effective correction she positions herself so that, relative to her, the "stuffing" moves from the outside of the horse's body toward the inside of his rib cage, shoulder, and neck, encouraging him to reach into the inside rein. Her outside thigh, seat bone, shoulder, elbow, and hand limit the bulge on the outside of his body; it is as if she makes a wall with her outside aids, bringing his forehand into a position which veers toward shoulder-in, so that his hind legs step beneath the bulk of his body and the gait has much more gymnastic value.

Counter canter (where the horse leads with his outside foreleg, and maintains a slight bend toward that leg) can also help to straighten the horse, but it needs to be ridden with care, and only after suitable preparation. It is not easy for the rider to stay with the horse in counter canter, and like all the more advanced movements, it puts her and the horse into a more stressful position. It requires an enormous amount of impulsion for him to maintain the gait, and some riders make it even more difficult for him by flexing him *too much* toward his leading leg. Done badly, the advanced movements are like the razor in the monkey's hands, and they entice the horse into more subtle, complex evasions. He simply becomes more clever in his ways of evading the strain, and the more wantonly ambitious the rider becomes, the more likely she is to find that even the easier work just becomes progressively more and more difficult.

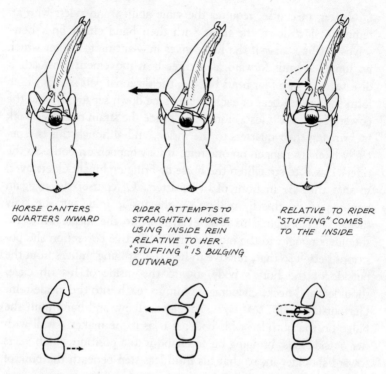

HORSE CANTERS
QUARTERS INWARD

RIDER ATTEMPTS TO
STRAIGHTEN HORSE
USING INSIDE REIN
RELATIVE TO HER.
"STUFFING" IS BULGING
OUTWARD

RELATIVE TO RIDER
"STUFFING" COMES
TO THE INSIDE

51. Straightening the horse in canter. Again, you will tend to straighten the horse by using your inside rein, and this will bring your pelvis out of alignment. Only when you stabilize your own body position can you rearrange the "stuffing" relative to yourself, and reposition the horse's shoulders. (A similar correction is often required in half pass.)

Awareness Questions and Imagery

• When you ride the lateral movements, do you find yourself using prolonged, forceful aids? In response, do your horses set themselves up against you and attempt to pull their way out of the movement, or do they slow down, so that their gait "disintegrates"?

• Where does your attention go? Can you maintain the overview which allows you to maintain impulsion, to keep taking the horse, and to shape him so that the circuit stays complete? Or is all your attention consumed by one factor—perhaps in battles with your hand, or in the process of trying to push the horse over with your leg?

If your leg aids do not have much effect, and if your body feels either rigid or like a series of disconnected pieces, it is highly likely that you have lost the pinch feeling. Finding the optimum position for your thighs and pelvis is not easy, but it immediately makes everything else fit into place, so that you and the horse can remain in one piece. When you become causal you will have a much clearer feeling of the horse's movement, and of your seat bones as they go with him.

- Imagine the framework of iron bars through your backside, down each thigh and through the horse's barrel in between your knees (see Figure 33). Which parts of the framework do you tend to lose? Emphasize the bar down your thigh on the side of your direction of motion, making sure that you hold it parallel to the horse's side, and think of this alignment originating *behind* your seat bone on that side. How does this change your position on the saddle? You will only become causal when each thigh makes a V at exactly the right angle. To find this optimum positioning you may need to bring your two thighs in closer together—imagine doing this by decreasing the width of your pubic bone. If you are new to lateral work, or if it has always befuddled you, begin by working in walk, and establish your ability using leg-yielding; reverse shoulder-in, done with the horse's head toward the wall, can also be useful.
- If you are a more skillful rider, do you find it more difficult to ride shoulder-in, traverse, or half pass?

In all these movements, it is imperative that you first create a bend to the inside, so that the horse is clearly reaching into the outside rein. This makes your pelvic positioning much easier, helping you to sit toward the horse's direction of motion. This in turn makes it possible for your inside hand and outside leg to be the dominant side.

- Can you ride both sides of the horse at once, or is your attention continually drawn to your inside hand? If it is, your pelvis is still misaligned, and you are very likely to be collapsing your hip. Ask someone to give you feedback from the ground about whether or not you are sitting straight. She may also be able to help as you pay more attention to the pinch feeling, your seat-bone placing, and your "aikido leg." Experiment with them, until you find the positioning which renders you causal.

- Is it more difficult for you to position the horse into the movement, or to make corrections as it progresses, or to finish it well? To what do you attribute these problems?

- When you are riding, can you differentiate between a three-beat and a four-beat canter? Do you notice when a horse is cantering with his quarters "in"? How much influence do you have over his straightness; can you adjust the position of his shoulders relative to his quarters? As you do this, think of positioning his shoulders relative to yourself, and in a position which veers toward shoulder-in. Imagine that you want to make him feel as if he is cantering between shafts, and with a clear contact into the inside shaft. Whereabouts in your body do you feel the strain of this correction?

- In counter canter can you keep taking him, so that he moves in one piece? Can you sit to his counter canter as well as you can sit to his canter? If not, you are very likely to be tipping forward.

- Does riding counter canter improve the true canter, or have an adverse effect on it?

To make constructive use of the time you spend schooling is indeed no easy task. It requires you to have a clear understanding of what you do to the horse and of what the horse does to you, and to recognize and honor the edge of your stretch zone. With this clarity, and the ability to focus your attention on ways of completing the circuit (rather than on your worries, or the end result), you can use the various school movements to help you in certain specific ways—rather than doing them because they are demanded by teachers or dressage tests.

As an example, let us take the way that I have ridden and used transitions during various stages of my learning. During the stage when I avoided them, I knew that they did little to enhance my horse's training; later, though, when I was spared the pulling match, halts became challenging and enjoyable, and I found them a helpful way of bringing the horse into an outline. At that stage, I tended to overuse them, and although I knew in theory that it was better to shape him during forward movement, this did not seem to be the case in practice. My need to use the walk-halt transition was merely a demonstration of my inability to work the horse in the more impulsive gaits; now that I can do this much better, I practice less often the transitions as such, and I trust that they will emerge as proof of the pudding when my work in the basic gaits is correct. I also know when not to use them; if any attempt to halt correctly would only compound a green horse's evasions, it is wiser to use the voice to bring him gently to a stop. Later, when the horse is more established, I may use the halt to confront his evasions, and to help lower his croup. The halt has become an exercise which I use to further the horse's gymnastic work; I know when it is relevant and useful, and I know what I hope to achieve by riding it. I am working from my own inner knowledge and authority, rather than riding transitions because somebody, or some theory, has told me that I should do so.

It is the presence of this inner knowledge which marks those riders who are able to do productive work on their own. I can remember a time when I used to wander round the riding school when I was working (like a free-range hen, as one of my teachers used to say), trying a bit of this and a bit of that, in the hope that *something* would eventually work and "get my horse going." My theoretical knowledge and my conscience dictated the exercises I should ride; I did them because they were what one did when one went into the riding school, rather than an expression on my own inner knowledge; and when nothing worked as I wanted I would get fed up and so bored that sooner or later I would give up and go out on the trail. Riders with little understanding of the "how" of riding are rarely highly motivated; often their bodily use is so inefficient, and their breathing so shallow, that they quickly run out of energy—and they do not experience the rewards which might encourage them to draw on their reserves. When the rider is working with *process* rather than *product*, on the other hand, she understands the structure of what she is doing, and this gives her the equivalent of a light at the end of the tunnel—as well as a lot of little rewards along the way. With these to offer strength and encouragement, it is worth expending some more energy; but without this light (or faith), wandering lost in a fog, it can feel pointless to continue.

It is interesting to realize that in Germany and Austria, for example, riders tend to work their horses for shorter time periods than in England. Their attitude is that once the horse has worked well and achieved what the rider wanted, he might just as well go back to the stable. Riders who lack a sense of purpose and direction quite often wander aimlessly round and round a riding arena without having the circuit complete, thereby giving themselves the ideal opportunity to confirm and ingrain the breaks in it. Riders who do not know if they are achieving anything measure a work session by time spent out of the stable, rather than by useful gymnastic effort, structured to achieve a certain result. Ideally, the rider uses the minimum amount of work to the maximum advantage. She structures her sessions so well that each step builds on the last, and this kind of build-up makes even the most difficult exercises seem comparatively much easier. She achieves her aim without any unrealistic goals threatening either herself or the horse, and this requires her to base her work on a recognition of the horse's needs and limitations, rather than focusing solely on her own. Her attention shifts away from herself to the horse. And thoughts such as, I wonder if I can get this horse going as well as I did yesterday, or, I'm not going to give up until I've put those extensions through, are replaced by, He's bound to feel stiff today, so I must work him lightly, or, If he feels ready, I'd like to work again on the extensions. Now the rider does not sense the horse as a threat to her ability, and she does not need to prove her competence. Instead, she works him partly in his stretch zone and partly in his comfort zone; she knows when to confront him and when to ease off. She has a far more genuine love for the horse and can put herself in second place, knowing that the time she spends preparing the soil will result in a strong and beautiful plant.

This requires the quiet confidence that only comes with doing rather than trying. Our cultural ethos so extols trying that those riders who do not actually give up continue to struggle with their horses day after day, making heroic efforts in which both they and the horse suffer, and find that the work becomes a grind. When the rider misjudges the edge of the horse's stretch zone, and continues to work until she proves her point, not only can the fight-or-flight reflexes become involved, but the body also suffers the effects of fatigue.

In *Basic Training of the Young Horse*, Reiner Klimke points out that although you may get obedience from a tired horse on one day, you will not succeed on the next. This is another manifestation of the learning-performance-enjoyment triangle which we discussed in Chapter 5, and which collapses whenever the rider works the horse rather rigidly, continually pushing herself and him beyond the limits of their stretch zones. If the muscles controlling a movement become tired, others are substituted, and inefficient, awkward movement results, in which neither the fatigued nor the substituted muscles get the proper training. When the rider becomes stressed, her kinesthetic sensations get so jumbled that she loses her clarity *and* her skill. Both she and the horse are often left with actual physical pain, and unpleasant memories which make even the prospect of the next work session daunting.

At one time, I was determined to keep the horse in front of me, but because of the way I put him under stress, I created situations in which this became more and more impossible. If I had a particularly difficult evasion on one circle, for instance, I would ride it time and time again; this can become rather like picking at a scab (and making it worse), and it is far better to use the whole school and a variety of movements, so that you diminish rather than intensify the resistance. When I had the horse going particularly well, I would also repeat movements again and again—delighting in the feeling I had created—but this kind of repetition leads to staleness and eventually evasion. Thus, when a movement has been done well it needs to be done only once or twice more, in order to ingrain it as a right-brain feelage. (Contrary to popular belief, hours and hours of repetition are not necessary. You will, after all, recognize somebody's face again when you have seen her only once, and this is equally true of feelages—even though it may take you somewhat longer to streamline the process of groping your way back to them!) After doing the good movement just a few times, therefore, it is best to put it together with something else, or to stop.

I now believe that a large part of the rider's skill lies in knowing when to go into the arena, and when to get off the horse. In the initial stages of learning, I often advise riders not to try to school their horses when I'm not there, because they often only manage to get lost (like free-range hens) or do damage. Ironically, it is the skilled riders, who could possibly afford to school more often without causing damage, who realize that *more is not necessarily better.* Other riders tend to keep pushing themselves and their horses, riding more and more demanding movements, until they reach their level of incompetence—the point where it can only get worse.

When a rider does not know when to stop, it is highly likely that her perfectionist streak is so strong that she can never live up to her ideals; if settling for anything less than perfection feels to her like admitting defeat, she is likely to be an extremely hard taskmaster. Often, this kind of rider makes an agreement with herself: I'll be satisfied when I get x. But then, when she gets x she wants y, and when she gets y she knows that she will not feel satisfied until she gets z. Then she needs to go back again and check that she can still do y ... and on it goes. Only when her feelings of self-worth are not dependent on her performance can she put the horse first, and work him in a way that cultivates his willingness and generosity. Instead of trying to make each session into the ultimate experience she sees whatever happens here and now as one stage on a journey in which she and the horse both have so much more to learn, and so many more chances to surpass themselves; she recognizes that he reaches a stage in each session when he is fatigued, and that this is the time when it is prudent to stop work.

The ideal work session has several stages. Normally it begins with a walk on a loose rein, which allows the horse and rider time to settle to each other and their surroundings. Some riders then put the horse in front of them or onto the bit before they do any other exercises; others prefer to ride an easy rising trot and an easy canter in which they do not shape him at all. When they do shape the horse, some riders bring him straight into quite an upright carriage, others start in a longer, lower outline. The latter is quite controversial. Some say that it only serves to put the horse on his forehand; others say that lengthening the muscles, and working them at a lower tone, is a good way to ease stiffness out of the body, and to give it greater control and fluidity when the muscles are finally shortened. Personally, I find it extremely useful (although it can be difficult—and inappropriate—if the horse begins the session rather fresh). As long as his withers remain lifted, his forehand will still exert a carrying and not a pulling function. This means that he does not go unduly onto his forehand, and to my mind, the benefits far outweigh any possible disadvantages.

When the horse's body is warm, the rider moves to "supplying" work, which forms the major part of the session. The simple school movements are used to put the horse more solidly in front of her, until he reaches a stage where he gives up his resistances and moves forward freely, working equally well on both reins. As all of us know, this is easier said than done, and very often the horse flummoxes his rider with evasions, using these to withhold from forward movement, or to keep the circuit incomplete, or to retain his asymmetry. A skilled rider uses the simple school movements to work through these difficulties, and then to push the horse a little further—transitions, half halts, and variations in the length of the stride all help to move the horse's center of gravity back, lowering his croup and lightening his forehand. The horse is also asked to be more supple from side to side, through the use of changes of direction and bend, and smaller circles. Some riders include turns on the forehand and leg-yielding in this work; others believe that these have the effect of disengaging the horse's quarters. (Personally, I rarely use them.) The skilled rider will use whichever gaits and exercises most help each individual horse to put himself at her disposal.

Out of desperation, some riders resort to using shoulder-in at this stage; others use it more skillfully, often as part of their initial warm-up in walk—and with some rather old, stiff horses this can be very useful. Unless it is ridden well, however, it only serves to encourage the horse into the second-level evasions, and, like the other collecting exercises, shoulder-in is probably best left until the horse is already in the "blank check state." Then the rider can use the supplying exercises in a more challenging way, and by riding smaller circles, changes of bend, and more frequent transitions, she can also incorporate the lateral movements, rein-back, and counter canter. Now that the body is hot, its flexibility increases, but endurance and stamina are less. The horse worked in collection is under great pressure, and he is very likely to find subtle ways of coming back "behind the rider"; therefore, this kind of work should be interspersed with more forward-going exercises at lower tone—lengthening his stride, or possibly putting him forward and down into an extremely long, low outline. These both serve to ease his muscles, and to confirm that he is "in front of the aids."

After a period of challenging gymnastic work, most riders like to finish the session by working again in a longer, lower outline, stretching the horse's muscles and allowing him to cool down gently. A sudden change, and rapid cooling off do not allow the waste products produced during muscular effort to be removed by the bloodstream, and stiffness results. A few minutes of walking on a long rein, or a short trail ride, completes the session before the horse is taken back to the stable.

A rider who had the skill to come out and ride an ideal work session every day would be a master. I have known very few riders who are consistent in their ability to put the horse in front of them, and who can gauge their work in order to be able to find an appropriate balance between cruising along and easing him into more difficult movements. But the most successful riders structure their work within each session, and vary it from day to day, challenging the horse more on some days and less on others, so that they develop different aspects of his physique and ability. They also utilize the gymnastic work much less randomly than most people.

One type of muscular use prepares and makes the body fitter only in that pattern—trot work strengthens the body for trotting, and canter work strengthens it for cantering. When a horse is consistently worked in an inefficient movement pattern he develops the wrong muscles. Thus, riding endless circles on his stiff side is of no use at all, unless he has already rearranged his carriage, and is actually flexing to that side; similarly, hours spent walking up hills are far more beneficial if the horse moves in a way that maximizes the effect this has on the muscles of his quarters, back, and neck. But when a horse is worked consistently in an efficient movement pattern, his whole physique can change in only a few months, so that he develops muscle on his top line, and he looks like a far better horse. At the same time, his respiration becomes deep and regular, and his joints are saved from excessive jarring.

Whatever the horse's purpose in life, his rider needs to keep a balance between work done at trot and work done at canter, because working solely in the diagonal trot gait can make the canter mechanism more difficult for the horse (as well as the rider). Another balance is necessary between fast and slow work, even for the dressage horse. Each muscle contains fibers designed to contract with the force and speed needed for fast movement (called fast-twitch fibers), and also fibers intended for the more prolonged contraction that goes with slow movement (called slow-twitch fibers). If only slow-twitch fibers are developed, the body becomes muscle-bound, and so the horse develops muscles like a weight lifter, losing his ability to move with grace and fluidity.

Skillful riders design a work program for each horse which counteracts his weaknesses and finds the appropriate balance between complete opposites—lightness and power, forward movement and collection, relaxation and muscle tone. I often think of these opposing qualities as being rather like the ingredients of a recipe. The rider has to take the ingredients of power, ease, grace, lightness, and accuracy, put them all in the melting pot, and come out with just the right proportions of each of them for her particular horse on a particular day. In their sessions at home, some riders like to overcompensate for the horse's weaknesses, asking him to produce more of a certain quality than one would ideally expect to see. This means that her work might not necessarily resemble the finished product of an ideal dressage test. The horse might work faster, or slower, than the classical ideal; but as long as the path the rider is taking *does* complete the circuit, develop all these qualities, and—ultimately—lead to Rome, it would be unwise to quibble with her chosen route.

Awareness Questions and Imagery

• How much are you working in the dark during your schooling sessions? Do you have a clear idea of what you want to achieve, whether this is realistic, and how you intend to do it? How much is this knowledge based on your own store of feelages, and how much is it based on hearsay?

Planning your work is a left-brain function, but it is important that you can adapt your program to the here-and-now feedback you are getting from your right-brain feelages. Working the horse constructively requires the best of both brains.

• Do you tend to stick rather rigidly to your left-brain ideas of what should be, or to forget your plan and get completely carried away with your right-brain perceptions of what is?
• Are your sessions based more around your horse's needs, or your own? At the stage where you are struggling to ingrain useful feelages you have to put yourself first, but it is far better to do this sort of work out on trail than to do it in the riding arena, where you may overstress your horse's generosity.

If you still find, after this stage, that your concern is more for yourself than your horse, you may have to disentangle your feelings of self-worth from your performance.

• Do you give up easily and go out for a trail ride, or are you tempted to carry on, asking more and more until fatigue sets in, or something goes wrong? What would you need in order to be able to recognize the time when you have done good enough work, i.e., when it is appropriate to stop? What else would you need actually to stop then?
• Do you tend to work only with the things you and the horse can do well, or do you tend to focus too much on the things that you or he find difficult?
• Have you ever ridden or observed an ideal work session? How

precisely do you use the school movements, and how clear are you about the purpose of each one that you ride?

- Do you measure a work session according to time, or gymnastic effort?
- Do you have an overview of the work from day to day? How do you vary it, and what do you hope to achieve by doing this?
- Which of the qualities of good work are well established and which are lacking in your horse?
- How could you work at home to redress this balance, and bring him closer to your classical ideal?

10 Jumping

Jumping must evoke more racing hearts and trembling knees than any other facet of riding. Some riders love it, and some hate it— and some have mixed feelings as the butterflies gather in their stomachs, and they feel themselves teetering on the brink of delight or disaster. Jumping feels wonderful when you are with the horse, and horrible when you are not; consequently, riders who fear the unpleasantness of foundering about over an awkward jump tend to remain rather cautious. But those who have faith in their ability to make fluent approaches and secure jumps often become addicts, who delight in the exhilaration of flying.

Like people, horses vary enormously in the aptitude and enthusiasm that they show for jumping. As a species, they do not have the ideal physique for it, but nonetheless, many of them become remarkably agile and clever. Some critics of competitive jumping claim that it is a cruel demand which goes against the horse's natural instincts; they seem to me to be making a statement analogous to saying that people should never swim, because if God had intended them to swim, he would have given them webbed feet! (There are also some show jumpers who claim that dressage is the most cruel of the equestrian sports.) But despite their limitations, some people take to swimming—and some horses take to jumping —like ducks to water, while those who prefer to keep their feet planted firmly on the ground can be extremely difficult to persuade to do otherwise. Between the extremes of kamikaze bravery and the caution of always wanting to look before you leap, horses can present their riders with very different problems, and in solving these the best riders instill a note of realism, transforming their horses into athletes who use their brain and physique to their own best advantage.

Most authorities agree that what happens to the horse and rider over a fence is the direct result of what happens to them between fences. The quality of the jump is determined by the quality of the approach to the fence, which is itself determined by the quality of the getaway from the previous fence and the turns between the two jumps. Each of these is a vital link in the chain of events leading to a fluent, accurate jump, so that, as a show jumping round progresses, difficulties tend to compound. All too often we see horses and riders push-pulling their way around a course, producing an erratic performance which is almost painful to watch. What is it that goes wrong, and how can riders help themselves and their horses to produce show jumping and cross-country rounds that give the onlooker a feeling of delight?

Again, we can trace many difficulties right back to the early stages of learning, when the focus lies on developing a stable jumping position. The rider's folding-down action over a fence is her dynamic response to the force of the horse's takeoff, and its success depends on there being a difference in her balance *before* and *after* the moment of impact, when the horse's hind legs hit the ground and straighten up to propel him into the air. The thrust of the horse as he begins his jump automatically closes the angle of the rider's hip joint, making an almost instantaneous difference to the positioning of her center of gravity. When riders (especially small children) first learn, they are often encouraged to fold down *before* they get to the fence, or to fold down over a fence which is so tiny that the pony just trots over it. Pupils are often encouraged to do this as a preparatory exercise for jumping, but it does not prepare them well for bigger fences. When they fold down too early, their center of gravity comes so far forward that it is difficult for the horse to lift himself off the ground. Then, when he lands, they usually find themselves draped around his neck, an unpleasant experience which does nothing to improve anyone's nerve.

I often find it valuable to demonstrate the mechanics of the folding-down action while standing on my feet. It is very easy to simulate the approach to the jump by standing with my knees slightly bent, and my shoulders, knees, and toes in line. But then,

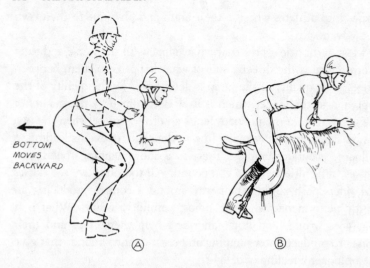

← BOTTOM MOVES BACKWARD

Ⓐ　　　　　Ⓑ

52. The folding-down movement that takes you from approach position to jumping position (A). If your backside moves forward rather than backward (B), you will have to balance yourself entirely by leaning on your hands and the horse's neck.

if I respond to the moment of takeoff in the same way as most riders, I find myself plummeting toward a head-first landing on the arena! The vast majority of people straighten their knee and throw themselves forward up the horse's neck on takeoff, and this results in their loss of balance; the more appropriate response (which takes far less effort) is to fold so that your backside actually moves *backward*, closing the angle behind your knee, and bringing your belly button near to the pommel of the saddle. If you try this standing on the ground, you will find that you can simulate the moment of takeoff while remaining perfectly balanced over your feet. As in a good jump when actually mounted, there is no movement in the rider's lower leg and foot. Throughout the flight, they provide her with a stable supporting base, and she neither falls forward onto the horse's neck nor has to support herself by using the rein. As many event riders will tell you, this secure base is the cornerstone of a jumping position which will withstand the rigors of cross-country riding. By supporting her own weight, the rider becomes a minimum encumbrance to the horse, able not only to leave his head and neck completely free, but also to adjust her center of gravity so that she keeps it in optimum alignment with his. Her adaptation to the jump requires her to ride with a shorter stirrup than she uses on the flat. This automatically closes the angles of her hip, knee, and ankle joints, making them into better shock absorbers and giving her a stable base of support both on the approach to the fence and throughout the flight. Most riders shorten their stirrups between two and four holes (using a slightly shorter stirrup for cross-country riding, where they have to maintain a forward galloping position between fences).

Since the time when the old-fashioned hunting seat was abandoned in favor of Caprilli's "forward" position, arguments have raged about how the rider can best position herself on the approach to a fence. The demand that she should not be left behind has perhaps meant that riding schools have produced several generations of riders who tend to have nurtured the opposite fault. Successful show jumpers are difficult to emulate, as they have such differing styles—more appropriate for the big tracks they meet in top-class competition (and rarely faced by the rest of us). Despite their individual preferences for leaning forward or staying more upright between fences, their most fundamental principle is that they *never jump before the horse* and "drop" him into the bottom of a fence. This is also the golden rule for event riders, who are less idiosyncratic in style, partly because it is more important in their culture to look right, and partly because show jumpers have to deal with the added problem of maintaining their balance on a horse who uses an enormous thrust to propel himself into an almost vertical takeoff. The show jumper's position has to allow the horse to jump high, whereas the event rider makes a lesser adaptation for a smaller jump, and stays closer to the saddle in mid-flight, using a stable lower leg for support so that she has the greatest possible security over solid fences and a less predictable terrain.

Traditionally, the arguments about the rider's approach position go like this: If she approaches a jump leaning slightly forward so that her backside is just touching or slightly out of the saddle, then she has less chance of being left behind over a fence. If the horse surprises her by taking off early, the results are less catastrophic than they might have been if she had been sitting deeper and more upright. However, this forward position reduces her effectiveness at driving the horse forward, and should he run out or refuse, she is in a more vulnerable position. The rider who sits more upright on the approach has increased security and effectiveness, but if she is to help the horse rather than hinder him, she needs to sit—as she does on the flat—in a way which encourages him to lift his back and engage his hocks underneath her. From this position, she has to make a bigger adaptation for the jump, and this gives her much less leeway for making mistakes—particularly if she is surprised by the horse's takeoff and makes the mistake of getting left behind.

Those who argue for an approach position in which the rider leans forward tend to assume that coming in front of the horse is a lesser fault than getting left behind. There may be some truth in this, especially for novice riders, but there are many riders who have their weight consistently in front of the optimum balance point, while very few remain consistently behind it. Skilled riders who are rarely left behind (and who can get out of trouble by slipping the reins when they are) almost always say that the worst mistake you can make is to anticipate the moment of takeoff and tip forward before it happens—putting yourself too far up the horse's neck. Lucinda Green claims that the secret of her success and stability across country lies in the fact that she always keeps her center of gravity a fraction behind her horse's, and she never takes off before he does. It is also wrong to assume that approaching a fence in a forward position automatically makes it easier for the rider to fold down and stay with the horse, because this actually deprives her of the chance to make a snap adjustment to her position in the moment of takeoff. Popular terminology often fails to distinguish between the rider's position in the approach to a fence and her position in mid-flight; both are loosely called "jumping position." Personally, I find it valuable to differentiate the two, and I encourage riders to approach fences sitting into the saddle, with a shoulder-knee-toe alignment, and with slightly more weight then usual supported on their thigh and stirrup. This provides a "middle place" from which they usually have no trouble staying with the horse; and later, if they want to, they can develop their own style, staying forward without coming in front of him, or staying back without being left behind.

In jumping, as in flat work, much of the rider's skill lies in preparation—in setting everything up so well that the jumping itself becomes easy. Many riders who would not dream of asking for a canter strike-off until they have set the horse up in a round, impulsive trot, with a correct bend, will send a horse into a fence when his trot or canter is all over the place! Skilled riders know not only when to jump, but also when *not* to jump. They know when discretion is the better part of valor, so they do not even put themselves and their horses into the situations which upset and frustrate beginners. Rarely, if ever, do they cling on for dear life while a horse who jumps without impulsion heaves himself into the air, founders through it in slow motion, and then flops to the ground on the other side. Rarely do they career toward a jump half out of control. The riders who *do* usually blame their misfortunes on the horse, without realizing that more skillful intervention could change his carriage and focus his attention to such an extent that he would automatically offer a much more calm, impulsive, athletic jump. For your own safety, it is important not to jump until your warm-up has put the horse in front of you, because only then can you trust that he is willing and able to draw on his reserves of power. You also owe it to yourself and to him to improve his athletic form on the flat, because only when he can turn well, and adjust his canter stride, can he make full use of his resources while jumping. (The lack of maneuverability in a green horse's canter is a very good argument for doing much of your early jumping from trot—and it is rarely wise to change pace while on the approach line to a fence.) As always, novice riders tend to accept as unchangeable many facets of the horse's behavior which a more skilled rider *can* influence; consequently, they struggle on, accepting his contorted efforts, and believing that "this is how he is," while a more skilled rider intervenes and is able to produce a jump which is far easier to sit on, and far more athletic.

Most teachers and event riders would say that the rider's job is to bring the horse into the fence in a form that allows him to jump most easily. This means having his attention, lining him up well for the fence, and bringing him into the fence with sufficient impulsion, in balance, and at a medium stride. The horse's job is then to sort his legs out and take the rider over the fence. Most people agree that four foot six is the height beyond which the horse's positioning for takeoff needs to be so precise that the rider must play a more dominant role in placing him (although specialist show jumpers with a very good eye for a stride may choose to place much more novice horses over smaller fences). Up to this height, the takeoff zone for the jump is so broad that the horse can easily clear the fence as long as the above criteria are met. The worst thing which can happen is that he arrives half a stride wrong, but even then, he should have the impulsion to take off from farther away or the ability to adjust his balance, put in a short stride, and take himself up and over the jump.

Difficulty arises when the stride is so long and the approach so fast that the horse has little room to maneuver. Some horses arrive at the fence so much on their forehand that the only way they can change direction from forward to upward is to put in a short stride. Others, instead of making this adjustment, launch themselves at fences from so far away that one day they are likely to overestimate their ability, and crash-land into the back pole of a big parallel. The opposite type of approach, which is tentative and lacking in impulsion, also leaves the horse with little room to maneuver. With no reserves of power he can neither take off from farther away nor bring his hocks underneath him to pop up and over the jump. This makes it impossible for the horse to bascule, showing the rounded arc which makes for the most neat and efficient jump. In order to lift his back end *up*, he first has to bring his head *down*, and on the last stride before takeoff he stretches his head and neck to look at the base of the fence so that he can judge his takeoff point. The rider has to keep her body in place, yet allow him complete freedom of head and neck once he is in the air. Horses who do not approach and take off in good style (or who are inhibited by their rider) trail their legs, launch themselves into space, or heave themselves over the fence, and all this results in awkwardness and loss of confidence which can undermine the enjoyment of both horse and rider.

Ideally, the horse approaches the fence with reserves of energy which make him like a coiled spring, and then the jump is like a controlled explosion. It used to be fashionable to overemphasize this, and to "bounce" the horse (so that he was cantering almost in place a few strides away from the jump) until the rider let him go, usually with a count of "three, two, one...JUMP!" Nowadays, both show jumping and cross-country rounds are ridden far more fluently, with an emphasis on maintaining a constant rhythm all around the course, so the approach strides in fact vary little from the others. The rider's role then is more to regulate the horse than to place him; basically, he places himself. I therefore suggest that the rider approach the fence on "red alert," ready to intervene if he should hesitate, but quietly and firmly in place rather than continually busy. For the novice, it takes great courage to begin to ride the horse positively as he approaches the fence. "Thelwellian" children are almost a tradition—they kick very hard thirty yards away from the fence, fairly hard twenty yards away, hardly at all when they are ten yards away, and then grind to a halt in front of the jump! Their speed, energy, courage, and determination all diminish gradually as they approach, but with age they get a bit braver and they learn to kick harder as they get closer. The danger is then that they overdo it, pushing the horse into a long flat stride, so that he has to either make a long flat jump, or put in a tiny stride to save himself. In fact, it takes quite some courage to drive the horse into a fence, but it takes even more *not* to over-drive him. Rather than pushing, the rider maintains rhythm, stride length, and impulsion, and waits (on "red alert") for the fence, almost as if she were waiting for the fence to approach her. Specialist show jumpers like their horses to make adjustments by "backing off" a fence and shortening their stride, while event horses will tend to lengthen into a fence—and many event riders bemoan their tendency to ride into show jumps seeing long strides. This fault is usually based on a degree of anticipation, and in his book *Riding and Jumping*, William Steinkraus (a brilliant show jumper who is now chairman of the U.S. Equestrian Team) states that the anticipation which leads to hurrying is "the most serious single fault of horses and riders." My belief is that it is almost always based on self-doubt.

Most riders who doubt their own or their horse's ability to jump overlay their worries with positive thinking. Overriding, and "chasing" the horse to take off a long way in advance, is an example of positive thinking which compensates for doubt—and teaches the horse to rush into fences as well. It is the same doubt

APPROACH   TAKE OFF   FLIGHT
                                    SHOWING GOOD BASCULE

MID FLIGHT   LANDING   GETAWAY

53.   The six phases of a jump, showing a good bascule and a well-balanced rider.

that encourages riders to "lift" the horse over the fence, drawing their hands up and back on takeoff, thus (supposedly) ensuring that the horse will lift and shorten his neck, as he must do in order to jump. William Steinkraus also says, "For a long time . . . I didn't really believe that a horse was capable of leaving the ground without some 'move'—at least a little one—on my part." His teacher had to hammer home to him that "[the horse is] larger than you are—don't try to carry him, make him carry you," and his present contention is that the rider has to do *absolutely nothing* as the horse leaves the ground, because her hip joint is closed, and her hand is drawn forward as a natural result of the takeoff. Riders who do not believe this, and/or who doubt the horse's intention or ability, tend to compensate with an extreme body reaction; they leave the saddle slightly before the horse takes off and throw themselves up his neck—almost as if they were saying, "I'm jumping, will you come too?" The old adage that if you throw your heart over the fence then your horse will follow undoubtedly has some truth in it; but "throwing your heart" does *not* involve throwing your body. I believe that "throwing your heart" means having the expectation that the horse will jump well, not because you are relying on his good will, but because you are sitting there making sure that he does. Relying on the horse's good will frequently leads to refusals—as many people have learned when their horse has stopped at the one fence they believed he was sure to jump—and especially across country, it can be helpful to think of riding every fence as if the horse will refuse it. But the most skillful riders do this in an attitude of relaxed concentration while they approach each fence on "red alert"; they are completely unhurried, relying on their stillness, their high muscle tone, and their quick responses. Even when they ride against the clock there are no panicky, hustled actions, and they always look (like all skilled performers) as if they have got plenty of time.

In contrast, the rider whose image of the jump involves some doubt about its quality has to "do something" to make sure that it comes out right—and most often, her actions substantiate her fears. In jumping, self-fulfilling prophecies abound, and the rider who does not really want to jump can easily communicate her intention to the horse, and ensure that he will stop. In her book *Up, Up and Away,* Lucinda Prior-Palmer tells the story of how she coped when her fear of Trakhener fences (which are formed by suspending a single telegraph pole over a large ditch) motivated her to go and practice jumping them, and a mishap then left her equally apprehensive. This preceded her ride at the Tidworth three-day event, and trainer Lady Hugh Russell insisted that she approach the Trakhener there with her gaze fixed solidly on the tree at the top of the hill beyond. As a result of not looking at the jump she eliminated the risk that she might "drop" the horse into the bottom of it, which she might otherwise have done, by looking there herself and surrendering her seat and hand just a fraction too early. Nothing is more undermining to a horse's confidence than being "dropped" at the last moment, and because this is the instinctive reaction of the frightened rider, her fears tend to produce refusals. Lucinda claims that she learned this lesson from her first pony, who stopped every time she tipped forward prematurely, and it is interesting to realize that having lined the horse up for the fence, so that *he* can see what he is doing, the rider does not actually have to look at it herself. The most skillful and confident riders always look over the top of the fence; they allow the horse to lower his head and neck just before he takes off, but as their hand lightens their body stays in perfect balance. Instead of tipping forward like a novice or nervous rider, they hold their seat throughout the last full canter stride until the horse's hind legs come underneath him again and hit the ground to provide the catapult mechanism necessary for takeoff... and this closes the angle of their hip joint.

Very often, the rider's fears have their origins in "What if..." fantasies, the catastrophic expectations which are so easily exaggerated by the mind. Real here-and-now danger is often present in jumping, but by magnifying our vulnerability or our inability, we distort reality. Many riders find that their fear is a rather nebulous thing, based on their worries about arriving right at the fence and maintaining a secure jumping position. The fear is a message to them that they have not yet ingrained effective ways of coping, and not a message about how stupid they are. In this situation it is helpful to use mental rehearsal to identify exactly what you are frightened of, and to work out exactly how you can avert your imagined trauma—and if you do not have sufficient knowledge to avert it, you may well discover what it is that you need to learn. It can also help you to ride as if you were not frightened, or as if you believed in your horse, for as William Steinkraus says, "... it is quite possible to have a low estimate of the horse's ability, or to be extremely apprehensive about the level of performance one will achieve; and yet if you ride confidently and well, and ask confidently and soundly for the horse's best level of performance, his response will be to the ride you give him, and not to your secret thoughts."

Awareness Questions and Imagery

- Do you enjoy jumping? If not, what would have to change before you did?
- How much faith do you have in your jumping position? Do you more often come in front of the horse, or get left behind; and is your balance least stable on takeoff, in mid-flight, or on landing? Does your lower leg provide you with a solid supporting base throughout the jump, or do you need to hold the mane or rest your hands on the horse's neck in order to feel secure?
- Can you clearly differentiate between your approach and mid-flight positions? As you fold down, does your backside move forward or backward, does your knee bend more or straighten? How close is your belly button to the pommel of the saddle?

If you find yourself feeling as if you are balancing on tiptoe, and/or coming a long way above the horse in mid-flight, you may have to go back a stage, and practice your approach and mid-flight positions in trot and canter. You need to sink your knee and heel farther down past the horse's sides, until you become completely stable over your feet, and feel as if you are more solidly wrapped around him.

- Before starting to jump, it is important to know that you have the horse in front of you, just as you would if you were working on the flat. How willing is the horse to move in a rounded carriage underneath you? Can you regulate his tempo, and hold the circuit complete? How responsive is the horse to your aids, and how easily can he adjust his stride?

If you have difficulties here, and if he wants to use your hand as a "fifth leg," you need to do more work on the flat. Examine your own seat and your driving aids, looking in particular for tension in your belly—because until you can produce good canter work, your jumping ability will always be limited.

- Do you know when discretion is the better part of valor? To what extent do you regard the difficulties you have in jumping as your own or the horse's?

The top event riders impress me tremendously with their skill and courage as they approach a difficult fence without interfering with the horse's rhythm, even though they know that his striding will not bring him in right unless he makes his own adjustments. They know how dangerous it would be to disturb him—that this would make it extremely difficult for him to engage his quarters and make a powerful jump bringing them right up out of the way. Instead, they sit upright and very still, allowing him to lower his head slightly and to adjust his own stride. As they train the horse they encourage him to develop his innate ability to sort his own legs out; some will even trot a young horse through uneven tree roots, and leave him completely to his own devices until he learns how to cope. They develop the skill of his right-brain computer, which (as a cybernetic system) can look at the environment and instantly compute how to position the body to best advantage. All it needs is sufficient information from previous successful performances, and for its owner to trust it enough to allow it to function without interference.

In doing this, the horse uses the same natural ability that we can all use to run over a rocky beach, jumping from boulder to boulder. If you make conscious decisions about where to put your feet you have to be careful and go slowly, and this encourages tentativeness and mistakes. But when you begin to trust your right-brain computer you can move at speed, with far more dexterity and safety, because you are using a process which goes way beyond the scope of your conscious resources. Self-doubt is banished as your eyes scan the environment and your feet instantly respond. As adults, many of us lose our childhood faith in our innate right-brain ability, but whenever you run down some steps, cross a road (making an instantaneous computation about the speed and placing of the oncoming traffic), and then jump up the curb at the other side, you are using the same skill. Danger only arises if you are in such a panic—or such a daydream—that your antennae do not register accurately all the information which contributes to your safety.

Similarly, the horse who is in a panic or a daydream will not attune himself properly to the fence—hence the importance of putting him in front of you before you even begin jumping—whereas the horse who has focused his attention, and who has both previous experience and faith in his right-brain ability, can be extremely clever. Even inexperienced horses can show remarkable dexterity, and ponies, in particular, have a knack of arriving right at fences. I have competed on several who would always place themselves beautifully as long as I did nothing to interfere with them on the approach. They gave me a clear message: "I know best, so leave me alone," and once I had learned to listen to them, we got on extremely well! Much of the difficulty that young riders experience when they make the transition from jumping ponies to horses arises, I think, because few horses have the same quick-thinking desire and ability to work it out for themselves. Some, in fact, seem positively thick, and most need help to attune themselves mentally. Ponies use their brains better—or perhaps they have better brains to use—and when it comes to making a jumper, this mental aptitude is far more important than the ideals of physical conformation.

Ponies, and some horses, frequently save the day and extricate their rider from whatever difficulties her continued interference got them both into; but many horses lose trust not only in her, but also in their own natural ability. When the rider does not believe that the horse can easily place himself correctly for fences, she tends to intervene, using crude conscious attempts to see a stride, and her mistimed efforts only serve to confirm and strengthen her fear. She continually puts the horse into positions where he doesn't have access to the physical resources he needs to extricate himself, disaster strikes, and soon a stage is reached when he loses faith in her, and she loses faith in him. They each approach the fence in a "will s/he or won't s/he" frame of mind, where each is tentative and waiting for the other. While they are each filled with self-doubt and wondering about the other, they do not perceive the feedback from each other and the environment which would allow their right-brain computers to get on with the job. This can lead to some big surprises—when the rider suddenly drops the horse, for instance, or kicks him, or when he suddenly takes off.

The ability to see a stride is one of those mysterious talents which some riders seem to have, while others do not, although my show-jumping friends support my belief that like other skills, it can be learned. For years I have wondered why it is that some riders can consistently arrive "right" at fences on horses they barely know, while others invariably make mistakes and put their horses into impossible situations. How much is this a statement about how well the rider sets up a horse so that he is physically and mentally in the optimum state to work it out for himself, and how much is it about how the horse subordinates himself to the rider, allowing her to organize and place him? Different riders would give different answers, and it is here that show-jumping technique differs enormously from cross-country technique, where the horse definitely does see his own stride. "Kick on!" is probably the best advice you can give a cross-country rider who is becoming over-concerned about the technicalities of jumping the fences; whereas your advice to the show-jumping rider might be more technical. In each case, however, the "talent" required is a process and not a thing. Horse and rider are exquisite cybernetic systems, offering feedback to each other through which they can both adjust their performances. Both need a more external focus of attention than they have in dressage work, because they are orienting themselves around an external objective. My belief is that the rider who consciously strains to see a stride sets herself up for failure, as this is way beyond the scope of her conscious resources; and by using her focused vision, she loses touch with the body sensation through which she perceives and regulates the horse.

As in flat work, the most skilled riders continually compare what is happening at present with the sensations they would ideally like to perceive; then they make whatever adjustments are needed to make the two feelages match. Specialist show jumpers do this almost unconsciously, and with such precision that they can tell if they are on a right stride up to six or seven strides away. They waste no time wondering, worrying, or imagining catastrophes; they just make it look and feel right—having enough previous experiences of success to know what "right" is. It is undoubtedly far easier to see a stride on a horse who "draws you into the fence" than it is on one who lacks impulsion. If you do not yet have this facility, therefore, your best bet is to set the horse up so that he draws you in, with the stride length, rhythm, impulsion, and balance which gives him the maximum self-control. Then, if you think you are more clever than he is, you can intervene, but otherwise let him get on with it, so he learns from his varied experiences, and can enhance his right-brain skill.

Horses and riders first develop their "eye" through grid work, using sequences of ground poles and low jumps which are placed at measured distances so that neither horse nor rider has to make adjustments to the horse's natural stride. (Many good books show how to build up athletic grids, and several are listed in the bibliography.) The predictability of the grid gives both horse and rider confidence. As they are guaranteed to arrive right for takeoff, many doubts and internal voices— Supposing he arrives wrong at this... What if I get left behind...—are quelled. The rider can perfect and ingrain her jumping position, until she trusts that it will automatically come right; and the horse can gain the athletic ability and perception necessary to deal with the problems posed by combination fences. When both have thoroughly grooved these basic skills they become able to devise their own approach. A single pole placed on the ground at nine to ten feet from the fence can be a useful intermediary stage, although working through a row of trotting poles on the approach to a fence is a far more difficult exercise than many people realize.

Interestingly, the use of grids and placing poles is far more prevalent among event riders and teachers in riding schools than it is in the world of show jumping, where riders tend to launch themselves and their horses straight into the job of jumping more sizable fences. To the beginner, "big" can be anything over one foot; to the event rider, "big" begins at about three foot nine, and to the serious show jumper, "big" is somewhere over four foot six. Not many show jumpers mess about with small fences, and not many other riders mess about with large ones. The difference in their approach is most clearly shown by the story of the candidate in an advanced riding examination who had to assess the jumping ability of an unknown horse. Because he insisted on jogging (rather than walking quietly) over a pole on the ground, she decided that he was not yet ready to begin jumping. In reality, the horse was a grade A show jumper, and he obviously did not have much time for such child's play. His training had put a lesser emphasis on submission and obedience, and a greater one on bringing out his natural flair for jumping. Jumping riders tend to have a more pragmatic approach than those who specialize in flat work, who must necessarily be more introspective. They get on with the job, and negotiate workable compromises with the horse in situations where the dressage rider would insist on submission. As a well-known show jumper said to me, "The horse has got to be a bit crazy to be good," and this is also true of most good event horses. When you attempt to bring out the best in a slightly crazy horse, you may need to deal very tactfully with his idiosyncrasies and kid him along, splitting the difference between your ideal and his. After all, what counts in jumping is the number of fences you can jump clear, and when correctness becomes an end in itself rather than a means to an end, it may not enhance your performance. In Neil French-Blake's book *The World of Show Jumping*, William Steinkraus notes that the rider's adherence to correct style, as an end in itself, can sometimes be at the expense of the horse, who never realizes his full potential. "The classical ideal," he says, "can be a millstone around the neck."

Most trainers believe that grid work and gymnastic exercises can improve the mechanism of the horse's jump, sharpening his reflexes so that he takes off with both hind legs together and snaps up his forelegs more quickly. When given freedom for his head and neck he can then produce the rounded bascule which enables him to bring his hind legs right up out of the way. Most horses like to jump fences cleanly—after all, it hurts when they hit them—and when horses consistently knock fences down, the problem often lies with the rider: in a bad approach, a loss of balance, or an unyielding hand. The ideal horse should be bold enough to attack his fences, but cautious enough to avoid hitting them. This is a delicate balance, because the most careful horses are often rather thin-skinned and sensitive, and sometimes not that bold. Despite this, many horses who are labeled "careless" would pick their feet up much better if given the chance. Eventers, who learn to skim over the top of cross-country fences, often try the same technique over show jumps, with the result that they rattle poles, and this means that they need particularly skillful riding. It is more difficult to influence horses who are lazy with their hind quarters than it is to influence horses who are slow or lazy in front, but (once you have determined that you are positioned on the optimum balance point) the skillful use of ground lines, placing poles, wide parallels, and combinations can all help the horse to bascule and jump cleanly, though some continue to insist forever on jumping far higher than is necessary while dangling their legs! Cross fences and "run-out" poles (running perpendicular to the fence, from the height of the jump to the ground) can encourage a horse to jump straight, and every trainer has her favorite exercises or "recipes" which she uses to improve the mechanism of a horse's jump.

Many eventers benefit from show jumping, but most show jumpers would throw up their hands in horror at the thought of taking their horses across country. The long distance between relatively low obstacles would encourage them to take off too early and jump hollow—thus undermining their ability to get up high—and the skill of show jumping lies in bringing the horse comparatively close into the fence. Show jumpers tend to lighten their hand a couple of strides away from it, earlier than event riders, and to give the horse maximum freedom to gauge his own takeoff by looking into the bottom of the fence. If they are riding a particularly talented horse who does not need to make much effort, they will deliberately take him in very close to the fence so that he has to pay attention, and extricate himself. In other situations, and particularly across country, this approach would not be appropriate. Show jumpers favor horses who are slow through the air because they will naturally go higher, while many event riders and trainers favor horses who are faster through the air. This is just one instance of the different ideals and approaches underlying two very different skills, and it is interesting to realize how few riders ever become highly proficient in both.

As well as varying enormously in *what* they jump, different riders also vary enormously in *how often* they jump. Throughout the horse world, the most skillful trainers use the minimum amount of work to produce the maximum improvement, so that the risk of overpushing the horse and making him stale is minimized. Many older, more experienced riders have said that they

54. A bad approach has made this horse jump awkwardly. The rider has not allowed his forehand sufficient freedom, and his jump is rather hollow; he has not taken off from both hind legs together, and his forelegs are "paddling."

now jump far less between competitions than they used to, and that there must be few horses who benefit from jumping more than twice a week. Novice horses obviously need more work at home; but even then, jumping two or (at the most) three times a week gives ample scope for polishing off old problems and tackling new ones.

A good jump jockey has to have full use of her sensing abilities right around a course, but the sight of even a small fence can be so overwhelming for the novice rider that her body goes into shock. She becomes paralyzed with fear, and if you ask her afterward what happened in the period between being a few strides before the fence and a few strides after it, she often has no recall of her experience. In popular terminology, one might say that she spaced out. An onlooker would probably see her freeze on the approach to the fence, scramble over it somehow, and eventually collect her wits and balance again a few strides later. Riding a course in this way is a hair-raising and dangerous experience, because the next fence looms up very quickly once the rider has come to her senses. Obviously, she is not safe until she has mastered the basics and can stay compos mentis, and I have found that riders with this problem benefit enormously from singing or talking as they go through a grid; if they do this they have to keep breathing, and this makes it impossible for them to freeze. Only from this baseline can they begin to refine their body control.

Once the jump itself ceases to be an overwhelming experience, riding courses becomes far less traumatic. First, the rider needs absolute faith in her jumping position, so much so that it functions automatically, without her conscious attention. Then she needs to ride each approach by comparing it with previous successful attempts, and with the faith and foreknowledge that this gives. "Will s/he/ or won't s/he?" and "What if . . ." turn into irrelevancies, and the rider can put the jump into a broader perspective. Then, instead of filling her consciousness so that she cannot think or see beyond it, the jump becomes relegated to the status of something that has to be got over while on the way to the next one. Once she has lined the horse up for the fence, she has enough surplus attention to be focusing on the next one, adjusting her approach if necessary, and knowing how she will turn the horse in the air, or rebalance him if he accelerates on landing.

It is especially important that all riders—and especially eventers—recover quickly after each fence, for anyone with tendencies to space out will lose one or two strides before she can react. This can have dire consequences in combination fences, when it is particularly important that the rider regain her seat quickly in time to ride the intervening stride(s). It is also important when the course demands a sharp turn, although a sophisticated rider can indicate this change of direction to the horse by adjusting her balance in mid-flight. The builders of cross-country courses often play on the rider's ability to keep her wits about her even over typically scary fences like ditches and drops. Often they state that the secret of their art is to build fences which scare the willies out of the rider without posing a particularly difficult problem to the horse. In eventing, taking the best line into a combination will usually result in straightforward distances between the jumps, but in show jumping, where more of the fences depend on each other, the distances between them are often designed to pose a particular athletic problem. Some riders who have specialized in show jumping have said that they never took to eventing because the fences were too low—and anyway, what was the point of having to gallop so far between them?

Whether you like to jump high, or whether you like to jump fast, the masters in each skill gain their supremacy by consistently offering the horse a ride which simultaneously gives him confidence and asks him for his best performance—whatever the rider's own "secret thoughts."

Awareness Questions and Imagery

- Both you and the horse have an optimum level of arousal which tunes and focuses you best for jumping. For you, is this higher or lower than your normal state, and how does it compare with your ideal state for flat work?
- How difficult is it for you to approach a fence on "red alert"; do you tend to over- or underride? Do you trust the horse's ability to sort his own legs out? If you have to "do something" to make sure that the jump comes out right, what kind of "something" do you tend to do?

Instead of overlaying your doubts with positive thinking, use mental rehearsal to clarify exactly how you would like to be able to ride the jump, and what you would like to feel on the approach.

- Can you keep taking the horse throughout the approach to a fence? Do you feel every beat of the trot or canter stride right up to the moment of takeoff, or is your attention sidetracked into your internal dialogue, or into crude conscious attempts to see a stride? If it is, concentrating on the horse's rhythm—or on your line as it continues on after the fence—may well help to quell your doubts. You could also try imagining that the fence is approaching you, rather than you approaching it.
- Can you maintain your approach position right up to the mo-

ment when the horse takes off? Do you feel him lower his head just before he does so, and can you maintain your seat as this happens?

If you have a tendency to drop horses, check where you look as you approach each fence—particularly any that worry you. Try riding as if you believed in the horse, or as if you were not frightened. Monitoring the front angle between your leg and your body can also help to ensure that you do not tip forward prematurely.

- How confident do you feel about riding courses? Is the jump itself an overwhelming experience, or can you put it into a wider perspective? How do you define "big," and how does the sight of a "big" fence affect your approach, your jumping position, and your recovery afterward?
- Are you satisfied to discover that you got over a fence and are still alive on the other side, or do you consider the detail of *how* you got over it? How concerned are you about the mechanism of your horse's jump, and about the part you play in improving or inhibiting it?
- What would you need to do in order to ride courses (and combinations) more fluently and confidently?

11 Competition

Riders have as many and varied reasons for competing as they do for riding. Some are attracted by the lure of a day out, the chance to meet friends and enjoy the atmosphere of the show ground; others are more concerned about the competition itself, and are keen to compare their horses and their skill with others by means of the challenge of a jumping round, or a dressage test. Some are intent on winning, and some are equally determined to enjoy themselves. Novices dream about the day when they will ride in their first competition, and more experienced riders practically move heaven and earth to try to make that vision a reality: hours of schooling at home, days of preparation, and prolonged periods of travel go into creating an experience in the ring which might only last a few minutes. Keeping a competition horse is an enormous drain on time, energy, and money; for some reason, however, more and more people find it worthwhile.

When I was eventing, the thrill of jumping, and especially of going across country, left me so elated that I was always desperate to get my next "fix." I was in danger of losing my sense of perspective, and my friends sometimes had to sit me down and talk sense into me, dissuading me from competing when my horse or I had minor—but significant—injuries. When asked, I used to say that I went to each show for the experience, in order that I would be better equipped for the next one, the next one . . . and the next one. My dream was about the day when I would win the ultimate competition—when I would really have made it; despite my enthusiasm, though, and my longing for this ego-boost, I actually lacked the will to win. I had been brought up to believe that it doesn't matter if you win or lose, it's how you play the game, so I would compete against a certain standard, and against my own previous best, without ever *going for it*. I was more concerned about style than I was about speed, and I always had a good reason for not pushing my horse to go fast. Many horses never live up to their early potential because their riders are too impatient—pushing them too hard, competing them too often, and doing irretrievable damage to their nerve or enthusiasm. But others never make the grade because their riders are always waiting for the right moment to go for it—and it never comes. Later when I won a series of dressage competitions, I realized that my reticence was based on a fear of winning. It seemed unfair on everyone else, and I was afraid of becoming unpopular or of discovering that other people's expectations of me might become impossibly high. The ups and downs of a life with horses are enormous for practically everyone, and this does not change if you make it to the top. In fact, the consequences of success can be difficult to bear—as difficult, perhaps, as those of failure and injury. They become even more difficult when the rider's sense of her own value is related to how well she performs.

Sports psychologists differentiate between "neurotic" and "creative" competitiveness. The "neurotic" competitor is not actually interested in the game itself, but rather in the attention and respect that supposedly go with winning. She uses the competition to prove how good she is, seeing if she can match up to some ideal that she either wants to be, or feels she ought to be. Thus, if she wins, she feels that she is a better person (who is more worthy of respect), and if she loses, she feels that she is a worse person.

Timothy Gallwey first became curious about competition and motivation at the age of fifteen and has since written extensively about it. It was then that he lost to a seeded player in the third round of the All American Junior Tennis Championships: he suddenly felt sorry for the eighteen-year-old he was about to beat, and having won the first two sets, he faltered at the moment of his first match point and continued to give the game away. His assumption that winning would make him more worthy of respect implied the belief (conscious or unconscious) that the person he beat must become less worthy. Later he shunned competition, believing that the only "creative" way to play was through pursuing excellence for its own sake and for the satisfaction which comes from playing beautiful tennis. But without the will to win, he found that he often lacked the necessary determination, and his game deteriorated.

Competition becomes "creative" when the competitor is primarily interested in the game itself, so that she competes not to *prove* who she is, but to *find out* who she is, by pitting herself and her horse against some challenge designed to give them feedback about themselves. Used in this way, the competition becomes a measurement of their development, which offers them the chance to surpass themselves. Only when called upon to use all their skill do they discover the true extent of their abilities, calling on reserves of courage, strength, and agility which as yet lie untapped.

Very often, however, our left brain assumes that the real benefit lies in winning. Many of us who spent our childhood striving for the benefits of "A" grades and honors continue in adulthood to value praise, recognition, and status above learning, understanding, and the overcoming of our internal obstacles; so we do not discover the difference between *proving* and *improving*. When we look at competition in such a way that our image and self-worth are at stake, other competitors become threats or victims, and the outcome shuffles everyone up or down on the who-is-the-most-valuable-person ladder. Those who are prepared to cheat obviously find the appearance of winning more important than their self-respect, and although recognition is a natural by-product of excellence, it is dubious as a goal in itself. Outsiders will probably praise you too highly for your good performances, and be blind to your faults, but they will also condemn you too strongly and without real reason for your poor ones, and they will have little time or respect for you as a has-been—a fallen hero. If you value this ephemeral praise (which society trains us both to seek and to offer), and you rate yourself according to other people's judgments about you, your performance is likely to be fraught with anxiety because so much is at stake. The final verdict is also dependent on many factors outside your control. The final verdict is up to you when the real satisfaction comes from how much you have learned, or how well your horse has gone, or how effectively you have utilized your skills. Setting inner goals for yourself helps to decrease anxiety, because it gives you so much more control over your achievements. In this way, although only one person can win, everyone still has the opportunity to learn something and to enjoy herself.

At times when you find yourself overidentifying with your performance, and suffering from the inevitable strain and pressure, Timothy Gallwey suggests that you ask yourself, What do I really win by winning? and What do I really lose by losing? Often we think that there is more to be lost or won than there actually is, and a healthy attitude toward competition treats it as a game—like Monopoly—which simulates the vicissitudes of real life, but does not actually matter. Then, as an Inner Game teacher once said to me, "You can know that it's only a game and *pretend* that it's important." This gives you the freedom to rise to the challenge, to enjoy the pressure, to learn more, to have more fun, and (paradoxically) to win more.

Few people would admit—or even realize—that they feel ambivalent about actually winning—or that they are more concerned with looking good and riding correctly than they are with achievement. Both of these different and often conflicting preoccupations draw their energies away from a concerted effort to win; they absorb so much energy that the rider can find herself pushing and trying hard in a determined effort to make up for her supposed lack of motivation. But when you stop working against yourself you free up an enormous amount of energy, so it is worth taking time to clarify your goal, and discover what winning means for you. The brain can then work singlemindedly, moving toward this goal with the efficiency of a servomechanism.

Of course, no one else can pinpoint the goal for you. All of us continually face decisions through which we define it: do we enter the lower grades of competition, where we may well find the acclaim of winning; or do we want to pit ourselves and our horse against some stiffer opposition, where the challenge is greater, and there is more to be learned? If we do that, will we overstress the horse? How do we balance our long-term goals with our short-term desire to ride for a win? If a course is flimsy and badly built, or if the going is appalling, do we scratch or go ahead? Actually riding a

course, the rider cannot afford reflectively to weigh up the alternatives; she has to be a gambler, to make split-second decisions, and
her ability to do this has a significant bearing on her success. Win-
ners are determined by what they accomplish, and not by what
they attempt.

For some riders, those few minutes in the ring are the end which
justifies the hours of work at home; for others, the competition
itself is primarily an opportunity to continue schooling. Either way,
the rider must not only keep her nerve while in the ring, but also
engineer the transition from the home to the competition environment so that she maximizes her chances of performing well. The
people who find this most difficult are often the perfectionists, the
riders who hate, on any occasion, to produce less than their best.
At home, therefore, they like to work in ideal conditions; but by
avoiding the irritating effects of distractions, and other horses, or
the added difficulty of working in an unfenced, grass arena, they
make the actual competition situation seem far more stressful.
Others who are more workmanlike simulate the competition environment at home, and accustom the horse to this (and to real
competitions) before they expect him to perform well in public.
Taken to its extreme, the approach of the idealist produces riders
who work quietly at home in the pursuit of excellence, and who
argue that only the riding of circles at home is pure art, while
competitive dressage is a distorted version of the real thing, and
competitive jumping is exploitation. In contrast, the pragmatist
argues for the importance of exposing and testing her work, even
under conditions which can be far from ideal—and some go so far
as to ignore the effect this exposure might have on the horse. The
most successful competitors find a middle ground between these
extremes. Like the idealist, they keep their beginner's mind, finding challenge and excitement in the familiar, so that this too is
done with full attention. (This is also the skill behind a good
groom, who notices tiny things wrong with the horse as she goes
about her daily tasks.) They have a very positive regard for the
horse, but like the pragmatist, they take the risk of exposure, of
being less than perfect, both in their work at home and on the
show ground. They do not let style become a millstone around the
neck, nor do they skimp on work which is, after all, the backbone
of any performance.

The transition from home to the show ring has a very different quality for dressage and for jumping. The lure of a jumping competition includes the attraction of jumping a new course of fences in a new situation—something one can rarely improvise at home. Furthermore, jumping cold-bloodedly at home is a very different (and often more terrifying) experience than jumping at the big occasion, when your "blood" (or adrenaline) is up. Competition makes the here-and-now situation so compelling that there is little room for fears which do not belong to it, and I know riders who are far more nervous and tentative when faced with one small schooling fence than they are when riding in competition. Often they repeatedly make mistakes over the practice jump and then, when they have succeeded in really frightening themselves, they go on to ride the competition course in good style. They need to experience a refusal, a run-out, or a fall before they pull themselves together and go on to ride well. These same riders often ride far better over cross-country fences than they do over show jumps; the here-and-now situation in show jumping is sufficiently safe that the rider can panic, and use it as a "coat hanger" for illusory fears which do not belong to it. In contrast, the same rider would know far better than to try "What if . . ." on the approach to a large and tricky coffin!

While competitive jumping encourages the rider to mobilize her resources, and perhaps to ride even better than she does at home, competitive dressage seems to do just the opposite. Few riders who regard each jumping competition as something unique and exciting would say the same about the dressage test; they are aware that at best they become tentative, and at worst paralyzed. Even if their work at home shows the flair which can only come from correct and skillful riding, their competition work is maimed by a sudden compelling need to keep the horse's head down. They exchange their positive approach for a passivity in which they sit and pray that nothing will go wrong, and of course, this guarantees that something will.

Part of the excitement of jumping lies in the danger involved; the dressage rider has no such challenge. The worst thing that can happen to her is that she does a bad test; her fear is fear of failing, of looking stupid in front of not only the judge but also her friends and rivals. Very few of the riders I meet claim that jumping rounds are more frightening to them than dressage tests, and usually these are the riders who would prefer to do anything rather than jump! Generally, the jumping rider transforms her fear into energy, and uses it to overcome the obstacle, while the dressage rider falls prey to the paralyzing effects of anxiety, which interfere with her concentration and coordination. It is far more difficult for her to blame the horse for her mistakes and as her fast reflexes become blocked, she loses the clarity of her bodily feelings and the courage of her convictions. It becomes impossible for her to ride with intention and purpose and correctly to evaluate her performance. In contrast, cross-country riding is so demanding that there is no time for paralysis by analysis, or worries about how you are doing—lapses in concentration are, after all, extremely costly. In dressage, you never pay for them with your life, as you might in jumping, and the dressage rider who falls to pieces does so because she has no such ultimatum; instead of focusing her attention on her task, she fritters it away on worries about herself.

I was at first very surprised to discover that at least one rider who has done both has said that she would rather be in the starting box at Badminton than about to ride down the center line at Goodwood! But ridiculous as the dressage rider's anxiety may seem, it is almost impossible to ride the horse as well in the competition arena as you can ride him at home. In jumping a clear round is at least a possibility, and the feeling that they have so little to lose fills some riders with gay abandon even before they enter the ring. In dressage, many riders *begin* their test feeling defeated—and the relief they feel as they come up the center line for the last time is displayed both on their faces and in their horse's trot. In this discipline the rider is marked against an impossible ideal, and anyone who aims to ride the perfect test from start to finish is bound to be disappointed. It is more realistic to ask, What would be a respectably good performance for the horse and me at this stage? and to look for how you can *pick up* marks—rather than panicking about the ones you are inevitably going to lose. However, even with this attitude, the stress of competition can have some quite debilitating effects. I recently heard a good rider say that she lost access to about fifty percent of her ability when she first rode in an international competition. When I am riding a test, I have often found that the corners seem to come at me far faster than they do when I am schooling at home, and this is not a statement about the speed of the horse or the size of the arena; it is a statement about the quality of my concentration, and my feeling of being not quite causal. Stress also has the effect of making your performance in competition lag several months behind what you are able to achieve at home. I can remember a time when I was beginning to sit with far greater control of my legs, and this was having a significant effect both on my effectiveness and of course on my horse's work. But when I was competing, my legs turned back to jelly again, and as I wobbled and flapped my way around the arena I felt rather helpless, and disappointed that I could not display in public more of what I wanted to believe was my true ability.

The most skillful competitors are aware of these discrepancies (even though they are minimized through practice), and they allow for them; they make sure that their horses are well used to the atmosphere of the show ground before they ever compete, and their work at home is likely to be several grades above what they show in public. They are the few whose horses often seem to go better in competition than they do in schooling sessions, because it is in the latter that they explore areas of difficulty, confronting the horse and making corrections; whereas their competition work consolidates a position, capitalizes on the horse's strengths, and attempts to hide and protect his weaknesses. (Once they have lost all chance of a ribbon, though, they are well able to change tactics, and use the dressage test or jumping round to teach the horse any lessons he needs to learn.) The idea of "ring craft" in showing has its equivalent in dressage, where "arena craft" is the ability to position your horse to best advantage, and to make use of optical illusions. But the rider is only able to do this once she has solved the most basic, practical problems posed by competition—as well as those which only exist in her mind.

In *Riding and Jumping*, William Steinkraus sums up his approach to competitive riding with the motto, "Know what you're going to have to do, and allow yourself plenty of time to do it in." Practically, the most effective way to minimize stress is to arrive early, with time to drive there safely, familiarize yourself with the surroundings, collect your numbers, arrange your equipment, and warm up. Most riders agree that having a friend or groom to back them up is an enormous advantage, and in the heat of the moment grooms become trainers, advisers, organizers, and dumping grounds for excess tension. (Having been on both sides of that fence, I have found that my friendships do not become damaged as long as we both appreciate the situation and can apologize afterward!) Having a competition routine streamlines your actions and provides horse and rider with a sense of security—sometimes to the extent that routines become rituals which must not be violated. If you feel better prepared when you wear your yellow socks and put your left boot on before your right, who is to say you are wrong? (A problem does arise, of course, when you need to have your lucky teddy with you, and you suddenly discover that you have left him at home!) Each person has her own idiosyncratic way of dealing with the competition environment, needing to be alone or to have company so that she can either bottle herself up or let off steam. Whenever we ride, we all need to find our particular place on the tension-relaxation continuum, finding the right-brain mode of relaxed concentration. Sometimes competition can affect us so profoundly that our usual route into our mode of relaxed concentration no longer works. (In desperation, some people try a quick gallop, or a slug of whisky!) There are riders who find it more easily in small competitions, and riders who find it more easily in large ones, and there are surprisingly few people who are able to produce their optimum performance regardless of how much or how little is at stake.

In an interview with *Horse and Rider* magazine, Chris Bartle (who came sixth in the dressage in the Los Angeles Olympic games) said, "If you are not affected in any way by a competition then it's probably time to give up competing." The competitor *needs* an increased flow of adrenaline, and she needs to become adept at channeling it to her own ends. Only experience with yourself and a certain horse will tell you what combination of activity and stillness calms and focuses you both best. However well you have prepared at home, and however well you have masterminded your transition into the competition environment, you need the versatility which allows you to respond to the new demands of a new occasion. Many riders thwart themselves by insisting on riding the horse in the way they do at home, even though he may be far more impulsive, and in need of very different tactics. Without the ability to differentiate between what *is* and what *ought to be*, they often do not realize when they have done enough, and by assuming that more must be better, they make themselves and horse tired and jaded. When warming up for jumping, many riders are tempted to jump just one more fence, and then just one more fence as if they have to keep convincing themselves that the horse has not forgotten how to jump! It can take courage to stop warming up, especially when your calculations have gone wrong because a class is running late; but it can pay enormous dividends at the end of a long, hot day.

Seasoned competitors become adept at planning each outing, minimizing the stress involved, and then dealing with it—reassessing their goals when necessary. But neither people nor horses are machines—they do not perform automatically—and Lucinda Prior-Palmer's books, *Up, Up and Away, Four Square,* and *Regal Realm,* as well as Virginia Holgate's autobiography *Ginny,* are full of stories about times when these two great riders did and did not succeed. It is apparent from their experiences that getting to the top is far simpler than staying there, and that this poses new challenges in terms of your attitudes and stamina. As well as enjoying the exhilaration of success, both of them have been through times of wondering whether to give up their sport, partly because of financial worries, and also because of their own losses of faith in themselves. In 1975, two years after her first Badminton victory, and after a series of mistakes which were caused primarily by her own inattentiveness, Lucinda reached a stage when, in her words, "I could see no reason for continuing to burden good horses with my presence. I trusted them, but I did not trust myself." As a junior competitor gaining experience in affiliated events it had taken a long time actually to win; on the morning of her first victory she had heard a voice in her head saying, "I think you might win today." The same aura surrounded her victorious 1973 Badminton, but in 1974, when she was defending the Whitbread Trophy, there were no such omens, and she and Be Fair had a terrible fall. As she was walking the course after his appalling dressage on the evening before the cross-country, her mind was still "smarting from the feeling of humiliation"; she decided to take the quickest and most difficult route through every cross-country fence where there were alternatives, and failed even to contemplate the slower route at the crooked S fence. This meant that she could not change her plans when she was advised to at the last moment, and the fall—as she says herself—was really the result of her attitude. "Previously I had not witnessed this particular kind of humiliation because I had always been an outsider coming from behind. If the dressage went well it was a pleasant surprise, and if it did not it was nothing unusual and went unnoticed. There was never any question of Be Fair having to pay for a bad performance."

Those of us who dream of making it do not usually stop to wonder what might lie beyond the initial exuberance that accompanies the ultimate success. Apparently, we would have to be even more dedicated, able to withstand the pressure of trying to live up to not only our own expectations but also other people's, while simultaneously maintaining a good enough performance level to keep us at the top. Attempting to remain on the top of the pinnacle can also give rise to a feeling of insecurity; teams and individuals who have in the past been successful often have difficulty retaining their form because they perceive themselves no longer as having something to fight for, but instead as having a status to defend.

Competitive riders live in a world which is full of elation and disappointment, victory and defeat, good luck and devastating blows. Those who bounce back and retain their form usually have immense self-discipline, an enormous amount of courage, and a very philosophical attitude. Lucinda says that her main fear in eventing is not of injury, or of looking stupid, but of letting her horse down; although she admits, "There's a special feeling attached to having no one else in front," she also says, "My principal ambition is one day to be able to step on to any horse and feel how to ride him to the best of his ability in a matter of days as opposed to years. This goal has always held greater significance than that of ephemeral victories: the attraction lies in its infinity."

Skilled competitors go into a competition with a feeling that they are causal; they can quickly assess a situation and use it to their advantage. Instead of perceiving the environment as an automatic handicap, they explore possible solutions to the problems it presents: they notice a quiet corner of the field that no one else has found, or they ride in with such aplomb that everyone else gets out of their way. Many competitors feel, however, that they are at the mercy of the riding conditions, and their fellow competitors. Although the way you feel about other people is based not so much on what you see but on what you *imagine* about what you see, and while you cannot change the external conditions, you can change the way you respond to them. In a jumping competition where all the other horses are at least one hand higher, it is tempting to believe that their jumping ability must match their size, and to feel more daunted. This imagined logic is not necessarily the truth, but the anxiety it generates is likely to have a visible and damaging effect on your performance. In a dressage competition where all the other horses seem better bred and more expensive, or where you are pitted against seemingly more professional riders, it is tempting to count yourself out of the running before you have even started, and therefore not to draw on the resources which make your performance creditable. The mere presence of onlookers who may seem to be there solely to judge your performance can provoke such a sense of inadequacy that your energy is turned away from your task and onto distracting thoughts. But even though you may never have had the experience and good fortune to hear your internal voice predict that you might win today, it is important to realize that you may have other, hidden, advantages.

Great competitors, like the tennis player Björn Borg, achieve their greatness at least partly through their exceptional ability to concentrate. When he was competing it made no difference to Borg whether the crowd was cheering or booing, whether he had just made a good shot or missed an easy one. He wasted no energy at all, but focused his attention entirely within a very narrow band of consciousness. If he could get his opponent to break *his* narrow band of concentration, so that he started to worry about his performance, or the crowd, or the next game, then Borg had the game as good as won. Cameramen at many different kinds of competition report that the only time a player complains about their presence is when he is losing—when his concentration is already broken, and external events he otherwise would not notice become annoying and distracting.

So, faced with the demands of competition, what can you do to help yourself? Riding in as if you were a seasoned competitor or using the numbering technique can work wonders for your concentration, and as the tension mounts you need to pay more and more attention to your body, deliberately taking time to re-create the feels which you identify as landmarks in your work at home. If you still feel inhibited, John Syer and Christopher Connolly, authors of *Sporting Body, Sporting Mind*, suggest that you try "energizing the opposite"—pretending that you love to be the center of attention, and to show off your work to an audience. So before you begin warming up, imagine how you would feel and look and think if you took on this role—and then try it on for size. Similarly, if you feel daunted by other competitors, take time to identify the qualities which they have and which you seem to lack; these may include self-confidence, relaxation, or the ability to ride more aggressively. We are actually only able to recognize such qualities in other people because we also have them in ourselves. Focus on them one at a time, therefore, imagining that each quality flows back from your opponent into you (perhaps through a shaft of light which connects you both), and feeling how it infuses your performance. Identify the difference that each one makes to the way you carry yourself, the way your horse moves, and the way you approach the test or course you're about to face.

These suggestions are actually very creative ways of using mental rehearsal, and they are based on the realization that our attitudes to ourselves, our environment, and our opponents *are just attitudes* —subjective—and not "the truth." As such, they can work for or against us; they can be out-of-date, exaggerated, or comparatively useful; and they can be changed. By consciously altering the subjective content of our experience we can also find new ways of responding to situations which seemed initially to contain inherent limitations. Thus we become more fully empowered and realistic.

Mental rehearsal plays a more commonplace role in course walking, and many competitors use it regularly, without really realizing that the benefits go way beyond a mere check that they know the way. When walking a course for the first time you see it as the horse will see it—complete with the element of surprise—and then, if you walk it again after you have had time to practice riding it mentally, you can check on your precision. Many people find that the object of their fear decreases in size as they familiarize themselves with it, so courses often look much less daunting on the second walk-through. If your early previews include grinding to a halt in a difficult combination, it is important that you take this as a warning signal which motivates you to rewalk the alternatives and determine the best line of approach—if necessary, by watching other competitors. If watching still leaves you in doubt about the best way to ride the fence, mental rehearsal can clarify how the alternatives would feel, and save you from falling into the awful trap of approaching the fence still undecided, and riding half of each! If your worst fears have still not abated, deliberately edit and reedit your mental ride until you can do it perfectly, and then practice the final version. It is also helpful to realize that you will not meet that "impossible" fence at number fourteen unless you have successfully negotiated all the previous ones, and by then it could look very different. If it does still seem overwhelmingly huge, and you cannot find it in you to attack it, you can always retire; but once your "blood is up" it is rare that "impossible" fences seem so impossible. When you are really anxious, mental practice becomes doubly important, because it generates a variety of different responses from which you need to choose one when you are put to the test. Imagine yourself riding each jump looking over the top of the fence, concentrating on the feel of rhythm and stride, and maintaining your seat right up to the moment of takeoff.

Lucinda Prior-Palmer, in particular, is a master of mental rehearsal. She developed this skill as a child, when she would walk a course and then go home and tell her pony Be Fair all the intricate details of the fences they were about to face. Other riders use it less systematically, and it is far more often associated with jumping than it is with dressage. In his interview with Horse and Rider, however, Chris Bartle also said: "Before a major competition I ride the test through in my mind a hundred times—step by step, half halt by half halt, imagining how the horse is going, and riding through the corrections I will have to make as we go along. . . . The best results that I have achieved have been when I have concentrated on following my plan to the nth degree rather than worrying about whether anything I ask is going to come off." Note that although he does not allow the idea that his corrections will not work, he *does* ride corrections. His preview is not an idealized fantasy, but a realistic, accurate, and detailed simulation of the difficulties he is going to meet in competition. As a general rule, the more closely your mental preview duplicates what you will see and feel in practice, the more useful your preparation will be.

Very soon after you have finished one competition preparation can begin for the next, and perhaps it is here that the most opportunities are lost. Neither winning nor losing is necessarily the same as producing a satisfying performance in which you meet some of your inner goals, and whatever happens it is worth asking, What did I do well? What could I improve on next time, both in my preparation at home and on the show ground? Were my expectations/objectives realistic? How should I modify them next time? Where are my strengths and weaknesses in terms of my physical, mental, and emotional preparation—that's to say with fitness and warm-up; with goal setting, planning, concentration, and mental rehearsal; with motivation, calmness and arousal, and the use of ritual? Just after the competition feelings can run so high—or low —that a detailed analysis is neither possible nor sensible; but once the feelings have been digested it is time to begin assessing tactics and techniques. The right brain can help here too, because a realistic mental review of your performance can tell you as much as or more than a video, since you also experience the subjective feelings of the event. (Beware, though, of recriminations. Continual replaying of a fall or bad jump does not help, and neither does telling yourself, If only I'd...; it is more helpful to discover exactly what went wrong, and then to reedit your mental ride so that you know exactly when to substitute exactly which response.) Reviewed in this way, any performance can become a learning experience, telling you of the strengths you need to build on, and the patterns you need to change.

In essence, the difference between "neurotic" and "creative" competitiveness lies in the way the rider feels about her horse. Riders often forget that the horse is not interested in their ambition, and they use him as a plaything to fulfill their desires. In some cases the horse becomes merely a rung on the ladder of their own personal success. This often has disastrous consequences, and the limitations and setbacks that can affect especially the one-horse owner can feel devastating. The higher levels of competition subject both horse and rider to some considerable strain, and one can justifiably question whether horses are subjected to stresses which are more than their systems can reasonably be expected to bear. Are we morally justified in continuing to organize competitions which are so arduous that only a few horses can compete at top level for more than a few seasons? How else might we challenge horses and riders, and encourage skillful riding, other than by insisting that they jump higher fences at greater speed? For somewhere there must be a limit, and the closer we get to this, the greater the stresses which both horse and rider must overcome. This was clearly apparent in the Three Day Event World Championships in Kentucky in 1978, where the high temperatures and humidity made a difficult course almost impossible. Few of the horses who took part ever regained their form in top-class competition, and since they had received such a physical and emotional punishment for their efforts, one can well understand why. Some event riders have suggested that perhaps their sport should be an individual and not a team competition at international level, because that would avoid the danger of a rider feeling compelled to push her horse too hard because she is carrying the fate of her country. It takes more skill, courage, and endurance to overcome them, and thus the likelihood of failure increases.

For a time when I was disillusioned with my riding, I began wondering what right I had to ride horses at all, let alone to ask them to compete. But as my skill increased, this conflict faded. I concluded that any horse who wants to be alive on this planet has to earn his keep—and given the choice, I would rather ride him than eat him. The horse pays for his bed and board by being my partner, and many riders I know also negotiate with their horses along the lines of "I do this for you, so you can do that for me." Although their horse may not appreciate being stabled, clipped, rugged, and corn fed as much as they think he ought to, the negotiation seems to produce a peaceful and workable solution. But the work itself can be far more rewarding than this. If, through my riding, I can communicate well enough with the horse to make him more calm and trusting, encouraging him to make better use of his body and mind, and to come closer to fulfilling his potential, perhaps I have done him a real favor. As the horse's grace, power, and agility increase, who is to say that he does not feel more proud through the physical act of carrying himself more proudly? Horses are extremely sensitive to atmosphere, and winning (or rather, the aura that surrounds it) can have a magical effect on a horse's personality. While some would say that horses love competition, that they rise to the occasion and thrive on the atmosphere, others would say that it is exploitative. Personally, I believe that both possibilities exist. However, if I am motivated in my work by my love for the horse, and not by the desire to prove—at all costs—how good I am, then perhaps the journeys we make together in horse trailers can be as much for his benefit as mine.

12 Inner Learning

Looking back over my learning process, I realize that it has been rather like doing a jigsaw puzzle. To begin with, it is relatively easy to find the corner pieces, and the edge pieces, and to sort out some of the obvious colors. Then, as you look more at the detail of individual pieces, it becomes more difficult; but sometimes, putting in one piece immediately allows you to add others, or to join up parts which were previously disconnected. Gradually, the more obscure parts fit into place, and as you near the end it gets easier, because you already have a framework into which the new parts will fit; you have an overview of the puzzle, and practical experience which boosts your faith that you can do it. Unlike riding, the puzzle is finite; but like riding it can only be done through trial and error, by learning to make fine distinctions with your senses. Few riders use and exploit their kinesthetic sense in the way that jigsaw enthusiasts use their visual sense, and most of us are so removed from our bodies that our kinesthetic sense is much, much less well developed than our ability to work with images and words.

Unfortunately, this problem begins in school, and in our word-oriented culture we are taught to believe that we automatically know all about something once we can give it a name. This supposedly eliminates the need to explore it further with our senses. The greatest riders, however, are the ones who *do* explore further, and those whose skill goes way beyond the average verbal description into the realm where the ultimate aid is to "make it feel right." We often forget that the multitude of tips and sayings that abound in riding all began, once upon a time, in someone's experience; that whoever first coined the idea that you should push your heels down used this phrase to delineate a certain feeling which was helpful for her in a certain context. But treating this idea like a universal rule and using it indiscriminately in any context, leads to all sorts of misconceptions (and can be rather like believing that all blue parts of every jigsaw must be part of the sky!). So the skill of the teacher is basically to be the tactful diplomat in an equestrian environment—knowing how to intervene by doing the right thing, at the right time, and in the right way.

Some teachers tackle the problem by concentrating their attention on the horse, while making the rider work through a series of gymnastic exercises which, if the teacher herself were riding, would bring about the desired improvement. However, this approach loses sight of the fact that the pupil is someone different—and probably someone with far fewer internal resources. Others tackle the problem by focusing on the rider, working on the details of her position as if it were an end in itself, rather than a means to an end. I believe that effective change can only happen by working on the interface through which the rider communicates with the horse, beginning necessarily by increasing the quality of the rider's tools (her concentration, breathing, body alignment, muscle tone and control, sensitivity, and so on) and then immediately applying them to the job she has to do (feeling the horse's movement, regulating it, shaping him, holding the circuit complete, and then working him through the various movements). By developing her inner resources the pupil discovers exactly what she does to the horse and what the horse does to her, and this offers her the kinesthetic clarity which is the backbone of skill. The teacher influences the horse most effectively by going through the medium of the pupil—for as long as the rider keeps bumping on his back, the cramping and deadening reflexes will continue to be brought into play, and the execution of the movements themselves will not change his way of going. Only her inner learning will lead ultimately to a viable outer result.

Practically all of us have grown up with the belief that knowing about a bad habit should be enough to enable us to change it. For centuries, teaching methods have been based on this premise, and few of us have questioned it. (I ought to be able to keep my hands still, we tell ourselves. What in heaven's name is wrong with me?)

Only recently has research shown that we are not, in fact, so stupid as we have often been led to believe—and I, for one, was immensely relieved to discover that there is a proven scientific reason for why my theoretical understanding of *what ought to be* never made a jot of difference to my practical influence over *what is!* You can take it as an established fact (and not merely a quirk of your own experience) that the body does *not* obey orders, regardless of whether they come from your teacher or from your own internal voice. Furthermore, the act of giving or receiving them blocks out your other senses, making it impossible for you either to perceive kinesthetically what is happening or to use the images which can have such an astounding effect on your muscle use. The primary key in riding lies in *how and where you focus your attention.* If you concentrate on the outside world, on what you look like, or on the product you want to achieve, rather than the process of how you get there, you will completely miss the necessary feedback from your body; you are effectively stopped from learning, and the phenomenal power of both brain and body go untapped.

In essence, there are two strands to learning. One is to improve your physical functioning, and the other is to improve your mental functioning, minimizing the crippling effects of left-brain interference. Moshe Feldenkrais, who was famous for his rehabilitation work with injured athletes, was one of the first to realize that awareness is the link which primes both mind and body. He stated, "If you know what you're doing, you can do what you want"; and the knowledge he meant is the right-brain awareness which enables you to revamp your crude neurological wiring in order to find new solutions to old problems. This new wiring makes breakthroughs far more frequent, and learning far less tedious; it not only breaks the grip of bad habits, but also allows you to re-create those exceptional rides which "just happen," and which it is tempting to attribute to the horse, or the weather, or some other factor completely beyond your control. I, for one, am often very slow to realize that whether or not I achieve these rides is not a matter entirely in the lap of gods, and that instead of treating them like an unaccustomed luxury, I must set about discovering the part I am playing in producing them. My contribution usually turns out to be far greater than I had at first imagined, and the discovery allows the good rides to become an ingrained part of my repertoire, which I can increasingly call upon at will.

Riders who base their work on ideas rather than tangible break-throughs often find themselves caught between conflicting bits of advice—should they sit up or sit down, face into the circle or out of it? In riding, the best judge is not the rational mind but the *body*—the right-brain sense of fitting—which discriminates between different feels and says, "Aha! This one works better." Effective change usually takes place through a series of distinct leaps, which provide answers that banish the mental confusion, and leave you in no doubt that you are learning. (If you are in doubt, you almost certainly are *not* learning.) Of course, the rider will experience some bodily confusion during the stage of breakthrough when she is neither here nor there, when she is abandoning the old way but has not quite discovered and ingrained the new one. She may no longer be satisfied, for instance, with what she used to class as a decent shoulder-in, but her attempts to grope her way toward a new ideal may feel extremely unsettling. This bodily confusion is actually very fertile soil from which new skills can grow, and even if the conscious mind does not understand, the body (in its own peculiar wisdom) always manages to find a more effective solution to the problem.

It is valuable to realize that the *process* of change remains the same regardless of the *content* of the changes. Knowing this enables sports psychologists to coach people in disciplines where they themselves have no formal training, and no knowledge of content or techniques—and I can verify from my own experience the remarkable effectiveness of their work. There are five steps in creating change. The first is to recognize what it is that you actually need to change. This involves differentiating causes from symptoms, so that you can answer the question, What *exactly* is happening? Often we do not make this initial diagnosis with sufficient precision. It is not enough to say, "My sitting trot is bad." How exactly is it bad, and where is the problem located? Is it based in the rider's stomach, seat, hand, or leg? How is she affecting the horse, and how is the horse affecting her? Often, once the problem is identified and the rider's awareness brought to it, the solution seems obvious. Change can then be made surprisingly easily.

The second step is *acceptance* of the habit, so that you look at it in a nonjudgmental way. Hating a bad habit, regarding it as an enemy, berating yourself for having it, and using willpower to try to change it, only tends to ingrain it more—because it fights back. It is helpful to realize that the bad habit is not there just because your body is trying to be perverse. Usually the part of the body which is causing the problem is only functioning in this way because another part is not doing its job, and the system as a whole is presenting the best solution it can to the problem. The habit therefore has a legitimate underlying cause; it represents an unsuccessful attempt to meet a need. Once this need is identified and met in the *right* way, the area which originally caused a problem actually recovers its *intended* function. As the habit is no longer able to serve a useful function, it ceases to exist of its own accord—without any conscious effort from the rider.

The third step is to change the way of functioning that is perpetuating the problem, and this is where the eye of a good teacher can prove invaluable. Since problems which manifest themselves in the extremities of the body usually have their origin somewhere nearer the center, you may have to focus on an area some way away from the apparent difficulty; and if you cannot identify this, or are not exactly sure what needs to change, some experimentation may be needed. The solution may lie in redirecting your attention, improving your concentration, increasing or decreasing your level of arousal, using imagery, or working more directly with body awareness. It may require a change in attitude toward yourself or your horse, or an analysis which reevaluates your performance and sets more realistic goals.

The fourth step is that, once discovered, the new technique needs to be integrated into your whole performance, so that it is gradually ingrained as an automatic response. This phase requires you consciously to inhibit the old responses in favor of the new one, and to keep reminding yourself about it—as you prepare in advance. Sometimes the change can be made with little conscious effort; sometimes it involves mobilizing parts of the body and mind which find the new effort very strenuous. At this stage, the rider often feels physically quite strange, but the new coordination renders her so much more effective that the rewards are instantaneous.

The fifth and final step is to experience the new pattern meshing perfectly with other aspects of your performance, creating a new whole which is a synthesis of these different parts. The rider has then transcended her former limitations, and new qualities emerge in her work. Often she finds that other problems are automatically solved, or that she also has access to other new abilities. This can lead to what Abraham Maslow calls a "peak experience" —a ride in which the barriers she was struggling with have completely melted away, revealing a whole new landscape and ultimately a new set of challenges.

Paradoxically, the learning process proceeds far more easily and quickly when you begin from the admission that it is difficult, and that it does take time. Good teaching believes in the potential of the pupil, but realizes that she has to learn step by step. The teacher aids this learning by using what is already correct as a base, and then expanding it by pinpointing the factors which are ripe for change. She has realistic expectations, and a variety of techniques which she can use to achieve them; and she always differentiates between time spent *doing* (working in the awareness mode) and time spent *analyzing* (talking about the experience in a left-brain mode). In the most efficient teaching, she defines her objectives extremely precisely and has the sensory acuity to know when she has achieved them; and when she loses track of what is happening she asks the pupil for her perceptions rather than just struggling on blindly.

Very often, I have found myself making some astounding assumptions about my pupils, and I know that other teachers do the same. One of the most common is for the teacher to assume that she knows what a pupil must be feeling in a certain situation, although her guess is based on a knowledge of what *she* would be feeling if she were riding. But even if her "eye" is good enough to pinpoint what is happening in the pupil's body, how can she know what is happening in the pupil's mind? The pupil may be feeling it in a different way, or she may not be feeling it at all; often, it pays to ask her.

I can usually tell when someone is working in a state of relaxed concentration, both from her riding and from the look on her face. Before we reach this stage, though, I can be way off beam. Many times I have heard teachers (and myself too) tell a pupil to "Come

one more time," and then to "Come just once more, . . . " and each
time the teacher keeps going in the belief that the pupil must get it
right next time. Her fantasy is based on the fact that if *she* were
riding, she *would* get it right next time; the pupil, however, who is
using different neurological pathways and a different coordination,
may not be so adaptable. She is probably grappling with her bad
habits in some rather ineffective ways, and consequently the more
the teacher pushes her, the more stuck and frustrated she becomes,
and the more she falls prey to the debilitating effects of fatigue.

The art of getting a different response from your pupil (or your
horse) lies in having the versatility to *do something different yourself*,
so that you meet her (or him) in a place where she (or he) is ready
and able to change. Many teachers who expect their pupils to be
extremely adaptable are actually very unadaptable themselves, so
that when their techniques do not work, they keep on doing exactly the same thing. As riders, they do not have the versatility in
their behavior that they are demanding from their horse (who is
supposed to listen next time). And they are supposed to be the
more intelligent partner! A friend of mine hit the nail on the head
when she quoted the saying: "If you always do what you always did,
you'll always get what you always got." Riders and teachers would
both get much further if they understood their horse's or their
pupil's responses as comments on *their* communication, rather than
as statements about their prodigies' stubbornness or inability.
Teachers, for instance, will often simply tell a pupil who is ingraining a new response to use it—and then they are surprised when
everything else falls to pieces. Instead of getting impatient with her
inability to add the new coordination to the old, it would be far
more useful if they remembered to help her; instead of just saying,
"Use your legs," they might say, "Keep making that same feeling
under your seat, and hold it as you add in a leg aid." Then they
would get a very different response, and would considerably reduce
the time it takes for the pupil to make this link for herself.

The more effectively a teacher can work, the less intrusive she
needs to be—the less she feels as if she is bashing her head against
a brick wall, and the less resistance she evokes in her pupils. The
teacher's choice is either to try to make the pupil obedient, so that
she can control her and turn her into something she is not, or to

interact with her in a way which increases the pupil's control of herself—mainly by offering amplified feedback which she would not normally have. It is well known that biofeedback machines can help teach us to influence our skin temperature and heart rate, which have previously been thought to be beyond conscious control; when the teacher acts like a biofeedback machine for the pupil, she can help her to increase her autonomy in similar ways. In practical terms this is the difference between giving her the order, "Sit still!" and saying, "Focus your attention on the underneath of your seat, and notice how much movement there is. What happens to your seat bones... are they bumped off the saddle? How much does your flesh get in the way? Is one side more stable than the other?" This gives the pupil information (from the pupil's own experience) which she would not get if she just tried to sit still (using brute force, ignorance, and a demoralizing internal dialogue), nor if she listened to the teacher's analysis of what was wrong with her.

Sometimes the pupil can get even more information by exaggerating the problem, finding out what she needs to do in order to increase and decrease it, or by using the numbering exercise. The teacher can suggest images and attitudes that might help her, and when the pupil finally finds a coordination which works, it is useful to say, "That's right! Keep on doing whatever it is that you're doing now," giving her encouragement, and feedback that this is a desirable state (as this may not be immediately obvious to her). After working, when they talk about their perceptions, the teacher can find out more about what the pupil feels she actually did, and this may offer some images or body feelings which will be extremely potent because they are *her own*, and which it can be useful to feed back to her while she is riding. By acting as a biofeedback device, the teacher amplifies things which are true, exaggerating the feedback which helps the pupil to learn like a servomechanism, and to function with more refinement. She joins forces with the pupil, and is both extremely precise and artfully vague, so that she does not contradict what the pupil knows—or feels she knows—to be true. This will strengthen her credibility, so that her pupil will come to trust and believe her even in times of confusion and stress.

In essence, helping people and horses to rearrange the ways in which they use their bodies is rather like trying to change the course of a river. One way is to dam it, opposing its flow directly; but this takes enormous energy, because it requires you to resist its full force. The alternative is to join it for a while and go with the flow, gradually rearranging its course from within. It is this way that the teacher and the pupil, or the rider and the horse, best work together, finding new pathways around old obstacles, making maximum use of their combined resources, and finding the state of relaxed concentration.

It is interesting to note that our bad habits always go together with our self-image, that we have them because they fit us. When we develop more useful habits, our self-image changes too; but often we are so fixated in a certain view of ourselves that this in itself presents a barrier to change. We tell ourselves, I can't ride that type of horse, . . . I always mess up when I'm put under pressure, . . . I'll never be able to ride good lateral work . . . ; and as we prepare to face the worst and think, Here goes . . . we galvanize all our resources in a way which is bound to provoke resistance in the horse, and make the prophecy self-fulfilling. (By now, you are familiar with the idea of feedback. This process, through which we create our own future, could well be called "feedforward.") In a battle between the will (which wants to) and the imagination (which knows it cannot), the imagination will always win—and that is why riding "as if . . ." is a far more potent tool than trying, forcing, and willing. The function of our individual fears is to keep us enclosed within the bounds of a self-image which (even if it is painful) is at least safe and familiar. As well as fear of falling, and fear of failing, many of us also experience fear of "flying"—of suddenly discovering that we have abilities far greater than we had realized. The truth is that we hang on to our bad habits as hard as they hang on to us, in fear and awe of the whole and empowered person we would become if we released them. When we transcend our self-image barriers in riding, it is usually when we are completely engrossed in our work, and so well entrenched in a state of relaxed concentration that we do not even realize what we are doing. One of my most beautiful experiences of this happened one day when I was working a horse who, after showing some considerable reluctance, had begun to produce some quite respectable medium trot. On this particular day, the work was going very well, and as another rider came toward me I circled away in medium trot without thinking what I was doing. Two-thirds of the way round the circle I thought, But we can't do this yet, and immediately the whole trot fell to pieces!

Many people view learning as a process of *addition*, in which we add qualities to a self which is perceived as being full of deficiencies. We tell ourselves how we should be, and feel inadequate because that is not how we are. But if we thought of the qualities as goals rather than "shoulds," we could work toward them, using them as fuel which enlivens our performance rather than dampening it. Many riders, regardless of their level, are struggling to become one of the "initiated"—whether that means moving from the three o'clock to the two o'clock lesson, having their own horse, training for a career with horses, or entering bigger, more prestigious competitions. If they do not immediately succeed, or if somebody else succeeds before they do—which, of course, inevitably will happen—they consider themselves inferior, primarily because they have been measuring themselves by *somebody else's* yardstick . . . and by that measurement, they could have done better. The fact that they are inferior as mathematicians and weight lifters does not bother them; the conviction that tells them that they should be better riders leads them eventually to conclude that there must be something wrong with them, and that they are second-rate people.

The person who believes she is inferior inevitably tries to make up for her lack by struggling to achieve superiority. But in reality she is neither inferior nor superior: she is just herself, at her own particular stage of development. When a teacher and pupil recognize this, and both trust in the potential of the pupil, she can learn, not by addition, but by *subtraction*, removing one by one the internal obstacles which currently make it impossible for her to express more of her potential and "fly."

Ideally, the teacher-pupil relationship is like an apprenticeship, in which the teacher is the pupil's guide and mentor. Because she has traveled the same road, she knows some of the pitfalls and difficulties involved, and she can help ensure that the pupil does not take any wrong turns. Her role is largely to hold the pupil within the bounds of her stretch zone, so that she sets herself realistic goals, and can learn primarily from the horse and her experience. The teacher is also a model, because the standard of the work that the pupil expects to produce will be limited by the standard of the work she has seen. At the same time, it is helpful if the gap between their respective abilities is not too large—children will often learn mathematics from one of their classmates far more easily than they would learn from a university professor, because their friend, who has recently grappled with the problem, has a student's-eye view of it. The really skillful teacher can enter even the most inept pupil's world, but the larger the gap between their respective abilities, the more difficult the bridging of the gap becomes. Good teacher-pupil relationships, in fact, are not all that common. A friend of mine, who is a renowned sports psychologist, went recently to a Young Riders' International Dressage competition at Goodwood, and asked the British riders, "What is the greatest source of stress throughout your training and competition work?" Independently, they all answered, "My trainer."

In devising your own training program, it is important to realize that your needs change as you improve. At times it is helpful to ride many different horses, but it is also important to have a continuing relationship with one in particular. As William Steinkraus says in Riding and Jumping: "Many riders only start really to think about their sport when they have to utilize time with some economy and make the most of limited opportunities," and in my experience, there is a lot of truth in his words. People who have lessons every day rarely value them sufficiently, and often, in long periods of intensive instruction, all that happens is that teacher and pupil both become resigned to the pupil's faults. The greatest amount will always be learned in the initial spurt and in the end spurt which accompany any program of instruction, and this is a very good argument for arranging periods of intensive instruction in a larger number of shorter chunks.

The other advantage of this is that it allows time for the integration of new material. Riders who are beginning to be skillful in their own right need time to digest what they have learned and to explore on their own, but this is rarely allowed when they are actually in training. I have often found that I make the most significant progress just *after* a period of intensive instruction, when I can work with the teacher's input in my own time and my own way. I also benefit from the increased confidence I feel when I can show off my newfound skill to the world, and am no longer in the role of pupil—where I (and many others) easily lose autonomy and become the "underdog." Incidentally, this balance of power is often encouraged by teachers who like to be the "top dog."

One of the results of effective instruction is that the pupil becomes progressively more independent of the teacher. In the early stages she needs frequent sessions, or she will fall back into her old ways between them. Then, as she internalizes the teacher's knowledge, she becomes able to do productive work on her own; she will benefit from alternating periods of intensive instruction with times when she works mostly alone. The pupil who gets this balance right can avoid many of the pitfalls of learning; she can use her in-depth work with the teacher to open dramatic new doors, and be sent away with enough new material to keep her busy for a while.

Riding, as an art form, does not yield its secrets very easily, and the varying approaches of different teachers only serve to intensify the enigma. Each one has her own interpretation of the tenets of whatever school she follows, but adherents of the doctrines of different schools all believe that *their* approach is "right," and that others are "wrong." Arguments rage over which is the most classical, emphasizing the differences between the various schools, and in the world of horses there is an awful lot of backbiting. I frankly find it more helpful to identify the underlying *similarities*. As most people are aware, many roads lead to Rome, and it is obvious that there are a few "talented" individuals in each school who succeed (by whatever methods) in producing beautiful work. What we need is to find out what they have in common, discovering the similarities in their internal approach—the quality of their concentration, where they focus their attention, how they use imagery, muscle tone, and so on—rather than arguing over the external differences in the exercises they use when they work the horse. It is very tempting to attribute a rider's success to the outer rather than the inner tools which she uses in training. When some riders swear that one should start each work session by working at a posting trot, while others swear that it should be begun in sitting trot, I find it most appropriate to take these as statements about what each of those *individuals* does best (and therefore finds more helpful), rather than as conflicting generalizations about how to work horses. By looking for inward similarities, rather than outward differences, I feel that we come much closer to discovering which roads lead to Rome and which ones do not. The underlying determinants of skill can be packaged in ways which make them look very different, but without them, whichever route you choose will certainly prove abortive—however well it works for someone else.

The masters in all the various schools are marked by their ability to transcend conflict with the horse, putting him in front of them so that they can draw out his most efficient and beautiful movement. While the essence of this remains the same in each school, the qualities valued most highly by the varying schools are not shared. If we think of power, ease, lightness, grace, fluidity, and precision as ingredients of a recipe, the final blend which each individual regards as preferable is probably a matter of tradition and personal taste. The various riding cultures have all grown up around a particular type of horse, and a particular people, and each has evolved an ethos which capitalizes on their strengths. For example, the qualities of the Andalusian horse helped to form the ethos of the old French school, which is currently exemplified by the work of the Portuguese. The horses have short, elevated strides, and are far more suited to collected work than they are to extension. Their riders work them at comparatively low muscle tone in gaits which show relatively little suspension, but with qualities of ease, grace, and lightness which are often missing in the modern German school of competition riders. The German horses, which are larger, longer-striding, and more powerful, have influenced the fashions in modern competition work, with certain winning combinations like Christine Stuckelburger and Granat, and Anne-Grethe Jenson and Marzog, helping to set new trends. Swedish, German, Dutch, and Danish horses go in and out of fashion according to which are winning most at the time, and although a competitive sport requires rules through which one can define excellence, one's response to a horse and rider (as to any form of art) is bound to be subjective. Personally, for instance, I often find that horses I have enjoyed watching at Prix St. George level disappoint me when they reach Grand Prix; with the heavier demands of extreme collection, their movement loses the fluidity which is part of my personal definition of beauty. But when we compare the various riding cultures, who is to say which is "right" and which is "wrong"? We choose to evaluate modern competition work by means of a certain set of criteria, but I have found that there is an immense amount to be learned from the other traditions whose ideas and horses do not fit. The French, Swedish, German, and Spanish schools all carry a history and an ideology which is deeply rooted in antiquity, and the masters in each utilize the same inner principles which are the essence of skill, regardless of how—individually—they package their work.

In their relationship with the horse, the masters of riding take on many of the attitudes and stances of another set of masters—the martial artists whose disciplines originate in Asia and Japan. They all have their roots in Zen philosophy, and consequently the artists embody attitudes to life which make them extremely difficult to unbalance. The martial artist never directly opposes her opponent's power; instead, she channels it to her own ends. Rather than hitting back, for instance, she uses her partner's momentum to throw her in the direction she was already moving in. The challenge to the rider is to blend with her horse's energy in a similar way, channeling it so that he can never get himself into a position from which he can use his power against her, and make her reactive rather than causal.

Many riders expend their energy opposing that of the horse, or trying to stop him from having it in the first place. Riders who do not have the subtlety to let their work be guided by their reflex interactions with the horse, and who base their work on the stick and the carrot, often fall into this trap—and their work suffers as a result. By appealing to the horse's rational mind, and insisting on submission and obedience, they lose many of the qualities which accompany a live interchange, when both parties concentrate fully. (As one of my old teachers used to say, "The horse already knows how to be a horse"; and the last thing he needs is for us to try to teach or subdue him, in an attempt to make him more or less than he already is.) While the rider is primarily the brains of the partnership and the horse is basically the brawn, the best work happens when they blend their abilities and strengths into a greater whole, attuning their wills in harmony. First the rider must center herself, focusing her attention and tuning her own will, and then, as she persuades the horse to join her, a new creature emerges, whose whole is far greater than the sum of his parts.

The most outstanding riders are able to work horses so that they can consistently find this union. In practice, I have met very few who can, and although most of us uphold the same ideal of "effortless effort," those "exceptional" rides in which it is manifested are indeed the exception. The problem arises largely in the attitudes that horse and rider bring with them to each session; driven by their determination, or their fears and doubts, they often produce something far from beautiful. Either the rider bullies the horse, or the horse bullies the rider, while the subtle communication in which they neither fight, nor play dead, nor merely go through the motions requires them to leave behind the limitations of their preconceived ideas. When riders are in a low, it tends to have begun from a state of defeat, and they often imagine that this state will last forever; conversely, when they are on a streak, they either fall into a lackadaisical contentment or they imagine that it cannot last. Either way, it does not. A rider whose horse worked well yesterday will generally try to do the same movements again today before she has successfully centered herself and put the horse in front of her, so of course her attempts are doomed. She may also overstress the horse, continuing until fatigue sets in, and he uses resistance to tell her about his problems. Alternatively, she will just work on the things that both of them can do well, and not expose or confront their areas of weakness; in time, this will have the same effect as her taking the good work for granted. As she does this the rider gradually loses concentration, and leaves the horse some loophole that he can dive into and then use to come back "behind her." When she finally realizes what has been happening, the chances are that she will have to have a massive confrontation with him in order to put him back in front of her again. The work proceeds much better when it involves a series of tiny confrontations, which are really just a part of the way that horse and rider hold each other within the confines of their stretch zones.

Very few riders can perform consistently, largely because so few realize that riding consists of a continuous series of moments, in which you have to keep putting the horse in front of you completing the circuit and "making it feel right." In a way, it is as if you are having a tennis match with the horse—you correct an evasion (fifteen, love), then he finds a new loophole (fifteen all). You close that, and then go a stage further (forty, fifteen). But the most magical moments are like a long rally, where no one scores any points but both of you are determined to keep the ball in play. In contrast, one of the biggest dangers lies in thinking that you have "got it now": this is rather like trying to catch running water and put it in a bucket; the moment you do this, it is not running water any more. Denise McCluggage expresses the same idea when she says, "Getting there is not only half the fun, it is all there is"; and arriving, it seems, is an illusion. The moment you believe that you have "got it," you no longer have a goal to strive for. As Maxwell Maltz says in *Psychocybernetics*, the human being is designed as a goal-striving mechanism, "somewhat like a bicycle... [which]... maintains its poise and equilibrium only as long as it is going forward toward something." When you attain your goal you become static, and you are likely to topple off your pedestal; you may also find that this wonderful achievement is not all it was once cracked up to be. From the perspective of those dizzying heights, the horse and other riders are more likely to become a threat to your image, and you experience frustration in the negative sense through not being able to live up to your ideals, rather than in the positive sense of having something to strive for.

The masters do not fall into this trap. They retain their beginner's mind and get onto the horse without preconceived ideas, remaining as curious and as interested in him as they were on the day when they first rode him. They realize that they must begin each ride right from the beginning, as if there had been no yesterday; they go through the processes of centering themselves and putting the horse in front of them all over again. They hold themselves in a dynamic interchange with him, channeling his power like a martial artist, submitting themselves to a constant demand on their concentration, presence, and alignment, and ultimately transcending it, so that they slide into the state of "effortless effort."

I doubt very much, however, if there are any riders whose work proceeds without frustration. None of us (and no horse) can function at our optimum all the time, and even though the most skilled riders can step into a state of relaxed concentration almost at will, it is still bound to be easier on some days than others. Some years ago, I would find that my riding varied enormously from day to day, and often I had no idea what to expect. I had no conception of how to center myself (in fact, I did not even know what that meant), and a minimal understanding of how the horse and I were affecting each other. I knew far more about what *should have been* than I did about what actually *was*, and this discrepancy lay at the root of the problem. The riders who are the most consistent and the least frustrated are the ones who are aware of subtle differences in themselves and the horse both from moment to moment, and from day to day; they respond to those differences realistically, always aiming to hold the horse in front of them with the circuit complete, but recognizing the times when really good work is not possible. Whoever it was who first said, "The best is the enemy of the good," was making a very valuable point. If you refuse, on all occasions, to be satisfied by anything less than perfection, you are liable to give yourself and your horse a really hard time. The real problem lies not in whether or how often you feel frustrated, but in *how you feel about feeling frustrated*—if you are frustrated by your frustration, you are doubly likely to vent your feelings on the horse. The most consistent riders view their frustration with equilibrium, and by accepting it, and the situations which produce it, they find that it diminishes in size and importance.

At times, I think that the onlooker watching a combination of horse and skillful rider is witnessing one of the greatest optical illusions of all time. It looks so easy, as if the rider has a magic touch, and as if she is doing nothing to achieve those incredible results. I used to imagine that those results just dropped down from the sky, and that one day, I might be lucky enough to be in the right place at the right time so that they might also drop down onto me! I was so taken in by the illusion that I had to give up riding in despair before it began to dawn on me that the answers were not going to come from the sky, a teacher, or a textbook, but only from within myself. Now I know that "talent" is nothing more than creating the internal environment which allows learning—

and magic—to happen. It means discovering that true control can only be gained through surrendering the desire to control, whether this be the control of the left brain, which so likes to believe that it can dominate the body, or an attempt to control the horse, limiting his power with the hand instead of containing and channeling it with the seat. The learning process requires such an enormous adaptation from our reflex reactions, and the normal ways of using our minds and bodies, that it is immensely confrontational: in Zen philosophy, the beginner and the master who lie at both ends of it are seen as being very close together. The beginner knows no technique, and the master has transcended technique; but in all the stages between, technique is the framework which fits parts into wholes, and offers a working knowledge of cause and effect.

Essentially, the lessons are those learned by students in many other disciplines, who also have to center themselves, to overcome their limiting beliefs, to value their potential, and to trust the power of the right brain, and of subtlety. Riding feels to me like a microcosm of life, a small part in which I have a skill, an awareness, and a way of relating, and this I can learn to adapt to other areas. It shows me how different my experience is when I am causal as opposed to reactive. It illuminates my strengths and weaknesses, and it teaches me acceptance—as well as the potency of the change that this can generate. In particular, I find it fascinating to realize just how much say I have in creating my own future; if the way I visualize a movement I am about to ride can have such a resounding effect on the outcome, how else might this principle of "feedforward" operate in other areas of my life? How do I visualize other aspects of my future, what other fears do I limit myself with, and perhaps more importantly, what is it that I would really like to create for myself?

This book suggests that each one of us is both the vehicle for fulfilling our own unique potential, and the victim of many current limitations and obstacles which often seem to exist not in us but in the horse and the outside world. Paradoxically, accepting these as our own (and accepting our own inadequacy) is the first step toward a solution. When learning from an inner perspective, the first problem comes with learning to quiet the mind and to develop our concentration. This is considered by many to be the master art, because all other arts depend on it, and athletes, artists, and mystics, and well as many ordinary people, have all come to realize that our occasional moments of wholeness—our "peak experiences"—lie not in the external world but in our state of mind. This suggests that learning to be at peace with ourselves is one of the first steps not only to improved riding, but also to a fuller, richer life, in which we will appreciate the world and those around us. In describing the "inner game," Timothy Gallwey writes: "Eventually some players come to realize that relaxed concentration is more important to them than a good backhand. Instead of playing the inner game to reach an outer goal, they play outer games only to help them reach an inner goal." This is equally possible with riding. The rider who has transformed herself through learning becomes a truly wise person, able to live each moment fully, and to be responsive to herself and those around her. She "wins" in the game of life . . . and she knows that she is forever only getting there.

Bibliography

BANDLER, RICHARD, and GRINDER, JOHN, *Frogs into Princes* (U.S. distrib.: Real People Press, 1979).

——, *Trance-formations* (Real People Press, 1981).

BARLOW, WILFRED, *The Alexander Principle* (London: Arrow Books, 1975).

BLAKESLEE, THOMAS R., *Right Brain* (London, The Macmillan Press Ltd., 1980).

British Horse Society, *Equitation* (London: Country Life Books, 1982).

CADE, MAXWELL, and COXHEAD, NINA, *The Awakened Mind* (Aldershot, Hampshire, England: Wildwood House, 1979).

CROSSLEY, ANTHONY, *Training the Young Horse* (London: Stanley Paul, 1978).

DECARPENTRY, *Academic Equitation* (London: J. A. Allen and Co., 1971).

DIAGRAM GROUP, *The Brain: A User's Manual* (London: New English Library, 1984).

EDWARDS, BETTY, *Drawing on the Right Side of the Brain* (London: Souvenir Press, 1979).

FRENCH-BLAKE, NEIL, *The World of Show Jumping* (Pelham Books, 1986).

GALLWEY, W. TIMOTHY, *The Inner Game of Golf* (London: Jonathan Cape, 1981).

——, *The Inner Game of Tennis* (New York: Random House, 1974).

——, *Inner Tennis* (New York: Random House, 1976).

GALLWEY, W. TIMOTHY, and Kriegel, Bob, *Inner Skiing* (New York: Random House, 1977).

GELB, MICHAEL, *Body Learning* (London: Aurum Press Ltd., 1981).

GERMAN NATIONAL EQUESTRIAN FEDERATION, *The Principles of Riding* (Threshold Books, 1985).

GREEN, CAROL, *Jumping Explained: Horseman's Handbook* (London: Midas Books, 1976).

HARRIS, CHARLES, *Fundamentals of Riding* (London: J. A. Allen and Co., 1985).

HENDRICKS, GAY, and CARLSON, JON, *The Centered Athlete* (Prentice-Hall Inc., 1982).

HERBERMANN, ERIK F., *The Dressage Formula* (London: J. A. Allen and Co., 1980).

HERRIGEL, EUGEN, *Zen in the Art of Archery* (New York: Vintage Books, 1971).

HOLGATE, VIRGINIA, *Ginny* (London: Stanley Paul, 1986).

HYAMS, JOE, *Zen in the Martial Arts* (New York: Bantam Books, 1982).

JENSEN, CLAYNE, and SCHULTZ, GORDON, *Applied Kinesiology* (New York: McGraw-Hill Inc., 1977).

KAPIT, WYNN, and ELSON, LAWRENCE, *The Anatomy Coloring Book* (New York: Harper and Row, 1977).

KLIMKE, REINER, *Basic Training of the Young Horse*, trans. S. Young (London: J. A. Allen and Co., 1985).

———, *Cavaletti: Schooling of Horse and Rider Over Ground Rails*, trans. D. M. Goodall (London: J. A. Allen, 1973).

LEONARD, GEORGE, *The Ultimate Athlete* (New York: Avon Books, 1977).

LEWIS, DAVID, *The Alpha Plan* (London: Methuen, 1986).

MALTZ, MAXWELL, *Psychocybernetics* (New York: Pocket Books, 1960).

MASTERS, ROBERT, and HOUSTON, JEAN, *Listening to the Body* (New York: Delacorte Press, 1978).

McCLUGGAGE, DENISE, *The Centered Skier* (New York: Bantam Books, 1983).

MOREHOUSE, LAURENCE, and GROSS, LEONARD, *Maximum Performance* (London: Mayflower Books, 1980).

MUSELER, WILHELM, *Riding Logic* (London: Methuen London Ltd., 1983).

PODHAJSKY, ALOIS, *The Complete Training of Horse and Rider* (London: George C. Harrap and Co., 1973).

———, *The Riding Teacher* (London: George C. Harrap and Co., 1973).

PRIOR-PALMER, LUCINDA, *Four Square* (London: Pelham Books, 1980).

———, *Regal Realm* (London: Pelham Books, 1983).

———, *Up, Up and Away* (London: Pelham Books, 1978).

REES, LUCY, *The Horse's Mind* (London: Stanley Paul, 1984).

RISTAD, ELOISE, *A Soprano on Her Head* (U.S. distrib.: Real People Press, 1982).

RUSSELL, PETER, *The Brain Book* (London: Routledge and Kegan Paul Ltd., 1979).

SEUNIG, WALDEMAR, *Horsemanship* (New York: Doubleday and Co., Ltd., 1976).

SIVEWRIGHT, MOLLY, *Thinking Riding, No. 1* (London: J. A. Allen and Co., 1979).

————, *Thinking Riding, No. 2: In Good Form* (London: J. A. Allen and Co., 1984).

SMYTHE, R. A., and GOODY, P. C., *The Horse, Structure and Movement* (London: J. A. Allen and Co., 1975).

STEINKRAUS, WILLIAM, *Riding and Jumping* (London: Pelham Books, 1971).

SWIFT, SALLY, *Centered Riding* (London: Heinemann, 1985).

SYER, JOHN C., and CONNOLLY, CHRISTOPHER, *Sporting Body, Sporting Mind: Athlete's Guide to Mental Training* (Cambridge, England: Cambridge University Press, 1984).

TOTKO, THOMAS, and TOSI, UMBERTO, *Sports Psyching* (Los Angeles: J. P. Tarcher Inc., 1976).

Index

311